Mrs Brown is a Man and a Brother

First published 2004 by
Liverpool University Press
4 Cambridge Street
Liverpool L69 7ZU

British Library Cataloguing-in-Publication data
A British Library CIP record is available

ISBN 0-85323-738-7 cased
0-85323-748-4 limp

Typeset by XL Publishing Services, Tiverton
Printed and bound in the European Union by Biddles Ltd, King's Lynn

In memory of my grandmothers and my great-aunt who,
as Margaret Piercy, Catherine Hughes and May Cowman,
would have watched much that is described herein.

Contents

Acknowledgements

This book has been part of my life for a very long time, and many people have helped its progress. My first thanks must go to Carl Levy and Pat Thane, who persuaded their underconfident MA student that doctoral research was an achievable aim. The thesis on which the book is based was painstakingly supervised by Jane Rendall and Joanna de Groot and examined by June Hannam and Mary Maynard; more importantly their continued interest in the project as it progressed towards publication offered me much appreciated support and an aspirational model of feminist working practice.

The Economic and Social Research Council funded the original research; further work was supported by the University of York and Leeds Metropolitan University. The knowledge and help of staff at a variety of libraries and archives, mentioned in the bibliography, has been indispensable.

Many historians have been extremely generous in sharing work with me, or pointing me in unthought of but fruitful directions. I am especially indebted to Heloise Brown, Elizabeth Crawford and June Purvis. Several people have been invaluable sounding boards during the writing of this book, listening patiently to my enthusiasms, reading drafts of chapters or paragraphs, and allowing me to declaim endlessly the unassailable importance of Liverpool women and their political tangles. For this, thanks to John Belchem, Kelly Boyd, Claire Cross, Anna Davin, Simon Ditchfield, Mary Eagleton, Claire Eustance, Laura Gowing, Sue Grace, Simon Gunn, Sylvia Hahn, Karen Hunt, Phillipa Levine, Jon Lawrence, Hugh McLeod, Jim McMillan and Tim Meldrum. Particular thanks must go to Sandra Stanley Holton and Louise Jackson. Sandra's pioneering work in the field of suffrage history has not prevented her from still being more than generous to younger scholars with both her knowledge and her time, and the keenness with which she would respond to yet another set of queries re-motivated me on more than one occasion. Louise, as well as offering academic support and expertise, has shared an office with me during the final stages of this writing, giving practical advice on the finer points of preparation and a constant sympathetic ear.

The years during which this project has evolved from thesis to book have also brought changes in my own life which deserve mention. My parents, Joan and Arnold Cowman, have been constant in their endorsement of the work. My husband, Jim Sharpe, has consistently displayed an interest in the

research despite being forced to read countless redrafts. Moreover, his practical help has enabled me actually to finish the work. My final debt is to my
children, Guy and Elfreda. Guy's birth coincided with the completion of the
original thesis, and Elfreda's with the manuscript. They have both lived all
their lives with this work, eaten and torn portions of it, wondered over its
ability to spill into every space in which they might wish to play, and have
more cause to resent it than most. I hope that, when they finally read it, they
feel that it was worthwhile.

Introduction

In 1928, in the preface to her history of the British women's movement, *The Cause*, Ray Strachey observed that

> The sudden development of the personal, legal, political and social liberties of half the population of Great Britain within the space of eighty years… [has meant that] the true history of the Women's Movement is the whole history of the nineteenth century: nothing which occurred in those years could be irrelevant to the great social change which was going on.[1]

Twentieth-century historiography shows Strachey's enthusiasm to have been somewhat misplaced. Early participatory accounts of women's part in achieving these liberties were joined by other attempts to broaden knowledge of women's contribution to the nation, notably those produced by women scholars associated with the London School of Economics.[2] The writers were products of 'first wave' feminism, university educated and seeking paying and fulfilling careers. Yet the presence of their works in academic libraries did little to alter the overall construction of the discipline of history, which remained largely gendered as male. Only with the emergence of 'second wave' feminism in the 1970s were sustained attempts made to establish women's history as a distinct category, first in challenges from the margins of academia – women's groups and adult education departments – and then

---

1 Ray Strachey, *The Cause: A Short History of the Women's Movement in Great Britain*, London, Virago, 1988 [1928], p. 5.
2 Early participatory accounts include E. S. Pankhurst, *The Suffragette*, London, Gay & Hancock, 1911; E. S. Pankhurst, *The Suffragette Movement*, London, Longmans Green & Co., 1931; E. Pankhurst, *My Own Story*, London, Eveleigh Nash, 1914; M. G. Fawcett, *Women's Suffrage: A Short History of a Great Movement*, London, T. C. & E. C. Jack, 1912; M. G. Fawcett, *What I Remember*, London, Fisher & Unwin, 1924. Non-participatory early women's histories include B. L. Hutchins, *Women in Modern History*, London, G. Bell & Sons, 1915; A. Clarke, *Working Lives of Women in Seventeenth Century London*, London, Routledge & Sons, 1915; I. Pinchbeck, *Women Workers and the Industrial Revolution, 1750–1850*, London, Routledge & Sons, 1930; B. Drake, *Women in Trade Unions*, London, Labour Research Department, 1920. For a broad overview of both categories, see J. Purvis, 'From "Women Worthies" to Poststructuralism? Debate and Controversy in Women's History in Britain', in J. Purvis, ed., *Women's History in Britain 1850–1945*, London, UCL Press, 1995, pp. 1–22.

increasingly from within established history faculties.[3]

The most urgent project for the new discipline was to identify and recover its subjects. Although some broad overviews emerged, the nineteenth century, as Strachey had predicted, was identified as 'a turning point in the history of women' and received special attention.[4] Particular changes in women's status were assessed, often within the categories identified in Strachey's preface. The 'personal' and 'legal' liberties were comparatively easy to chart, resulting from steady campaigns that improved women's legal status and widened their opportunities through removing existing boundaries in education and the professions.[5] 'Social' liberties, although more difficult to quantify, have begun to be investigated. However, it is the 'political' category that has so far invited the most attention. From the suffrage movement onwards, histories of women's politics and the history of women have often appeared inseparable.

The main explanation for this lies in the concerns of the historical subjects themselves. An interaction with the political can be traced in the lives of many nineteenth-century women. Reforms in divorce, education, child rearing or the right to enter professions all required political legislation. Yet, although historians such as Sandra Holton have done much to alert us to the shifting concerns and fluid alliances of nineteenth-century women's politics, the majority of these political histories remain focused on individual and distinct campaigns and organisations.[6] A key line of investigation has consequently

3   Recent British investigations into the discipline of history which recognise both the category of women's history and its origins include J. Tosh, *What is History? Present Aims, Methods and New Directions in the Study of Modern History*, London, Longmans, 1984, pp. 6–8; L. Jordanova, *History in Practice*, London, Arnold, 2000, pp. 43–44. For a more detailed overview see C. Hall, 'Feminism and Feminist History', in C. Hall, *White, Male and Middle Class: Explorations in Feminism and History*, Oxford, Blackwell, 1992, pp. 1–42.

4   G. Fraisse and M. Perrot, 'Oracles and Liberties', in G. Duby and M. Perrot, eds, *A History of Women in the West Vol. IV: Emerging Feminism from Revolution to World War*, Cambridge, MA, Belknap Press/Harvard University Press, 1993, pp. 1–14, especially p. 3. Broad overviews include S. Rowbotham, *Hidden from History: 300 Years of Women's Oppression and the Fight Against It*, London, Pluto Press, 1974. For accounts that commence in or focus on the nineteenth century see J. Lewis, *Women in England 1870–1930: Sexual Divisions and Social Change*, Brighton, Wheatsheaf, 1984; M. Vicinus, *Suffer and Be Still: Women in the Victorian Age*, London, Methuen, 1980; S. Alexander, 'Women's Work in Nineteenth Century London', in S. Alexander, *Becoming a Woman and Other Essays in Nineteenth and Twentieth Century Feminist History*, London, Virago, 1994, pp. 3–56.

5   For medicine, see, for example, E. Moberley Bell, *Storming the Citadel: The Rise of the Woman Doctor*, London, Constable, 1953; C. Blake, *The Charge of the Parasols: Women's Entry into the Medical Profession*, London, Virago, 1990. For education reform, see C. Dyhouse, *No Distinction of Sex? Women in British Universities 1870–1939*, London, UCL Press, 1995; F. Hunt, ed., *Lessons for Life? The Schooling of Girls and Women 1850–1950*, Oxford, Blackwell, 1987. Accounts of the removal of legal disabilities include L. Holcombe, *Wives and Property*, Oxford, M. Robertson, 1983.

6   S. Stanley Holton, *Suffrage Days: Stories from the Women's Suffrage Movement*, London, Routledge, 1996, pp. 1–2.

been those aspects of political activity that united women in purpose or membership. Initially, work concentrated on working-class women and socialist politics. This tendency, largely peculiar to Britain, arose from the early links between women's history and socialist history.[7] Early projects by Anna Davin, Jill Liddington and Jill Norris, and Sheila Rowbotham among others performed essential recovery work, shifting forgotten figures from the historical margins.[8] In common with many of its subjects, this work took class as its primary analytical category. As an indirect result, many middle-class women were sidelined and their political organisations largely ignored, with the consequence that we have national studies of women within many major socialist organisations but little material on Conservative women and as yet no monograph on the Women's Liberal Federation (WLF).[9]

More recently, attempts have been made to probe the difficulty of imposing a one-dimensional class analysis on all women socialists, especially when coping with those activists whose origins lay firmly in the middle classes but whose association with socialism challenged their respectability, a key facet of middle-class identity. The work of June Hannam and Karen Hunt in particular has provided a welcome reinterpretation of the complex composition of many socialist groups.[10] For the early nineteenth century, Amanda Vickery and Kim Reynolds have begun to investigate middle-class women's politics.[11] Against this, historians such as Olive Banks and Dale Spender have

7   See S. Leydesdorff, 'Politics, Identification and the Writing of Women's History', in A. Angerman, G. Binnema, A. Keunen, V. Poels and J. Zirkzee, eds, *Current Issues in Women's History*, London, Routledge, 1989, p. 11; also Hall, 'Feminism and Feminist History'.

8   Examples include A. Davin, 'Foreword', in D. Nield Chew, ed., *Ada Nield Chew: The Life and Writings of a Working Woman*, London, Virago, 1982, pp. ix–xxiv; J. Liddington and J. Norris, *One Hand Tied Behind Us: The Rise of the Women's Suffrage Movement*, London, Virago, 1978; S. Rowbotham, *Women, Resistance and Revolution*, London, Penguin, 1972.

9   Work on socialist movements includes C. Collette, *For Labour and For Women: The Women's Labour League 1906–18*, Manchester, Manchester University Press, 1989; J. Hannam, 'Women and the ILP 1890–1914', in D. James, T. Jowitt and K. Laybourn, eds, *The Centennial History of the Independent Labour Party*, Halifax, Ryburn Academic Publishing, 1992, pp. 205–28; K. Hunt, *Equivocal Feminists: The Social Democratic Federation and the Woman Question 1884–1911*, Cambridge, Cambridge University Press, 1996. For Conservative women, see J. Robb, *The Primrose League*, New York, Armstrong Press, 1968 [1942]. For the Women's Liberal Federation, see C. Hirshfield, 'Fractured Faith: Liberal Party Women and the Suffrage Issue in Britain, 1892–1914', *Gender and History*, vol. 2, no. 2, summer 1990, pp. 173–97; L. Walker, 'Party Political Women: A Comparative Study of Liberal Women and the Primrose League', in J. Rendall, ed., *Equal or Different: Women's Politics 1800–1914*, Oxford, Blackwell, 1987, pp. 165–91.

10 K. Hunt, *Socialist Women: Britain, 1880s to 1930s*, London, Routledge, 2001.

11 A. Vickery, *The Gentleman's Daughter: Women's Lives in Georgian England*, London, Yale University Press, 1998; K. D. Reynolds, *Aristocratic Women and Political Society in Victorian Britain*, Oxford, Clarendon Press, 1998.

shifted the focus away from the arena of party politics and sought to redefine all female political activists as primarily feminist, concerned with advancing the cause of women above that of political parties.[12] This trend can also be found in the work of non-feminist historians such as Brian Harrison, whose article in the *Historical Journal* explores the category of 'Women MPs'. An acceptance of gender differences and an assumption that women's politics is inherently different from men's lies at the heart of such work, while the fact that many women joined political parties and thus directed some of their campaigning energies against other women in opposing parties is given little consideration.[13]

Both of these approaches to women's politics are problematic, placing heavy emphasis on what are identified as factors unifying early female activists without seeking to locate them in any particular context. As a result, the concerns of all women involved in political campaigns can be presented as identical, and two oppositional 'correct' models for female political involvement emerge, those of the class-centred party activist or the woman-centred feminist. These models are presented as dominant and typical, and accordingly neither affords much space to women who question or differ from them. I have tried to take this into account in this book, which aims to uncover both unifying and divisive factors within women's political involvement.

As well as considering the shifting points of conflict between women in politics, my intention is to move away from national studies of organisations in order to consider how political involvement functioned for women who fitted it in around the concerns of paid and domestic employment, family and friendship. I have attempted to avoid constructing a political narrative centred, in the words of Georges Haupt, on 'congresses, good or bad leaders, right or wrong decisions' at the expense of the experiences and perceptions of the membership on whose behalf such high political agencies purported to act.[14] For many rank and file members, the presence of friends or the quality of dances were as important in deciding their choice of political identity as events on the national political stage. This consideration of politics as a recreational or cultural activity has been an important strand in European

---

12 See, for example, O. Banks, *Faces of Feminism*, Oxford, Martin Robertson, 1981; O. Banks, *Becoming a Feminist: The Social Origins of First Wave Feminism*, Brighton, Wheatsheaf, 1986; D. Spender, ed., *Women of Ideas and What Men have Done to Them*, London, Routledge, 1982; D. Spender, ed., *Feminist Theorists: Three Centuries of Women's Intellectual Traditions*, London, Women's Press, 1983.

13 B. Harrison, 'Women in a Men's House: The Women M.P.s 1919–1945', *Historical Journal*, vol. 29, no. 3, 1986, pp. 623–54.

14 G. Haupt, *L'Historien et le Movement Social*, p. 12, cited by M. A. Garcia, 'The Gender of Militancy: Notes on the Possibilities of a Different History of Political Action', *Gender and History*, vol. 11, no. 3, November 1999, pp. 461–74, p. 461.

labour history.[15] Historians such as Mary Nolan and Tony Judt have found that the methodology of a local study has been particularly useful in this approach, allowing for careful comparison of the appeal of particular socialist or union groups and for detailed mapping of the movement of individuals between them.[16] Eleanor Gordon and Patricia Hilden have extended this analysis into socialist women's politics and demonstrated how theories regarding women's involvement that emerged at national conferences translated into a variety of practices within particular locales.[17] In the United States, others including Carole Turbin and Elizabeth Faue have extended the local study successfully to consider a range of women's political activities and have found that the format allows them to engage closely with the themes of unity and division and to map the complex 'short-lived alliances' that were part of the day-to-day experience of politics.[18] Here, I have attempted to make similar use of this methodology. My purpose is to present, through a close examination of the activities of those political organisations that recruited a female membership, a detailed picture of the breadth of political activity available to women in the Merseyside area between 1890 and 1920.

The format of a local study moves interpretations of political activity from the decisions and alliances of a small number of national leaders to an investigation of how these affected the actions, priorities and affiliations of large numbers of individual members. It also allows a broad range of political organisations to be considered, and some conclusions to be drawn about their relative effectiveness when operating within the same geographical boundaries. Obviously, such boundaries are inherently specific, and I am not suggesting that the picture that I present for Merseyside would hold for the rest of Lancashire or Cheshire, let alone Britain. However, the breadth of activity that can be considered within a small area allows such issues as cross-

---

15 For example, C. Waters, *British Socialists and the Politics of Popular Culture 1884–1914*, Manchester, Manchester University Press, 1990; K. Callahan, '"Performing Inter-Nationalism" in Stuttgart in 1907: French and German Socialist Nationalism and the Political Culture of an International Socialist Congress', *International Review of Social History*, vol. 45, pt 1, April 2000, pp. 51–88.

16 T. Judt, *Socialism in Provence 1871–1914: A Study in the Origins of the Modern French Left*, Cambridge, Cambridge University Press, 1979; M. Nolan, *Social Democracy and Society: Working-Class Radicalism in Dusseldorf 1890–1920*, Cambridge, Cambridge University Press, 1981.

17 P. Hilden, *Working Women and Socialist Politics in France 1800–1914: A Regional Study*, Oxford, Clarendon Press, 1986; E. Gordon, *Women and the Labour Movement in Scotland*, Oxford, Clarendon Press, 1991.

18 C. Turbin, *Working Women of Collar City: Gender, Class and Community in Troy, New York, 1864–1886*, Chicago, University of Illinois Press, 1992, pp. 150–51. See also E. Faue, *Community of Suffering and Struggle: Women and the Labour Movement in Minneapolis 1915–45*, London, University of North Carolina Press, 1991; C. Stansell, *City of Women: Sex and Class in New York 1789–1860*, New York, Alfred A. Knopf, 1986.

organisational activity to be studied to an extent that would prove unmanageable on a national scale.[19] Organisations that have been presented as welcoming women on a national scale can allow individual members to erect unexpected barriers at branch level. Similarly, others that have appeared insignificant across the country can produce surprising centres of strength when viewed through the local lens.

The success (or lack thereof) of an organisation is particularly difficult to quantify. Electoral fortune is an obvious yardstick for political historians but is not particularly helpful in assessing the pre-franchise era of women's politics, or in considering organisations such as the WLF that did not seek independent office. Longevity might be another useful tool, although this too is less reliable when attempting to assess many suffrage organisations where largely single-issue campaigns floundered after the first moves towards enfranchisement in 1918. One factor common to all the organisations in this book was a desire to open up the formal world of public politics – street meetings, the public platform, the political column and the world of party organisation – to women. What I have attempted to do here, therefore, is to evaluate success in these fields by considering how many women were brought into political activity by particular bodies.

The Issue of Ideology and Practice

When considering why some organisations became much more effective at opening up the world of public politics to women, attention must be paid to the complex relationship between political theory and organisational practice. In the case of political organisations, ideology does not merely display psychological power;[20] rather, it influences debates that in turn prescribe organisational practices.[21] While this relationship is implicit throughout my text, my interpretation of different ideologies may require further clarification at this stage. The numerous political organisations available to Merseyside women between 1890 and 1920 can broadly be seen to be conforming to three ideological models based on theories of separate spheres,

---

19 For specific discussion of the local study and its role within suffrage history, see K. Cowman, '"Crossing the Great Divide": Inter-Organisational Suffrage Relationships on Merseyside 1895–1914', in C. Eustance, J. Ryan and L. Ugolini, eds, *A Suffrage Reader: Charting Directions in British Suffrage History*, London, Leicester University Press, 2000, pp. 37–52; also J. Hannam, '"I had not been to London": Women's Suffrage – A View from the Regions', in J. Purvis and S. Stanley Holton, eds, *Votes for Women*, London, Routledge, 2000, pp. 226–45.

20 For a discussion of the psychological power of ideology, see P. Levine, *Victorian Feminism*, London, Hutchinson, 1987, p. 13.

21 For a useful discussion of ideology and practice, see M. Povey, *Uneven Developments: The Ideological Work of Gender in Mid-Victorian England*, London, Virago, 1989, especially p. 3.

socialism and the more radical 'sex-class' analysis developed by some suffrage groups. I am acutely aware that each of these definitions has been the subject of much challenge, revision and debate over recent years. While they are far from perfect, they do offer a convenient means of encapsulating a broad spectrum of late nineteenth- and early twentieth-century debates, which might briefly be classified as follows.

Separate spheres: This once universal categorisation of women's position in the nineteenth century has undergone significant revision.[22] As a result, it is increasingly apparent that the rhetorical construction of distinct male and female worlds was at its strongest at the point at which its nebulous reality had been challenged to the point of collapse. Yet despite the increasing difficulty of identifying exactly how to ascribe boundaries to the dichotomous worlds of public and private in the nineteenth century, there remains a clear acknowledgement of such a divide within both the writings and the lives of many nineteenth-century women. Often this was far from submissive. Rather, as Pat Thane has explained,

> An important characteristic of many of the women who sought to promote women's causes [in the late nineteenth century]... was their acceptance of such essential elements of the ideology of separate spheres and their determined reinterpretation of it as a basis from which to promote the notion of *female superiority*.[23]

There was a tremendous paradox to be overcome by any woman attempting to justify her involvement in public politics by means of the theories of separate spheres, which generally stressed her unsuitability for this area. The ideology consequently fostered the development of a variety of models of political organisation for women. Each held in common an acceptance of essential biological differences. These could facilitate the formation of cross-class or cross-political alliances such as those that formed within the women's trade union movement, where all women were perceived as having some common interests. The Merseyside work of Jeannie Mole, wealthy

---

22 See, for example, A. J. Vickery, 'Golden Age to Separate Spheres: A Review of the Categories and Chronology of English Women's History', *Historical Journal*, vol. 36, no. 2, 1993, pp. 383–414; L. Kerber, 'Separate Spheres, Female Worlds, Women's Place: The Rhetoric of Women's History', *Journal of American History*, vol. 75, 1988, pp. 3–39; J. Rendall, 'Women and the Public Sphere', *Gender and History*, vol. 11, no. 3, November 1999, pp. 475–88; L. Davidoff, 'Regarding Some "Old Husbands' Tales": Public and Private in Feminist History', in L. Davidoff, *Worlds Between: Historical Perspectives on Gender and Class*, Cambridge, Polity Press, 1995, pp. 227–76. For a succinct overview, see R. Shoemaker and M. Vincent, eds, *Gender and History in Western Europe*, London, Arnold, 1998, pp. 177–80.

23 P. Thane, 'Late Victorian Women', in T. R. Gourvish and A. O'Day, eds, *Later Victorian Britain, 1867–1900*, London, Macmillan, 1988, p. 186.

socialist benefactress of many causes, and her Liberal colleagues who worked together towards the early unionisation of Liverpool's women workers, fits well into this pattern. However, Merseyside models were rarely cross-political. Local Conservative women's organisations drew their inspiration from the rhetoric of separate spheres, arguing that all women were by their very nature Conservatives who opposed the immorality of radicalism.[24] Simultaneously, the WLF based much of its local election work on the notion that their gender made its candidates ideally suited for local government work. The influence of this ideology appears the most deeply rooted of the three positions that I have identified, and enjoyed the greatest degree of longevity. Hence, having been vital to the model of organisation enjoyed by women trade unionists on Merseyside in the 1890s, it also underlay women's relief work during the First World War.

The socialist model: While some women considered their gender to be central to their political identity, many working-class women found themselves more attracted to the socialist movement whose rhetoric emphasised the primacy of class. The model of organisation that socialist parties developed for their female members rested on a particular understanding of gender oppression as being analogous to class oppression. The theoretical premise for this came from two texts, August Bebel's *Women in the Past, Present and Future* (1879) and Frederick Engels' *The Origins of the Family, Private Property and the State* (1884).[25] Bebel's text was initially made available in English through a series by Eleanor Marx and Edward Aveling in the *Westminster Review* and was mentioned as a popular work among Liverpool socialists in the 1890s.[26] Both *The Origins* and *Women* drew heavily on new anthropological data to provide a materialist interpretation of women's oppression, placing its emergence alongside the development of class society.

Male and female socialists were becoming increasingly suspicious of the growth of feminism, which was seen as an ideology that would benefit bourgeois women in the long term, while having the short-term disadvantage of turning working-class women away from socialism.[27] A theory that empha-

24 See G. Samuel, 'Women's Franchise: A Safeguard Against Socialism', *Conservative and Unionist Women's Franchise Review*, Issue 3, May 1910, pp. 30–31.
25 The dates cited are for the English editions. For an excellent discussion of the content of these texts and their implications for British socialism see Hunt, *Equivocal Feminists*, pp. 23–29.
26 E. Marx Aveling, 'The Woman Question', *Westminster Review*, New Series, LXIX, January 1886, pp. 207–22. For Liverpool, see *The Clarion*, 19 October 1895; also letter from Moira Anderson to Joseph Edwards, 3 February 1894, mentioning her correspondence with Bebel about his book, Joseph Edwards' Papers, Liverpool Record Office.
27 See R. Evans, *Comrades and Sisters: Feminism, Socialism and Pacifism in Europe 1870–1945*, Brighton, Wheatsheaf, 1987, p. 3; C. Sowerwine, *Sisters or Citizens? Women and Socialism in France since 1876*, Cambridge, Cambridge University Press, 1982, p. 88.

sised the common origins of class and women's oppression fostered the development of an ideology that held that class emancipation would bring women's emancipation along with it. Several prominent European socialists took this further, promoting policy issues that had previously been dismissed as feminist distractions. Women's suffrage, for example, was adopted as policy by the Second International in 1900, while the idea for an International Women's Day was taken up from the suggestion of Clara Zetkin in 1911.

Debates on these issues had indirect implications for the types of organisation offered to socialist women. Many parties offered separate women's sections that provided a space for members to select and organise their own campaigns from a socialist perspective.[28] These represented an important step forward for the politicisation of working-class women although the majority of middle- or upper-class women were excluded. Furthermore, in some instances, even separate women's sections were unsuccessful. Within Britain, the Social Democratic Federation (SDF) formed women's circles, but the Independent Labour Party (ILP) never achieved this aim, although its members could join the Women's Labour League (WLL) from 1906.[29] On Merseyside, the ILP recruited many women whose access to public politics depended on their successful competition with socialist men. The WLL only established itself successfully after the First World War while the SDF was never large enough to support a women's circle.

A 'sex-class': In the years immediately before the First World War, many politically active women found both of the preceding ideologies to be insufficient and began to develop an analysis of women's oppression based on the understanding that women constituted a distinct class. Although never formulated as explicitly as the separate spheres or socialist ideologies, its existence and progress is discernible in the writings of many suffragettes, especially in the Women's Social and Political Union (WSPU), and can still be identified in feminist thinking today.[30] It has been classified by Elizabeth Sarah as that strand of suffragette thought underpinned by 'an insistence on seeing *men* as the enemy and an autonomous feminist movement as fundamental to the challenge to male power'.[31]

This ideology drew important elements from the discourses of separate spheres and socialism. From separate spheres came the belief that biological

---

28 For a full discussion of the forms, sizes and relative successes of these, see C. Sowerwine, 'The Socialist Women's Movement from 1850 to 1940', in R. Bridenthal, C. Koonz and S. Stuart, eds, *Becoming Visible: Women in European History*, Boston, Houghton Mifflin, 2nd edn, 1987, pp. 399–428.

29 For the SDF see Hunt, *Equivocal Feminists*, pp. 217–50.

30 See J. Hanmer, C. Lunn, S. Jeffreys, and S. McNeill, 'Sex Class – Why is it Important to Call Women a Class?' *Scarlet Women*, vol. 5, pp. 8–10, n.d.

31 E. Sarah, 'Christabel Pankhurst: Reclaiming her Power', in Spender, ed., *Feminist Theorists*, p. 282.

similarities between women led to common experiences that transcended differences of class and race. Within the sex-class analysis this went beyond a belief that women were 'equal but different'. Many suffrage writings explain how biological differences make women superior to men, and refute calls for a secondary, supportive role for women. Dora Marsden, one-time organiser for the WSPU in Southport, explained that what was needed was a total transformation of society:

> We are conscious that we are concerned with the dissolution of one social order... Men are involved, but women differently from men because women themselves are very different from men. [This] difference... is the whole difference of a religion and a moral code. Men are pagans... women are wholly Christian.[32]

The importing of elements of socialist thinking clearly differentiates sex-class from separate spheres analysis. From the socialist model came the language of class along with the concept of class as a unifying factor. The oppression of women was no longer seen as simply analogous to that of the working class by the ruling class. Instead, women were conceived of as oppressed by a different ruling class, that of men. The economic concepts of class were taken, broken down and rearranged into new ones based wholly on gender, rendering class divisions between women irrelevant. The appropriation of the language of class gave a new edge to the rhetoric of sex-class feminists, who began to argue for a sex-based revolution:

> The sex war is going to be the biggest thing that civilisation has seen – big, that is, as far as the consequences are concerned. The... effects will be gigantic. And let [no-one] be deceived by the circumstances that men are fighting on women's side and women on men's here and there, in meetings and societies, in articles and what not. The great mass of armies on the two sides are similar. Men are on one side, women on the other. Watch for the clash.[33]

Sex-class ideology has the most obvious organisational implications of the three ideologies considered. Separate spheres ideology led to single-sex organisations, but also to mixed ones where men and women worked together to promote women's input in certain fields. The socialist position allowed women some separate space, but auxiliary to what were seen as the main parties and groups. Accepting sex-class ideology removed such ambiguities. Women were to unite in political organisations only with other women. These, it was anticipated, would provide them with unique opportunities to access the political sphere and affect a feminist transformation of

---

32 D. Marsden (possibly with M. Gawthorpe), editorial, *The Freewoman*, vol. 1. no. 4, December 1911.
33 'V. I. R.', *The Freewoman*, vol. 1, no. 4, December 1911.

society. On Merseyside, the WSPU offers the best example of organisational practice derived from this theory. Although a very small number of men were accepted as supporters of this group they were never admitted to formal membership, removing all gender-based competition for public space, with some interesting results.

* * *

Finally, I must offer some words about the organisation of this book. There are problems with limiting a study to organisations where membership involved a formal act of enrolment. Much recent work has concentrated on the importance of networks in women's politics, which demonstrate, in the words of Catharine Hall, the 'power that collectivities of women could have, whether in friendship groups... or in informal... organisations'.[34] However, while recognising that women had to challenge many sites of political power within and outside the state in the period, I believe that those within formal political organisations provide us with valuable insights into women's *collective* strategies when faced with an organised, gender-based opposition in a way in which the individualism of informal networks cannot. For this reason, I have selected a definition of public political activity based on that which involved women acting from within organisations where formal membership was a necessity. Reluctantly, I have therefore excluded the work done by Merseyside women on the School Boards and the Boards of Guardians, although a handful of individuals achieved local successes on these bodies prior to the First World War.[35]

Initially, my text was conceived as an investigation into the class composition of the suffrage movement on Merseyside, following the work of Liddington and Norris in the north of Lancashire. However, as the project progressed, I became more aware of, and concerned with, the ways in which women chose different political priorities at different times, and were able to move between issues of class and gender in ways that did not appear to be available to male activists. For this reason, I have spread my work from 1890 to 1920, enabling the full effects of both the struggle for the vote and the First World War to be considered. This book is organised in both a chronological and a thematic fashion. This is mainly due to the impact of the suffrage campaign, so vibrant and persuasive in the region, on local women's poli-

---

34 Hall, *White, Male and Middle Class*, pp. 14–15. See also E. Ross, 'Survival Networks: Women's Neighbourhood Sharing in London Before World War One', *History Workshop Journal*, 15, Spring 1983, pp. 4–27.

35 The Boards are studied in more detail in K. Cowman, 'Engendering Citizenship: The Political Involvement of Women on Merseyside, 1890–1920', unpublished DPhil thesis, University of York, 1994, Chapter 2, '"There are many Ladies who can do Useful Work": Women on Liverpool's Local Government Boards, 1890–1914', pp. 65–87.

tics. So many changes were brought about in local political groups through the efforts of the suffragettes that it proved impossible simply to chart the chronological development of individual organisations. This is most apparent in the case of the political parties that make their first appearance in Chapter 3 and return in Chapter 7. I hope that readers will find that the intervening discussion of suffrage politics enables the later party political problems that women faced to be viewed in context.

CHAPTER ONE

Introduction to Merseyside

'Merseyside' is a recent conception, a product of 1970s local government reorganisation. At the start of the nineteenth century the area covered by today's county boundaries belonged to south-west Lancashire and north-west Cheshire, two counties separated by the River Mersey. Yet a definite sense of 'Merseyside' is discernible in the 1890s, and the term itself was in common use after the First World War.[1] A sense of corporate identity emerged among the inhabitants of the Lancashire and Cheshire banks of the Mersey, helped by demographic relocations of the later nineteenth century, when wealthy individuals left the urban centre for the villages that became Merseyside's suburbs. For those who moved west across the river, Liverpool remained 'the city' just as it did for those who migrated north, south or east. Liverpool's business centre made and controlled their fortunes. Its cultural opportunities provided their leisure. Its shops clothed them and furnished their houses and its churches and chapels remained the focus of their spiritual lives. Consequently, many of the political organisations in this book that grew out of the personal networks of early members grew as Merseyside, not Liverpool or Wirral branches. So although much of this work concerns Liverpool, the somewhat anachronistic term 'Merseyside' is also used, particularly when dealing with organisations such as the suffrage groups whose membership spanned the Mersey. For the political parties that aimed at the city council, local government boards and parliament, Liverpool's municipal boundaries defined their spread and form my focus here.

As Tony Lane has pointed out, 'Liverpool is the only city in Britain… upon which other Britons have definite opinions.'[2] Yet while there are no end of recent newspaper articles tracing the industrial decline and urban

---

1   See, for example, A. Holt, ed., *Merseyside: A Handbook to Liverpool and District Prepared on the Occasion of the Meeting of the British Association for the Advancement of Science*, Liverpool, Liverpool University Press, 1923. The British Library also holds handbooks for various societies such as the Merseyside Rugby Union and the Merseyside Aquarian Society dating from the mid-1920s.
2   T. Lane, *Liverpool, Gateway of Empire*, London, Lawrence and Wishart, 1987, p. 13.

problems of the region, academic histories of Liverpool are scarce.[3] Compared with the self-conscious chronicles of municipal greatness that proliferated in later nineteenth-century Liverpool, the twentieth century rests largely unresearched, although there are works dealing with specific aspects of local history.[4] One exception is the substantial work of P. J. Waller which provides 'a history of over a century of recent political life'.[5] Waller adds much to our understanding of the development of Liverpool's political map, but says nothing specifically about how women contributed to this. Few women appear within his work, and no women's organisations are mentioned in the index, not even those affiliated to the local political parties that are so richly detailed. His main focus is 'sectarian conflict [which] especially injected political life with unusual intensity and moulded the popular Conservatism and immature Labour Party which were the hallmarks of Liverpool before the Second World War.'[6] Religious sectarianism remains a byword for Liverpool politics. Despite the recent challenge of John Belchem that in many areas of local life, 'the unbridgeable division was not sectarian, but sexual', there has been little attention paid as yet to the role of women in local politics.[7] Yet, in later Victorian Liverpool, women formed an increasingly visible group in many key areas of public and political life.

Later Victorian Liverpool had achieved international status through a

3   Newspaper articles generally follow events that bring Liverpool to national prominence. See, for example, British national press coverage of the Toxteth riots, August 1981; St Saviour's School, February–March 1982; the Heysel Stadium disaster, May 1985; the stand-off between the city council and central government, August–November 1986; coverage of the Hillsborough tragedy, April 1989.

4   Late nineteenth-century works include J. A. Picton, *Memorials of Liverpool, Historical and Topographical*, London, Longmans, 1875; R. Muir, *History of Liverpool*, London, Liverpool University Press, 1907. For works on specific examples of Liverpool see, among others, W. Hamling, *A Short History of the Liverpool Trades Council 1848–1948*, Liverpool, Liverpool Trades Council and Labour Party, 1948; Lane, *Gateway of Empire*; H. Hikins, ed., *Building the Union: Studies of the Growth of the Workers' Movement: Merseyside 1756–1967*, Liverpool, Toulouse Press, 1973; G. Anderson, *The Service Occupations of Nineteenth Century Liverpool*, Salford, Salford Papers in Economics, 1981; R. Holton, *British Syndicalism 1900–1914*, London, Pluto Press, 1976; M. Brogden, *On The Mersey Beat: Policing in Liverpool Between the Wars*, Oxford, Oxford University Press, 1991; E. Taplin, *Near to Revolution: The Liverpool General Transport Strike of 1911*, Liverpool, The Bluecoat Press, 1994; J. Belchem, *Merseypride: Essays in Liverpool Exceptionalism*, Liverpool, Liverpool University Press, 2000.

5   P. J. Waller, *Democracy and Sectarianism: A Political and Social History of Liverpool 1869–1939*, Liverpool, Liverpool University Press, 1981, p. xiv.

6   Waller, *Democracy and Sectarianism*, p. xv.

7   J. Belchem, 'Introduction: The Peculiarities of Liverpool', in J. Belchem, ed., *Popular Politics, Riot and Labour: Essays in Liverpool History 1790–1940*, Liverpool, Liverpool University Press, 1992, p. 7. For sectarianism see F. Neal, *Sectarian Violence: The Liverpool Experience 1819–1914: An Aspect of Anglo-Irish History*, Manchester, Manchester University Press, 1988; B. Whittingham-Jones, *The Pedigree of Liverpool Politics: White, Orange and Green*, Liverpool, privately published, 1936.

combination of innovative engineering and good geographical fortune that combined to make it the largest port in Britain. The increase in trade brought an impressive increase in population, which stood at 223,000 by 1841.[8] Much of this arose not from an increasing fecundity among native Liverpolitans, but from in-migration. Lancashire, Cheshire, Wales, Scotland and Ireland provided most of the first wave, who were joined by some from further afield – refugees from Europe or sailors from China and Africa who settled when in port. Although many of these newcomers found in Liverpool a poverty as vicious as anything they were attempting to escape, for others it represented a place of new opportunity. New to the area, and in some cases to wealth, they rapidly established themselves as a local aristocracy controlling civic affairs in a way that belied the fact that few of them could trace their roots back beyond three generations.[9] The rapid growth of Liverpool offered them a blank municipal canvas on which they could create themselves as gentry.

Although it was not until 1880 that Queen Victoria saw fit to grant the 'gateway' of her Empire city status, the local municipal elite had long anticipated the elevation and prepared accordingly. Sir James Picton, architect and councillor, published proposals for civic improvement in 1853 that aimed to 'render the external appearance of the town worthy of the exalted rank she seems destined to fill in the commerce of the world'.[10] These were enthusiastically taken up, alongside similar ventures. Radiating out from the centre, older buildings were demolished to make way for development befitting a grand city: a new Town Hall encasing what Edward VII reckoned 'the finest suite of rooms in England'; St George's Hall, claimed as one of the world's foremost neo-Grecian buildings; a magnificent round library; art galleries; an acclaimed museum; and a thriving Stock Exchange.[11] Fifty years after his original proposals, Picton surveyed the new Liverpool and spoke proudly of 'the radiance of [its] municipal glory... bright with the promise of success'.[12]

The civic leaders were equally keen to look to their own comforts. By the later nineteenth century many of the larger mercantile properties were being abandoned as increased trends towards suburban living saw a displacement of the middle classes from the city centre to large, opulent mansions mainly

---

8 M. Power, 'The Growth of Liverpool', in Belchem, ed., *Popular Politics*, p. 23; M. Simey, *Charitable Effort in Liverpool*, Liverpool, Liverpool University Press, 1951, p. 7.

9 Lane, *Gateway of Empire*, p. 53.

10 J. A. Picton, *Liverpool Improvements and How to Accomplish Them*, Liverpool, E. Howell, 1853, p. 24.

11 G. Chandler, *Liverpool*, London, Batsford, 1957, p. 213. For details of civic buildings and their dates see also Lane, *Gateway of Empire*.

12 J. A. Picton, *Memorials of Liverpool, Historical and Topographical, including a History of the Dock Estate. Second Edition Continued to the Reign of Queen Victoria*. Liverpool, Gilbert G. Walmsley, 1903, p. 550.

in the south. These openly aped the stately homes of the English country-side, and it is estimated that more of them were built in Liverpool than in any other city of the Empire, excepting London.[13] There were obvious geographical limits to this expansion. The River Mersey, despite a regular ferry service, was an impenetrable barrier as far as building was concerned; even the self-styled local aristocracy could not walk on water. Large mansions were also built on the Cheshire side of the river, but land everywhere was increasingly at a premium. The lack of available land close to the port coupled with new waves of work-seeking immigrants led to the growth of slums in the city centre and towards the north. Unscrupulous builders capitalised on the necessity for affordable housing and the notorious courts developed, bringing an unprecedented juxtaposition of extremes of wealth and poverty.[14]

Liverpool's new citizens had a wealth of political organisations from which to choose, party based or otherwise. Reflecting its tendency towards differ-ence, Liverpool retained a Conservative administration from 1890 to 1920 (and beyond), excluding a brief Liberal interlude from 1892–95. Local Conservatives masked class distinctions with 'a conspiracy of social breezi-ness' appealing to merchant and worker alike.[15] Local Liberalism presented a less fluid class profile. Its failure to achieve a significant base among the working class was largely due to the few grand families that personified Liberalism in Liverpool. Mostly these were recent arrivals who saw civic duty as a crucial part of their identity as a new municipal elite. Indeed, their very names became public projects, with Holt, Bowring, Rathbone and Picton enshrined in streets and buildings. This set who 'neither worked hard at elec-tions nor saw the need to do so' were more Whiggish than radical, tainted in the eyes of many fellow merchants through their family opposition to slavery, a position akin to heresy in a port so closely linked to the African trade.[16] They were joined in the later nineteenth century by a younger generation including the Muspratts, the Brights, the Crosfields and the Cherrys, who were slightly less patrician in outlook and keen to include women in their family-based politics, yet still rigidly rooted in their own class.

---

13 Lane, *Gateway of Empire*, p. 66. For a broader discussion of suburban living and respectability see L. Davidoff and C. Hall, *Family Fortunes: Men and Women of the English Middle Class 1750–1850*, London, Hutchinson, 1987, especially Chapter 8. For specific details on Liverpool see R. Lawton, 'Population Mobility and Urbanization: Nineteenth Century British Experience', in R. Lawton and R. Lee, eds, *Urban Population in Western Europe from the Late Eighteenth Century to the Early Twentieth Century*, Liverpool, Liverpool University Press, 1989, pp. 149–77.

14 See R. A. Armstrong, *The Deadly Shame of Liverpool*, Liverpool, G. Philip & Son, 1890, p. 4; Anon., 'Wealth and Want – Glitter and Grime', *The New Penny Magazine*, no. 216, vol. XVII, 1903, pp. 301–05.

15 Waller, *Democracy and Sectarianism*, p. 17.

16 Waller, *Democracy and Sectarianism*, p. 13.

Working-class political organisations also developed. The Liverpool Trades Council, founded in 1848, was active in building New Unionism.[17] An SDF branch formed in 1882, a non-party socialist group, the Workers Brotherhood, in 1886 and the local Fabian Society (FS) and ILP in 1892. All admitted men and women as members. Irish nationalism also had a formal party structure in Liverpool through the Irish National League of Great Britain which held council and parliamentary seats.[18] This organisation had strong roots among working-class electors, and returned Liverpool's first working-class councillor, J. G. Taggart.[19] Women were also able to organise through the Ladies' Branch of the Irish National League formed in 1891 by Miss Paul, daughter of a city councillor, but sadly no records of the activities of this organisation have been found.

For women of all classes, Liverpool offered many opportunities beyond their homes. As with other cities the public world of the streets was not rigidly masculine, but heavily contested. Working-class women, identified by dress and behaviour, found work on the streets as costers, hawkers or occasional prostitutes.[20] The street also formed the centre of their social world. The local paper, *The Liver*, in 1893 found thoroughfares impassable, 'crowded with the fair sex standing in groups from three to a dozen... laughing hilariously at each other as they relate "funny" stories'.[21] Middle-class ladies also found that the streets provided them with opportunities. Philanthropic work became increasingly public throughout the nineteenth century, and by 1893 the well-to-do members of the Food and Betterment Association had adopted uniforms when engaged in their work of taking 'food... to the homes of the sick poor and help where help is wanted'.[22] Equally visible was the local branch of Octavia Hill's Kyrle Society which gave the daughters of many prominent families their first taste of social work.[23] Gradually a more formal role also emerged as local government reforms opened up particular areas for women. Florence Melly and Ann Jane Davies served on the Liverpool

17 Hamling, *A Short History of the Liverpool Trades Council*.
18 For more detail of this organisation in Liverpool see L. W. Brady, *T. P. O'Connor and the Liverpool Irish*, London, Royal Historical Society, 1983.
19 See Waller, *Democracy and Sectarianism*, p. 100; R. Bean, 'Aspects of New Unionism in Liverpool 1889–91', in Hikins, ed., *Building the Union*, pp. 110–11.
20 On prostitution see Armstrong, *Deadly Shame*; W. Nott-Bower, *Fifty Two Years a Policeman*, London, Edward Arnold & Co., 1926, pp. 141–42; P. O'Mara, *The Autobiography of a Liverpool Slummy*, Liverpool, Bluecoat Press, repr. n.d.; P. Bartley, *Prostitution: Prevention and Reform in England 1860–1914*, London, Routledge, 2000, pp. 2–3.
21 *The Liver*, 21 January 1893.
22 V. Webster, 'What Women are Doing in Liverpool', *Womanhood*, vol. 6, no. 32, July 1901, p. 105. See also letter from H. Lee Jones, *Liverpool Daily Post*, 31 May 1895.
23 For the National Kyrle Society see C. E. Maurice, *The Life and Work of Octavia Hill*, London, Macmillan, 1913, pp. 317–18. For Liverpool see I. Ireland, *Margaret Beavan of Liverpool: Her Character and Work*, Liverpool, Henry Young & Sons, 1938, pp. 26–27.

School Board from its inception in 1870.[24] In 1893, Miss Jane Calderwood and Miss Johnson were elected to the West Derby Board of Guardians, to be followed by a steady trickle of female candidates across the city.[25]

Religion also offered opportunities for women to participate in public life. The strong element of Catholicism associated with twentieth-century Liverpool only emerged in the mid-nineteenth century. Prior to this, Liverpool had a Protestant lineage reaching back to the English Civil War. The influx of Irish immigrants from the 1840s added a particular edge to this, revitalising Orange Lodges which had formed in the early 1800s. The marching season became a time for prolonged battles involving men and women, including the infamous 'Belfast Mary' who allegedly required six policemen to arrest her.[26] Religious identities were also frequently assumed by women in their public work. Margaret Simey has shown Unitarians to be at the forefront of local philanthropy in the 1850s.[27] Over time their chapels at Hope Street, Renshaw Street and Ullet Road became key sites for radical philanthropy, often overshadowed by a Liberal philosophy. By the end of the century, these had been joined by more radical Baptist chapels. Of these, the most notable was Pembroke Chapel which soon came to represent much more than philanthropy, hosting many political meetings including suffrage and socialist gatherings. Women played a full role in the running of Pembroke; the suffragette and ILP member Hattie Mahood was a deacon there, and Ethel Snowden an active member of the congregation who once preached from its pulpit.[28] Philanthropy was not always immune from sectarian divisions, and women's experience of it was not universal. Within Catholic philanthropic enterprise a different view of gender prevailed as outlined in the work of Martha Kanya-Forstner, who has argued that women were more likely to be the recipients than the distributors of charity.[29] Yet religion was not always a divisive factor in women's politics. The personal affiliations of many individual women within particular parties or suffrage

24 On their work there see Cowman, 'Engendering Citizenship', Chapter 3; P. Hollis, *Ladies Elect: Women in English Local Government 1865–1914*, Oxford, Clarendon Press, 1987, p. 185; Simey, *Charitable Effort in Liverpool*, p. 115; *Liverpool Review of Politics, Literature and the Arts*, 30 July 1898; *The Liverpool Mercury*, 9 May 1901.

25 For women on the Board of Guardians see Cowman, 'Engendering Citizenship', Chapter 3; *Liverpool Review of Politics, Literature and the Arts*, 8 April 1893; 15 April 1893; 22 December 1894.

26 Whittingham-Jones, *The Pedigree of Liverpool Politics*, p. 52.

27 Simey, *Charitable Effort in Liverpool, passim.*

28 I. Sellers, 'Nonconformist Attitudes in Later Nineteenth Century Liverpool', *Transactions of the Historical Society of Lancashire and Cheshire*, CXIV, 1962, pp. 215–39. See also I. Sellers, *Salute to Pembroke*, unpublished typescript, Liverpool Record Office.

29 M. Kanya-Forstner, 'Defining Womanhood: Irish Women and the Catholic Church in Liverpool', in D. M. MacRaild, ed., *The Great Famine and Beyond: Irish Migrants in Britain in the Nineteenth and Twentieth Centuries*, Dublin, Irish Academic Press, 2000, pp. 168–87, especially p. 175.

organisations clearly demonstrate how religious differences could be subsumed into other causes.

For women seeking political activity, Victorian Merseyside offered many choices, often predetermined by external factors. Some women saw their primary allegiance as being to their class, others to their religion or to a political party (often dictated by class). These allegiances were not rigidly fixed: increasingly in the twentieth century a new group of women activists emerged who viewed gender as their main identity and sought organisations that would allow them to work with other women, regardless of their class, religion or political affiliation. Also, there were occasions when those who normally prioritised one of these identities chose to subjugate it temporarily in favour of another, as through the cross-class and cross-party alliances found in local suffrage groups. The politics of the workplace, frequently demonstrated through trade union activities, were important, as were the wider concerns of philanthropy and education. Yet all women seeking public political life in Liverpool in this period faced particular, common challenges. Many wider conventions had to be broken, whatever their personal perspective on their own activity might have been. The various routes that women adopted and adapted to overcome these were never straightforward or uncontested, as the following chapters will demonstrate.

CHAPTER TWO

'The workwomen of Liverpool are sadly in need of reform': Women in Trade Unions, 1890–1914[1]

The final decade of the nineteenth century witnessed two important devel-opments in attitudes towards the organisation of working-class women. The rise of New Unionism among unskilled and casual workers brought many women into trade unions where they received their first taste of public work.[2] In unions they united with other working-class women but often found that their first battles were fought not against capitalist employers but against male trade unionists fearful of the whole idea of women's employment.[3] Simultaneously, increasing public concern about sweated female labour encouraged many upper- and middle-class feminists to act to improve the lot of working women. Their heavily gendered approach, usefully described as 'social feminist', believed that women (often from upper- or middle-class backgrounds) were best suited to solving the problems of working-class women.[4] Social feminists used the techniques of investigation and publicity. Their campaigns aimed at small-scale reform and they avoided the larger economic critiques of New Unionism. Yet, faced with strong hostility from male unionists, many women workers found a sympathetic hearing from social feminists. Consequently, despite their solidly working-class member-

1 *Liverpool Review of Politics, Society, Literature and the Arts* (hereafter *Liverpool Review of Politics*), 13 September 1890.
2 See, for example, the route taken into politics by Ada Nield Chew or Julia Varley: D. Nield Chew, ed., *The Life and Writings of a Working Woman*, London, Virago, 1982; D. Thom, 'The Bundle of Sticks: Women, Trade Unionists and Collective Organization Before 1918', in A. V. John, ed., *Unequal Opportunities: Women's Employment in England 1800–1918*, Oxford, Blackwell, 1986, pp. 261–89. See also the links between trade unionism and suffrage cited in Liddington and Norris, *One Hand Tied Behind Us*.
3 For a discussion of male hostility see S. O. Rose, 'Gender Antagonism and Class Conflict: Exclusionary Strategies of Male Trade Unionists in Nineteenth Century Britain', *Social History*, vol. 13, no. 2, May 1988, pp. 191–207; S. Boston, *Women Workers and the Trade Unions*, London, Lawrence & Wishart, 1987, pp. 42–48 also explores this point.
4 For the term 'Social Feminist' see E. F. Mappen, 'Strategists for Change: Social Feminist Approaches to the Problems of Women's Work', in John, ed., *Unequal Opportunities*, p. 256.

ship, early women's unions were often based on alliances of gender rather than on those of class.

Women's unionisation did not progress equally throughout Britain, but neither did women's work patterns. As Jane Lewis has identified, there was no universal increase in female labour before the First World War.[5] The particular areas where women did form a mass female workforce within a dominant local industry such as the Lancashire textile factories or the Leicester hosiery trade have received much historical attention.[6] However, such large concentrations of women appear exceptional when compared with other urban centres such as London, Birmingham or the Potteries. Here, women were restricted to particular trades within industries or remained as outworkers in small units or their own homes. Unionisation was patchy in such districts, to say the least.

Against this overview, Liverpool appears less exceptional although very different from northern Lancashire. Unlike the cotton towns, women are barely visible in Liverpool's trade union history.[7] The city lacked a solid manufacturing base, and there were no large factories on hand.[8] There was a female workforce, estimated at 28,000 in 1895, mostly employed in small-scale or sweated trades such as tailoring, dressmaking, millinery, upholstery or book folding.[9] Other women relied on domestic service or on casual trades such as hawking. The worst conditions were undoubtedly experienced by those who sought work in the 443 known brothels, or in their vicinity.[10]

The notorious difficulty of organising casual trades coupled with the lack of large concentrations of women workers explain the weakness of female unionism in Liverpool compared with Greater Lancashire. Liverpool women's experiences contrasted markedly with those of local working men whose organisation dated back to the establishment of an embryonic Trades

---

5 Lewis, *Women in England*, p. 149.
6 For Lancashire see Liddington and Norris, *One Hand Tied Behind Us*; S. O. Rose, *Limited Livelihoods: Gender and Class in Nineteenth Century England*, Berkeley, University of California Press, 1992, pp. 154–84. For Leicester see, for example, N. G. Osterud, 'Gender Divisions and the Organisation of Work in the Leicester Hosiery Industry', in John, ed., *Unequal Opportunities*, pp. 45–70; also Rose, *Limited Livelihoods*, p. 6.
7 For national studies see Boston, *Women Workers and the Trade Unions* and S. Lewenhak, *Women in Trade Unions*, London, Ernest Benn, 1977, both of which comment on the lack of work on female unions when compared with that on male ones. For Liverpool see L. Grant's study 'Women's Work and Trade Unionism in Liverpool 1890–1914', *North West Labour History*, 7, 1980–81, pp. 65–83. Grant's findings form the basis of J. A. Golding's 'An End to Sweating? Liverpool's Sweated Workers in Legislation', *North West Labour History*, 21, 1996–97, pp. 3–29.
8 D. Caradog Jones, *A Social Survey of Merseyside*, London, University of Liverpool/Hodder & Stoughton, 1934, vol. 1, pp. 30–31.
9 J. Mole, 'Women Workers in Liverpool', *The Liverpool Pulpit*, no. 39, vol. 4, April 1895, p. 35.
10 The figure for 1889 comes from Nott-Bower, *Fifty One Years a Policeman*, pp. 141–42.

Council in 1848, formed to safeguard 'trades unions from suppression by the employers' use of criminal law'.[11] In the 1890s New Unionism encouraged this Trades Council to reach out beyond skilled trades, and it recruited 15,000 dockers and 13,000 firemen along with sailors and smaller tradesmen.[12] Local New Unionism in Liverpool encouraged a conciliatory approach from workers towards their employers, and adopted a radical Liberal as well as a socialist political character.[13] However, it reflected its national counterpart in attempts to reach unskilled workers, particularly women. There were precedents for this. In 1879 the London-based Women's Protective and Provident League (WPPL) helped to form the Liverpool Working Women's Union.[14] This had a brief success in organising tailoresses into a society based on mutual aid.[15] Financial problems (including embezzlement by a male trustee) confounded the society, and by the late 1880s both it and the Working Women's Union were in a moribund state, forcing organisers to begin again.[16]

Jeannie Mole and the Liverpool Workwomen's Society

The new campaign was initiated by Jeannie Mole, the acknowledged 'pioneer' of socialism in Liverpool.[17] Her second marriage to Keartland Mole, a fruit merchant, had brought her to Liverpool in 1879 at the age of 38. By then she was already a socialist and had worked in London slums and for black rights in America.[18] In 1886 she founded the Workers' Brotherhood, Liverpool's second socialist society and brought speakers of the calibre of William Morris and Edward Carpenter to its meetings.[19] Two years later she began the work with which she was to become synonymous – organising women workers.[20]

---

11 In 1888 this became the Liverpool and Vicinity United Trades Council. See Hamling, *A Short History of the Liverpool Trades Council*, pp. 15–18.
12 Bean, 'Aspects of New Unionism', pp. 99–120; Waller, *Democracy and Sectarianism*, pp. 102–06
13 Mersey Quays and Railway Carters' Union Statement, October 1890, in Bean, 'Aspects of New Unionism', p. 113.
14 Women's Protective & Provident League Annual Report, 1885.
15 *Women's Union Journal*, April 1881.
16 Women's Provident and Protective League Annual Report, 1882.
17 Grey Quill (pseud.), 'The Liverpool Fabian Society: Some Memories of Strenuous Days and Personalities That are Gone', undated newspaper article, Fabian Society Archives.
18 *The Labour Annual*, 1895, p. 180; *The Liverpool Labour Chronicle*, January 1896; *The Labour Prophet*, April 1896.
19 A branch of the SDF had been formed in 1882, but this appears to have collapsed. See H. Pelling, *The Origins of the Labour Party*, Oxford, Oxford University Press, 1965, p. 24. For the Brotherhood see Hamling, *A Short History of the Liverpool Trades Council*, p. 24; *The Liverpool Labour Chronicle*, January 1896.
20 See Obituary, *Liverpool Daily Post*, 23 April 1912; *Labour Leader*, 26 April 1912.

Although Mole's background was unremarkable, her second marriage brought her a degree of wealth.[21] Her insistence on combining this with socialism irritated some contemporary observers, and she and her husband were sometimes accused of hypocrisy, particularly in regard to employment practices in his fruit business.[22] Later accounts of her life have also dwelt on this point, emphasising her wealth to the detriment of her political beliefs.[23] Yet these approaches underestimate the complexities surrounding issues of gender, class and politics in the later nineteenth century, and give little indication of the importance or historical relevance of Mole's political beliefs. The Moles were comfortably off, with sufficient social status to access the elite networks around such institutions as the Rathbone Literary Club, of which they were briefly members.[24] However, rather than remain in fashionable society, Jeannie Mole chose to move beyond this, and, through her enthusiastic embrace of socialism, placed herself outside the bounds of conventional respectability.[25] If anything, her social position made this more difficult for her. As an early adherent to dress reform she consistently wore a rather peculiar version of a Greek gown which instantly distinguished her from Liverpool's fashion-conscious ladies.[26] One of her fellow activists later remembered the outcry when she marched unemployed workers along Castle Street in the heart of the business district, passing many of her husband's colleagues.[27] Nor was Mole shocked by the less pleasant features of working-class life. When a report in *The Liver* suggested that she was forced to 'retire in disgust' at the antics of three drunken men who were disrupting a meeting for the unemployed at which she was the only woman present, she wrote in their defence:

> I left... simply to catch the... train... It is not fair to speak harshly of working men because they are too talkative, like the rest of mankind.[28]

21 She was the daughter of a Warrington whitesmith. See biographical entries in J. Bellamy and J. Saville, eds, *Dictionary of Labour Biography*, vol. IX, pp. 220–23; also *New Dictionary of National Biography* (forthcoming).

22 See *The Liver*, 9 September 1893; 29 September 1893; *Liverpool Review of Politics*, 13 September 1890; *Porcupine*, 15 September 1894.

23 See N. C. Solden, *Women in British Trade Unions 1874–1976*, London, Gill & Macmillan, 1978, p. 31; Grant, 'Women's Work and Trade Unionism in Liverpool', p. 71; Bean, 'Aspects of New Unionism', p. 111; Hamling, *A Short History of the Liverpool Trades Council*, p. 24.

24 Rathbone Literary Club Minute Book, 16 December 1894, Liverpool Record Office.

25 For a similar analysis of a middle-class lady who espoused socialism at the expense of her social networks see J. Hannam, *Isabella Ford*, Oxford, Blackwell, 1989, pp. 46–47.

26 *The Clarion*, 12 March 1898. Jeannie Mole, who adopted the dress in the 1860s, gave the pattern to Caroline Martyn and Julia Dawson, both of whom also wore it.

27 Grey Quill, 'The Liverpool Fabian Society'.

28 *The Liver*, 17 February 1894.

Mole's socialism was broad and inclusive. She held joint membership of the FS, ILP and the SDF. She disliked any 'rabid denunciation of capitalists': her version of socialism was 'sufficiently inclusive to admit even the rich' but only if they were willing to build a new society rather than a reformed version of the existing one.[29] Mole realised that even 'model' employers like Lord Leverhulme made workers 'a mere part of a great machine'.[30] Consequently, the Workers' Brotherhood was committed to 'the overthrow of... monopolies which... brutalise the workers'. Yet Mole's socialism was also coloured by feminism, and she spoke movingly of the 'beautiful future which... Socialism will bring... [with] our women... in freedom, side by side with our men'.[31] Her fusion of socialism and feminism can be seen to good effect in her attempts to unionise women workers. In these campaigns, she articulated exactly what distinguished her approach from the social feminism of other middle-class campaigners. These, she felt, were 'fearful lest they should lose their position as alms givers and... naturally out of fellowship with working women'.[32] By contrast, Mole's socialism gave her an economic perspective which she believed helped to unite her in a common bond with working-class women, who she frequently referred to as her 'sisters'.[33]

As a socialist feminist she also had grand visions of the potential of unionisation for altering the lives of some of the poorest of Liverpool's women workers. The idea of a protective society was only a small part of her aims. More important to her was unionisation's potential to politicise women, widen their horizons and bring them into the socialist movement. First and foremost Mole stated that women workers ought to be 'more discontented... with a bad system' and wish to change it.[34] Yet, although she was clearly irritated by apathy, she realised that it was difficult to stand out against a system that placed individual workers in strong competition with one another, and recognised no common cause. If unions could inspire 'a spirit of loyalty to their comrades' or 'the spirit of comradeship that comes of labouring and suffering and rejoicing in common' then the problems of such selfishness might be overcome.[35] The key to achieving this, she felt, was to allow unions a social and recreational as well as an organisational function. If working-class women were given opportunity to meet together and encounter new ideas, their developing solidarity would both reinforce the union and extend the scope of what it could accomplish. Educational classes would be

29 *The Liverpool Labour Chronicle*, January 1896.
30 *The Liverpool Labour Chronicle*, February 1898.
31 *The Liverpool Labour Chronicle*, April 1897.
32 *The Porcupine*, 15 January 1894.
33 Jeannie Mole, 'Liverpool's Industrial Women', *The Liverpool Labour Chronicle*, October 1894.
34 *The Liverpool Labour Chronicle*, April 1897; October 1894.
35 *The Porcupine*, 15 September 1894

provided. Entertainments would also be offered, and families would be welcomed to encourage the spread of socialist ideals within households.[36]

It was in 1888 that Mole first began to put these ideas into practice with others from the Workers' Brotherhood. A campaign to unionise Liverpool's women workers was initiated. Fred Willis, Mole's son and a founder member of the Brotherhood, published a series of articles in *The Liverpool Review* containing the results of his investigations into conditions in local sweated trades. The series coincided with a large local demonstration against the sweating system at which Willis, in a letter, called for the establishment of a local committee of the WPPL.[37] This was an obvious step. The WPPL was a prominent national body, known in Liverpool for its earlier efforts among tailoresses. More importantly, it was well resourced and able to send Clementina Black to support the Liverpool initiative with a week-long campaign.[38] There was an implicit tension between Mole's socialist feminism, which envisaged unionism as an important means of politicising working women, and the aims of the League, established by middle-class feminists who were less concerned with changing women's lives beyond the workplace.[39] Nevertheless the campaign ensured that by May the plight of sweated women workers was being keenly debated locally, whereupon Willis wrote to the Trades Council 'suggesting the promotion of a Women's Protective Society'.[40] The Trades Council was not overwhelmingly enthusiastic, but agreed to appoint a small committee to consider the question.[41] The committee met regularly throughout the summer with Mole a keen co-opted attender. The following January it organised and sponsored the inaugural meeting of the Liverpool Workwomen's Society (LWS), affiliated to the WPPL, aimed primarily at unionising local women.[42]

Despite being the main force behind the LWS and serving as its secretary from 1889, Mole was unable to mould the entire committee to her socialist views. Prominent local welfare campaigners were drawn to the society, seeing in it the opportunity to encourage 'good' employers and harmonious industrial relations rather than use women's poor working conditions as a basis for drawing them into political consciousness. Local Liberals supported the LWS in the hope that it would 'ensure a decent… if a frugal existence' for working women rather than achieve any significant change in the social order.[43] Radical clergymen such as Canon Major Lester and the Rev. R.A. Armstrong, an anti-vice campaigner, hoped that the LWS would combat

---

36 See her advice to 'a neglected wife', *The Liverpool Labour Chronicle*, January 1896.
37 *The Liverpool Courier*, 24 May 1888.
38 Women's Trade Union League Annual Report, 1889.
39 Rose, *Limited Livelihoods*, p. 182.
40 Liverpool Trades Council Minutes, May 1888, Liverpool Record Office.
41 Liverpool Trades Council Minutes, July 1888, Liverpool Record Office.
42 *Women's Union Journal*, November 1888.
43 *Liverpool Review of Politics*, 26 January 1889.

prostitution by protecting against 'the temptations to which... working girls were subjected and the keenness which was given to their condition by hunger and cold'.[44] This, the Vice President of the Trades Council affirmed, ought to be its main role:

> The miserable wages given in some workshops to their women workers had to be supplemented in a way he did not dare to mention but which [the audience] would readily understand. This society will protect these young women.[45]

Male supporters of the LWS were also keen to remove any suspicion that it might be thought a feminist organisation. Rather than challenge patriarchy they hoped that it would eventually remove women from the workplace and

> immensely benefit the organisation of men... If masters found that a certain fair price had to be paid for an article, whether made by a man or a woman... the proper order of things would result – the man would be the breadwinner and the woman the housekeeper.[46]

Although Mole believed in 'giving... women... a recognised and honourable position as bread-winners' the majority of her LWS colleagues disagreed.[47] The organisation declared that in an ideal world a woman would be at home, able to 'minister directly to the needs of her own people'. Only because the present was far from ideal would the LWS attempt to assure working women of 'the advantages of mutual counsel and assistance'.[48]

While she refrained from public dissent, Mole, now the official organising secretary, hoped for far more from the LWS. To further her wider aims she devised ways to bring the newly unionised women together, fostering an associational culture in order to strengthen feelings of collectivity and comradeship. She encouraged an active view of membership, and received subscriptions at a weekly meeting where 'a few words of encouragement' could be passed on to newer recruits. She also realised the importance of shared leisure in advancing a sense of unity within the society. Weekly gymnastic classes were held, and the local Ruskin Society was invited to provide tuition in country dancing. A library was put together to encourage the women to take an interest in social and political affairs, and once a month an entertainment was provided.[49] To cement these initiatives Mole argued

44 R. A. Armstrong, quoted in unidentified press cutting, Liverpool Trades Council Minutes, 4 January 1889.

45 Unidentified press cutting, Liverpool Trades Council Minutes, 4 January 1889.

46 Unidentified press cutting, Liverpool Trades Council Minutes, 4 January 1889.

47 *The Porcupine*, 15 September 1894.

48 *Women's Union Journal*, November 1888.

49 *Women's Union Journal*, April 1889.

for the provision of a central building where all the unions could meet, something she felt 'would... give the movement stability'.[50]

Throughout the competing discourses of their organisers, the voices of the working women themselves remained notably absent. Recruitment was slow. After its inauguration, the LWS had targeted the likely trades of cigar making, bookbinding and tailoring. Seventy women enrolled in the first week, but two months later membership had barely doubled, standing at 25 tailoresses, 43 cigar makers and 104 book folders.[51] Mole blamed the lack of progress on the absence of suitable premises (they had only the schoolroom of a church) which thwarted her plans for a reading room and nightly drop-in centre, leaving the LWS 'unable to fulfil its mission to the thousands of industrial women in Liverpool'.[52] An appeal for funds was begun, but by June no premises had been found.[53] The target membership began to drift away, disillusioned. Significantly, their lack of input was not yet considered a major reason for the lack of success.

The Tailoresses' Strike

Matters altered in the following year when the first strike by local working women dramatically altered public attitudes towards them. In May 1890, the LWS organised the Liverpool Tailoresses and Coatmakers' Union among sweated workers. Spurred on by the recent unionisation of men in the same trade, which had achieved significant improvement in working conditions, 300 women signed up. With Miss Alice Duggan, a tailoress, as leader and Mole as secretary, the union looked to the LWS not for protection, but for support for direct action. On 10 June 1890, the new union led 400 of its members out on strike. Their demands were simple: a two-hour reduction in their working day with no associated loss of earnings, and the abolition of piecework.[54]

The strike faced ferocious opposition from employers who had combined themselves into a 'Master Tailor's Association' the previous year. Dismissed by the Trades Council as 'an association of sweaters', they worked closely together to break the strike, disputing claims of low wages in a statement that also promised 'a time reduction only with a wage reduction'.[55] Many attempts were made to combat the image promoted by the strikers of an exploitative, sweated industry. One Master said that his workers

50 Unidentified press cutting, Liverpool Trades Council Minutes, 1 February 1889.
51 WPPL Annual Report, 1889; *Women's Union Journal*, March 1889.
52 *Women's Union Journal*, April 1889.
53 *Women's Union Journal*, June 1889.
54 *Liverpool Daily Post*, 13 June 1890.
55 *Liverpool Daily Post*, 11 June 1890.

came late to work... and as soon as it got to half past twelve they began to send message girls round to see about their pies, puddings and other things... when it struck one o'clock they [stopped]... but it was five or ten minutes after two before they settled down to work... considering the time... they took up talking about novels, dresses, bonnets & etc... their day was not long.[56]

Others threatened to replace the women with men. Even the more conciliatory employers denied any problems in their trade. They dismissed the strikers as 'misled' by outside agencies, certain that they would capitulate if presented with 'the full facts'.[57]

Yet, despite their unity, the Master Tailors failed to convert public opinion. The LWS was largely conceived within popular discourse around the shameful aspects of sweated labour, and its unsuitability for a 'Great City' such as Liverpool. The fact that the striking tailoresses embodied this ensured them financial support from wealthy Liberals including the Muspratts and the Meade-Kings.[58] The strike was highly public, its associated spectacle removing the strikers from their dark backroom workshops. Once on public view, the strikers quickly recognised that respectability was essential to retaining public sympathy. An image of them as 'deserving' poor was carefully constructed. Alice Duggan, 'a smart business-like young lady' emphasised that the strike posed no threat to a social order based on sexual difference. Equal pay was never an issue, as her members were 'quite content' without it. They accepted that 'The only reason that a man gets more wages than a woman for doing the same work is that a man is a man and a woman is a woman.' The impression of the strikers as meek and exploited was so convincing that the public remained on their side when they moved into direct action, haranguing those who were still working at their workplaces. While the Liberal *Daily Post* was dismayed to find 'fair strikers... demonstrating in a somewhat hostile manner against those who do not fall in with their views', it was able to reassure its readers that the strikers still 'presented a very respectable appearance... [and were] a very intelligent class... much above the average working girl'.[59] This respectability ensured that 'the girls... were soon induced to desist from their efforts to bring out the black-legs', thus removing any fear that they may be developing a radical edge to their campaign.

The Trades Council also approved of the strike, and offered its support and experience. Both proved crucial when some of the women wavered and considered returning to work. Trades Council leaders urged them to 'stand

56 *Liverpool Daily Post*, 12 June 1890.
57 *Liverpool Daily Post*, 12 June 1890.
58 Balance Sheet, Liverpool Trades Council Records, June 1889–December 1890.
59 *Liverpool Daily Post*, 12 June 1890.

firm' against an offer of a one-hour reduction by middlemen.[60] A Mr Goodman addressed the girls personally on behalf of the Council and assured them that 'they had nothing to fear' in continuing.[61] His intervention persuaded the strikers to hold out, and by 20 June they returned 'very jubilant' to work having won 'two hours reduction in the day's work [and] no reduction in wages'.[62]

Yet, in the aftermath of its success, the Union floundered. Once the excitement of the strike had evaporated, the women quickly lost interest in weekly business meetings. In 1893, Alice Duggan attempted to reconstitute the Union, but without a grievance she was unable to persuade women of its relevance and it dwindled away to almost nothing. The LWS also suffered from the problem of convincing women to remain active in unions when there was no particular cause to be fought. The society had given much help to the tailoresses. Mole had been particularly active, but found that retaining women in the union proved impossible. Almost immediately after the strike Mole appealed to WPPL headquarters to save her society. A Miss Abraham and a Mrs Barber were sent to Liverpool where they found the position so serious that their advised course of action was to abandon the LWS temporarily until the Trades Union Congress met in Liverpool in September.

The Congress attracted large numbers of unionised women from outside the city, and the LWS organisers hoped that their presence would prove inspirational. They even went so far as to make and display a banner for a non-existent Liverpool Laundress's Union, hoping that the sight of it in the large closing-day procession would encourage laundresses to come forward.[63] A large fringe meeting was also held, where an audience of 3,000 saw the LWS relaunch itself as the Liverpool Society for the Promotion of Women's Trade Unions (LSPWTU) with Jeannie Mole as treasurer.

This second society was able to attract more solid political support, as well as philanthropic patronage. Socialism was a growing force in local politics. The Workers' Brotherhood had given way to the Liverpool Socialist Society which was formed in 1889 and closely associated with the SDF.[64] Branches of the FS and the ILP were formed in 1892 and 1893. A socialist newspaper, *The Liverpool Labour Chronicle*, provided each of these groups with a platform. The Trades Council was also keen to become more involved with the LSPWTU. Influenced by favourable impressions from the tailoresses' strike, it agreed to a request to admit women members.[65] Aside from a few minor dissents it was committed to this, going so far as to find a meeting place 'other

---

60 *Liverpool Daily Post*, 13 June 1890.
61 *Liverpool Daily Post*, 13 June 1890.
62 Women's Trade Union League Annual Report, 1890.
63 *Liverpool Review of Politics*, 25 October 1890.
64 *Justice*, 25 January 1890.
65 Liverpool Trades Council EC Minutes, 1 October 1890.

than a licensed public house' to encourage women's attendance.[66]

Mole now began a vigorous propaganda campaign to rekindle enthusiasm for unionisation among those trades previously organised by the LWS. New groups were also sought out, particularly in small workforces where the personal networks of employees might promote the associational culture that she thought necessary to maintaining interest in a union when no strike threatened. Fifty-three laundresses did come forward after the Trades Union Congress (TUC), and were unionised.[67] Meetings were also held among the sack and bag makers and marine sorters, who organised along with book folders and upholsteresses. Again, the main emphasis was on the protective benefits of combination through sickness and unemployment assistance, but again Mole sought to expand this, believing that a union ought to move beyond self-interest to develop 'many of the qualities which make good citizens in its members'.[68] She opened the Society's rooms in Wilton Street on Monday evenings to receive members' subscriptions and also to provide a recreational space with sewing and singing classes and a monthly entertainment. Yet, as with earlier attempts, women workers largely resisted these efforts and stayed away, seeing little benefit in unionisation beyond insurance or aid in particular campaigns.

Unsurprisingly, it was another strike that gave the LSPWTU its greatest success. This time an even smaller trade was involved, that of tobacco-roll spinning which employed only 361 women. This was a notoriously unpleasant occupation, carried out by gaslight in a cellar which had to be filled with steam to prevent the tobacco from drying out. Wages averaged five shillings a week, 'less than enough to buy plain food, clothing and shelter'.[69] Workers were also plagued by a system of fines which reduced their already meagre wages for inconsequential breaches of regulations. It was these fines that provided the main grievance in the strike. Organised groups of socialists moved in to help Mole, with the ILP and particularly the FS arranging collections and meetings which *The Liverpool Labour Chronicle* reported with enthusiasm.[70] With this help, the strikers won a small increase of a shilling a week in wages, and, more importantly, succeeded in abolishing the fines.[71]

---

66 Liverpool Trades Council Minutes, 3 October 1890.

67 *Liverpool Review of Politics*, 25 October 1890.

68 Pamphlet, 'Rules of the Liverpool Upholsteresses' Union established November 11 1890', British Library of Political and Economic Science; for unions formed at this time see monthly lists in *Women's Trade Union Review*, April 1892–January 1893; *The Labour Prophet*, September 1893.

69 *The Labour Prophet*, September 1893.

70 *Fabian News*, July 1893.

71 *The Labour Prophet*, September 1893. The LSPWTU also succeeded in obtaining a 2-hour reduction in the working day for coat makers, possibly through negotiation rather than strike. See *The Liverpool Labour Chronicle*, October 1894.

The Tailoresses' Union had become moribund after their strike, despite representing a reasonably large trade. Mole was becoming increasingly concerned about the prospects of retaining unions in tiny trades. Work among non-unionised women had alerted Mole to their isolation, which she felt encouraged an unpleasant selfishness in their attitudes. In their tiny workplaces, isolated from most other workers, it was difficult to politicise

> the fortunate daughter living upon her parents earnings [who] will willingly sell her labour for the price of a feather, a dance... a little pocket money without in the least suspecting that... she is snatching the lifebread that would save her poor sister from misery.[72]

Despite the untiring work of the LSPWTU, 'Unskilled workers [were] helplessly trampling each other down in their struggle for a living' with little prospect of this changing.[73] An episode shortly before the tobacco spinners' strike had added to her concerns. A group of needlewomen had approached the LSPWTU asking for help in unionising. It was decided that they were too few to sustain a branch and attempts were made to recruit others from the same trade, but the original girls became discouraged with the waiting time and fell away.[74] To avoid losing the tobacco spinners, Mole encouraged them to join the Gasworkers and General Labourers Union which they did, remaining organised but beyond her broader aims of union-based recreational culture.

Other observers were also beginning to despair of improving the lot of Liverpool's working women. The Trades Council complained that although it had made efforts to change and had helped with particular strikes, 'the female workers in Liverpool... hold aloof from our council'.[75] Liberals in *The Liverpool Review* opined that attempts to motivate women to organise would be useless unless they came from the women themselves.[76] *The Porcupine* also largely blamed the interference of 'middle-class theorists' although it also criticised 'excessive subscription rates... lack of organisation... [and] internal quarrels'.[77] Furthermore, *The Porcupine* failed to recognise Jeannie Mole's socialist-inspired attempts as being any different, naming her work as a prime instance of 'middle-class interference'.[78] Whatever the particular reasons, it was clear that the approach of the LWS and the LSPWTU had failed to promote and sustain unionisation. A new direction was needed.

72 *The Liverpool Labour Chronicle*, October 1894.
73 *The Labour Prophet*, September 1893.
74 *The Liverpool Labour Chronicle*, October 1894.
75 Trades Council Annual Report 1893–94 cited in Grant, 'Women's Work and Trade Unionism in Liverpool'. It was not until 1908 that a woman delegate was actually elected.
76 *Liverpool Review of Politics*, February 1895.

The Women's Industrial Council

In the face of failure and personal abuse, Mole's tenacious belief in the importance of a socialist-inspired organisation of working women held firm. She was, however, willing to vary her tactics. The formation of a Women's Industrial Council (WIC) in London in November 1894 inspired her next attempts. Mole's previous societies had only produced a handful of activists from each trade. She now believed that her best hopes of achieving her more ambitious aims for women's unions lay in a federation of all working women which would allow the keenest recruits from each trade to work together.[79] She hoped that a local branch of the WIC could function as just such a federation, avoiding the problems that isolation had caused in her earlier committees.[80]

In taking this step, Mole seriously overestimated the aims of the WIC.[81] Her error was understandable. Clementina Black, one of the main forces behind the WIC, had encountered similar problems to those that Mole faced in Liverpool when attempting to organise London women from a position outside their trades. Furthermore, although the WIC was explicitly independent of any political party, its early recruits included socialists such as Mary Fenton MacPherson and Margaret MacDonald, both of whom were known to Mole. What she failed to take full account of was the emphasis that the WIC placed on social science rather than a socialist approach to the problems of working-class women. Its main concern was 'systematic inquiry into the conditions of working women' providing accurate data to strengthen its role as a pressure group.[82] Despite its attraction for socialist feminists frustrated by the difficulty of sustaining women's unions or politicising the most downtrodden female workers, the WIC had no pretensions to act as an organising force. Mole's belief in the potential of federation led her unwittingly to subsume the LSPWTU into a national body which was every bit as troubled with tensions between socialists, liberal philanthropists and social feminists as her previous organisations had been.

This was not immediately apparent when the WIC appeared in Liverpool. It was launched amid civil disturbances and political tension. The winter of 1894–95 was particularly harsh in terms of economics and climate. Large numbers of unemployed gathered on the streets in freezing conditions where they were offered food by philanthropic groups, and soup and socialist

77 *The Porcupine*, 8 September 1894.
78 *The Porcupine*, 15 September 1894.
79 *The Liverpool Labour Chronicle*, October 1894.
80 *The Liverpool Labour Chronicle*, December 1894.
81 For the WIC see E. F. Mappen, *Helping Women at Work: The Women's Industrial Council 1889–1914*, London, Hutchinson, 1985; also Mappen, 'Strategists for Change', pp. 235–60.
82 *The Times*, 26 November 1894.

speeches by the ILP, the SDF and the FS.[83] The city council refused to intervene. When the Lord Mayor, William Herbert Watts, was approached, he
refused to consider emergency provisions, declaring that the unemployed
'could go to the devil'. Near riots ensued.[84] Therefore it was not surprising
that when the same Mr Watts insisted on chairing the public meeting at which
the WIC was launched, which coincided with the street disturbances, he was
subjected to a barrage of abuse from socialist and trade union speakers.[85]
This also detracted from Mole's stated but questionable aim of attracting
'men and women of all shades of opinion' into the WIC.[86] Although she was
keen to make use of the time and money of wealthy philanthropists, her ambitions for the new body were much more closely linked to party politics.[87]

Although it attracted reformers such as Rev. Canon Major Lester, the first
activists of the WIC were all socialists. Mole became its honorary secretary.
She was joined in her work by Eleanor Keeling, an enthusiastic and energetic
Fabian.[88] Keeling, who was shortly to marry *Labour Annual* editor Joseph
Edwards, had built up Socialist Cinderella Clubs in Liverpool, and attempted
to establish a Labour Church, as well as making a name for herself nationally as a speaker and inaugurator of the *Clarion* Woman's Column.[89]
Together the two women shared a political vision for the WIC. Its national
funding allowed for organisers to be sent into the regions for specific
campaigns. Mole and Keeling used these funds to bring socialists to
Liverpool. Rachel Macmillan came for much of 1895. Caroline Martyn
joined her in an initiative aimed at organising women workers rather than
investigating their working conditions.[90] Isabel Tiplady and Margaret
Macmillan visited the following year.[91] The financial backing of the London
WIC allowed the Liverpool group to take offices, and funded Keeling's
appointment as paid secretary from January 1896.[92] This combination of
funding, nationally recognised socialist organisers and local socialist backing

83 For details see *The Liverpool Labour Chronicle*, February and March 1895; *The Clarion*, 26
   January 1895; *Justice*, 16 March 1895.
84 For more detail on this see K. Cowman, 'The Battle of the Boulevards: Class, Gender and
   the Purpose of Public Space in Later Victorian Liverpool', in S. Gunn and R. Morris, eds,
   Making Identities: Conflicts and Urban Space 1800–2000, Ashgate, 2001.
85 *The Clarion*, 9 February 1895.
86 *The Liverpool Labour Chronicle*, February 1895.
87 *The Liverpool Labour Chronicle*, December 1895.
88 See G. Fidler, 'The Work of Joseph and Eleanor Edwards, Two Liverpool Enthusiasts',
   International Review of Social History, vol. XXIV, 1979, pp. 293–379.
89 *The Porcupine*, 27 January 1894; *The Liver*, 18 November 1893; *The Labour Prophet*, January
   1894; *The Clarion*, 9 February 1895.
90 See *The Liverpool Labour Chronicle*, May–October 1895; C. Steedman, *Childhood, Culture
   and Class in Britain: Margaret Macmillan 1860–1931*, London, Virago, 1990, pp. 28–29.
91 *The Liverpool Labour Chronicle*, February 1896.
92 *The Liverpool Labour Chronicle*, December 1895.

brought the WIC far closer to Mole's ideal federation than her previous committees.

Again it was a strike that helped the WIC to reach a group of previously unorganised workers. In April 1895, during Caroline Martyn's visit, trouble flared among ropemakers. The ropemaking industry employed almost 2,000 women in unpleasant and sometimes dangerous conditions for around nine shillings per week.[93] When Garnock and Bibby's ropeworks in Old Swan threatened to reduce the women's wages, socialists quickly became involved. Caroline Martyn and Jeannie Mole formed a union among the women which fought off the wage cut.[94] Bessie Kazier from the FS was appointed secretary and through her efforts the union continued to meet through the spring and early summer.

Socialists in the WIC concentrated most of their efforts on ropemaking and began to campaign around safety issues. Much of the machinery used was dangerous, but it was not until Mole intervened that a machine that had torn off a girl's finger at Jackson's ropeworks was protected. Then tragedy struck. On 27 July 1895 'Cissy' Louise Jane Muller, a 21-year-old spinner employed by Jackson's for nine shillings a week, broke a coil of rope off a machine. As she carried it across the factory floor on her arm, the loose end caught in 'a useless piece of revolving shafting' eight feet above ground. Cissy was drawn up to the ceiling and torn to pieces by the machine. The horrific accident was rendered more poignant by the fact that the main witness was Cissy's mother, Harriet, who worked alongside her. At the subsequent inquest she informed the coroner:

> I just turned, and there she was, looking so bonnie. She had a new blouse and shoes that morning, and a pair of earrings that someone had given her, and I turned my head away not to let her see how proud I was, when something happened. And oh, sir, it were Cissy! I heard a thumping against the ceiling and it were my Cissy! And I never saw her any more.[95]

Mrs Muller's account was supported by her foreman who told the inquest:

> I never saw an accident so bad before. The nearest to it was when a woman was scalped... [and] another woman was being drawn into a machine, and was just about to meet the same death, when her skirt gave way and down she fell.[96]

No other workmates were allowed to attend the inquest, despite their wish to help Mrs Muller through the ordeal. Mole was admitted and won tremen-

93 *The Liverpool Labour Chronicle*, September 1895; A. Harrison, *Women's Industries in Liverpool*, Liverpool, 1904, Williams & Northgate, pp. 40, 47.

94 *The Liverpool Labour Chronicle*, May 1895.

95 *The Liverpool Labour Chronicle*, May 1895. See also West Derby Coroner's Inquest Register (CR16/1/2), 31 July 1895, Lancashire County Record Office.

96 *The Liverpool Labour Chronicle*, May 1895.

dous sympathy from the workers for her efforts, which included adjourning the inquest until a factory inspector could attend.[97] She persuaded the jury to make safety recommendations, and had the union's solicitor arrange compensation for Mrs Muller. She also used the *The Liverpool Labour Chronicle* to publicise the horrific event and reprimand the local press, whose sensational accounts made little mention of the dangers of ropemaking, and did not question the notion of holding a closed inquest.[98]

Emboldened by such public and practical help from the WIC, ropemakers at Jackson's acted quickly in September when, less than a month after the inquest, an elderly woman arrived slightly late for work and was told that as well as losing the hours she had missed, she would be fined one shilling and eight pence for her misdemeanour. Complaints from the woman and her colleagues met with accusations of laziness from the employers. Mole was outraged, and rushed to their defence with an emotive picture of the women's lives:

> Many of [them] rise before five, tidy their little homes, prepare the day's food and pass the factory gate after a walk of two miles, before the steam whistle stops shrieking at 6.30... So many of them receive only a few shillings a week, and have to tramp a long way to reach cheap shelter, and are not able to afford out of their wages such food as would give them energy and vigour. Sometimes, then, it happens that a woman hears the dreaded whistle stop when she is a quarter of a mile away, and then she knows that some of her hard earned wage will be kept back from her.[99]

A second strike of ropemakers ensued, which again succeeded, and, as with the tobacco-spinners, the fines were withdrawn.

The union continued to meet weekly. Again, organisers attempted to fuse unionisation and recreational activities aimed at providing the women with a taste of a more pleasant lifestyle. Families were encouraged to attend to ensure that the union became a focus of family life rather than a cause of marital discord. Socialists who attended the weekly meetings noticed

> the tired faces of the men and women brighten as they listen to the music and song and watch the happy dancers. Mothers sit knitting and dreaming of their youth whilst the younger wives nurse their babies with sad yearnings for the future.[100]

'Great things are expected!' exclaimed James Sexton in *The Clarion*.[101]

Despite such expectations, the union had vanished by 1896. Organising

97   *The Liverpool Weekly Mercury*, 3 August 1895.
98   *The Liverpool Labour Chronicle*, November 1895.
99   *The Liverpool Labour Chronicle*, October 1895.
100 *The Liverpool Labour Chronicle*, December 1895.
101 *The Clarion*, December 1895.

women when there was no strike, safety issue or need for immediate action was almost impossible. Rachel Macmillan found 'Liverpool one of the most difficult districts in the country for socialist work' despite conditions 'worse than in... any town in England'.[102] The perception of many young women workers was that a union had nothing to offer them except when they had a particular problem in which case they could form one there and then. At other times it was at best irrelevant, at worst a potential source of trouble. Early in 1896 Keeling attempted to spread the union to Lodge Lane rope-works. She became exasperated by the attitude of the workers:

> Last time I only saw *two* and that was not enough and I was *very* disap-pointed. Besides these two were frightened and ran away. I wonder if they thought I was going to hurt them. Well I was not. I only want to talk to you about a union and see if we can start one. You know girls it would help you *so* much and it would be quite easy if you just made up your minds to have one.[103]

Aims to retain the WIC as a practical arm of the local socialist movement were further hampered by the increasing ill health of Mole. Early in 1896 she suffered a severe heart attack, and was forced to give up her work with the council for several months and travel abroad to recuperate. Although many of her co-workers in union organisation disagreed with Mole's political stance, it was very difficult for them publicly to criticise this indefatigable woman who almost single-handedly led their campaigns. Mole was not above calling on 'philanthropic gentlewomen' to join her work, but balanced their presence with her own politics, retaining a socialist base for the WIC's work.[104] The effects of her temporary withdrawal were compounded by Keeling's first pregnancy the same year, which left the WIC largely in the hands of 'an untried under secretary'.[105]

In October 1896 the WIC elected a new committee. This retained a place for Keeling but added a host of new names: Mrs Rendall, wife of the University Vice Chancellor, Mrs Allan Bright, Mrs Alfred Booth and Mrs Nessie Stewart-Brown among them. This formidable group of feminist philanthropists had remained aloof from the WIC and its predecessors within their separate Liverpool Ladies' Union of Workers Among Women and Girls, a society that had read papers about the unionisation of working women, but had taken no part in it.[106] Under their leadership it was decided

---

102 *The Labour Prophet*, November 1895.
103 Eleanor Keeling, letter to Lodge Lane rope workers, 18 March 1896, Joseph Edwards' Papers, Liverpool Record Office.
104 *The Liverpool Labour Chronicle*, December 1895.
105 *The Liverpool Labour Chronicle*, May 1896.
106 Liverpool Ladies' Union of Workers Among Women and Girls, *Women Workers: Papers read at a Conference Convened by the Liverpool Ladies' Union of Workers among Women and Girls November 1891*, Liverpool, Gilbert G. Walmsley, 1892.

that the WIC's priorities should be information gathering and dissemination rather than union organisation. Offices would act as a point of contact not as a social forum. They drew away from the ILP and worked more closely with the new local branch of the National Union of Women Workers, also dominated by Mrs Bright and Mrs Booth, in 'obtaining and supplying information concerning women's work'.[107]

The following year Lady Aberdeen became national president of the WIC. Liberal women in Liverpool now saw the WIC as belonging to them, and found no room for class conflict in its work. At its annual meeting Mrs Stewart-Brown complained about a 'misapprehension of what the council was formed for' among its 'advanced wing... [which] appeared to think that they did not go forward sufficiently fast enough'.[108] Mole and her supporters 'not being concerned in the giving of alms' severed all connections with the WIC and recommenced work under their previous name of the Society for the Promotion of Women's Trade Unions.[109] In 1898 Mole helped Jim Larkin to form a local branch of Tom Mann's Workers' Union, the group that aimed to 'salvage some of the... spirit of New Unionism' among the unskilled.[110] She and other socialist women attempted to turn this into the federation that she had hoped the WIC might become. She appealed in *The Clarion* for 'women workers to attend the meetings' noting sadly 'how few women are in [the] Union which only costs three pennies a week'.[111] She especially hoped that the tiny group of tailoresses, still working under Miss Duggan, would be among the first to benefit.[112] Yet, as with her other efforts, the women themselves still could not be persuaded to unionise. This was to be Mole's final effort in this direction. Ill and disappointed, she turned to other socialist work. Keeling left Liverpool for Scotland with her family and was unable to continue the work that she and Mole had begun.

The WIC achieved a better degree of longevity. The personal wealth and connections of its new leaders ensured it the permanent headquarters that Mole had wished for, but these were used solely for collecting and collating information and were unavailable to working women as a social or recreational space. An Inquiry and Employment Bureau for Educated Women was opened in 1898, which offered little to unskilled trades, being 'to assist the class who are called ladies in distress' to secure positions.[113] The WIC continued its investigative work in Liverpool until the First World War. Its

107 *Liverpool Review of Politics*, 31 October 1896.
108 *Liverpool Review of Politics*, 13 March 1897.
109 *The Liverpool Labour Chronicle*, May 1897.
110 S. Pollard, 'The New Unionism in Britain: Its Economic Background', in W. J. Mommsen and H. G. Husung, eds, *The Development of Trade Unionism in Great Britain and Germany 1880–1914*, London, George Allen & Unwin, 1985, p. 37.
111 *The Clarion*, 18 June 1898.
112 *The Liverpool Labour Chronicle*, April 1897; *The Clarion*, 18 June 1893.
113 *Liverpool Daily Post*, 19 May 1905.

achievements in this field were significant. Published reports such as those on the conditions of homeworkers (1909), widows under the Poor Law (1913) and the families of dock labourers (1909) ensured that the problems faced by working-class women continued to receive public attention.[114] Eleanor Rathbone, who authored some of the reports, made great use of their statistics in her work on the city council from 1909. But the WIC never again attempted to organise unskilled women workers.

In 1894 Mole had remarked that initiatives to form women's unions would only succeed if 'the call should come with the need from the women themselves'.[115] The pattern of local women's union involvement before the First World War reflected this judgement. After Mole's retirement, sporadic activity around particular issues continued to be interspersed by long absences of any significant numbers of women in unions. Women involved themselves in violent conflicts, attacking scabs during a docks strike in 1905, and joining events on St George's Plateau on Bloody Sunday.[116] Yet no sustained autonomous movement of women's unions emerged. If anything, women were more prone to join in strikes with men in the later period, as in the 1912 strike at Wilson Brothers' bobbin works, Garston. This strike among a mixed workforce saw women and men acting together in increasingly violent picketing against a group of strike-breaking women who travelled into the area daily.[117] The prospect of a mass union of all working women that would educate and politicise as well as organise its membership remained remote.

Unlike the Lancashire textile trades whose women unionists collectively organised around suffrage in the early twentieth century, Liverpool's women's unions did not develop a highly politicised membership. Here, as elsewhere in Britain, women's unions were small and sporadic. Much of their political dimension came from individual organisers whose ideology was developed through connections with other political groups prior to their

---

114 *How the Casual Labourer Lives: Report of the Liverpool Joint Research Committee on the Domestic Condition and Expenditure of the Families of Certain Liverpool Labourers*, Liverpool, Liverpool Women's Industrial Council, 1909; *Liverpool Women's Industrial Council Report on Homework in Liverpool*, Liverpool, Liverpool Women's Industrial Council, 1909; *The Report of the Liverpool Women's Industrial Council Survey into Widows Under the Poor Law*, Liverpool, Liverpool Women's Industrial Council, 1913.

115 *The Liverpool Labour Chronicle*, October 1894.

116 E. Larkin, *James Larkin, Irish Labour Leader*, London, Pluto Press, 1989, p. 8 details women's involvement in the dock strike. Photographs of women involved in Bloody Sunday can be found in Taplin, *Near to Revolution*. See also the leaflet 'Strike's Death-Roll: How the Children of the Poor Died – Dr. Hope's Terrible Indictment' by Dr. Hope, Liverpool Medical Officer of Health held in the Legge Papers, Liverpool Record Office. See also R. Holton, *British Syndicalism 1900–1914*, London, Pluto Press, 1976, pp. 100–01.

117 For more details of this strike see the *Liverpool Daily Post*, August 1913; individual testimonies of strikers can be found in the Liverpool Trades Council and Labour Party Papers, Liverpool Record Office.

contact with working-class women. Mole was active in several socialist organisations, and brought other women socialists into her trade union work. Similarly, the WIC became dominated by members of the WLF and the Liverpool Women's Suffrage Society (LWSS). It was from these other groups that the women who championed unionisation or worked with women workers drew their inspiration. Thus, from their different political perspectives, two distinct trends, both equally unsuccessful, emerged. One, informed by socialist theory, saw trade union membership as a starting point from which further education, politicisation and class consciousness could be achieved. The other did not seek to challenge existing orders of gender or class, but attempted to protect women from the worst effects of the systems that these orders promoted. To discover more about the broader arena in which Merseyside's women activists developed their particular perspectives we must move to the world of party politics, where many of the leaders of the LWS, LSPWTU and WIC began their political lives.

CHAPTER THREE

Early Party Activity, 1890–1905

By the end of the nineteenth century, the political party was an important site for women.[1] Liberals and Conservatives alike had been forced to reconstruct their organisations' appeal in the face of a rapidly expanding electorate. Both realised the potential of women campaigners and began to formalise female space within their ranks.[2] Simultaneously socialist parties were forming, influenced by ideologies that radically challenged existing orders of class and gender. From the outset they gave women and men equal membership rights. In Liverpool, women found that party politics now offered accessible routes to public activity. The local Liberal and Conservative parties opened branches of their national auxiliary women's organisations. Socialist groups were also forming which actively sought women members. The generation of female activists who joined these organisations in Liverpool held strong party-political convictions. These allowed for some circumnavigation of the traditional local political boundaries of class and religion as women activists placed their party identity above these. However, being a party member also meant giving up some personal autonomy; women were placed at the mercy of the vagaries of local and national party politics. There were some deviations from national trends. Particular local circumstances restricted the success of Conservative women's organisations. Women Liberals in Liverpool fared slightly better, but were nevertheless affected by their party's local decline. Socialist women achieved slightly more within their parties, but found that a lack of socialist electoral success limited their opportunity for public work as will be shown. Ultimately, in all political groups, women members were supposed to serve the interests of their parties and not the other way around.

The Primrose League

When the Conservative Party regained control of Liverpool City Council in 1895, a number of women were among those credited with achieving this

---

1 For a general discussion of this point see N. Kirk, *Change, Continuity and Class: Labour in British Society 1850–1920*, Manchester, Manchester University Press, 1998, p. 183.
2 See D. Rubinstein, *Before the Suffragettes: Women's Emancipation in the 1890s*, Brighton, Harvester, 1986, pp. 150–53; Levine, *Victorian Feminism*, especially Chapter 3, 'The Public Sphere: Politics, Local and National'.

victory.[3] They had organised through the local branches or 'habitations' of the Primrose League.[4] The League, founded in 1883, was closely associated with Conservatism although it eschewed overt party politics in favour of a vague ideology of Church, Crown and Empire. From 1884, it admitted women to its ranks, thus becoming 'the first body to recognise the usefulness of women in politics'.[5] Women members enjoyed autonomous organisation under the direction of a Ladies' Grand Council, but most of their actual activity was within local, mixed-sex habitations. Much of the League's theorisation of the role of its women members accepted a degree of sexual difference, emphasising the unique contribution that the female nature could make to politics. The Conservative woman ought not to

> emulate man in the many qualities he alone possesses; [but]… rather try to excel as woman in all that is most feminine and womanly.[6]

By 1891, the League's national membership stood at one million. It had established eight habitations in Liverpool. Toxteth, the most successful of these, had over 1,000 members.[7] While much habitation activity was socially oriented, it was not wholly apolitical, as this report from Liverpool's Rodney habitation explains:

> Apart from its pleasant social features, there is a deep feeling among members that they are united for a serious purpose, that is the maintenance of the Empire, the maintenance of freedom at home and abroad, the maintenance of religion and the furtherance of the constitution.[8]

This ability to create and sustain an associational political culture of the type that had eluded women's trade union organisers accounted for much of the League's success.[9] Women were fully involved, inspired by energetic activists such as the Baroness de Worms, Dame President of Toxteth habitation, who called for 'the right of women to uphold the principles of the League' at every available opportunity.[10]

The League's belief in sexual difference did not particularly limit these opportunities as its women members consistently sought to expand the areas

---

3 *The Primrose League Gazette*, December 1895.
4 See Robb, *The Primrose League*; M. Pugh, *The Tories and the People 1880–1935*, Oxford, Blackwell, 1985; B. Campbell, *Iron Ladies: Why Women Vote Tory*, London, Virago, 1987. For a comparison between the national Primrose League and the Women's Liberal Federation, see Walker, 'Party Political Women', pp. 165–91.
5 This is a phrase that occurs frequently in *The Primrose League Gazette*.
6 Lady Borthwick, 'English Women as a Political Force', *The Primrose League Gazette*, 15 October 1887.
7 *The Primrose League Gazette*, 10 November 1888; 9 February 1889. The other habitations were Rodney, Kirkdale, Exchange, Wavertree, Everton and West Derby, and Waterloo.
8 *The Primrose League Gazette*, 14 December 1889.
9 See Pugh, *The Tories and the People*, Chapter 5.
10 *The Primrose League Gazette*, 12 November 1887.

in which their influence might be exercised. Elections evidenced women's appreciation of their expanding role when initial opposition to their presence in 'the rough and tumble of the [electoral] contest' evaporated in the face of the success of female canvassers.[11] Liverpool women took active parts in elections throughout the city, even in the most difficult districts. In Kirkdale, during the General Election campaign of 1900, the Chairman of the polling district singled out 'the ladies... [as] responsible for returning the Conservative candidate... by such a splendid majority'.[12] Kirkdale was not an easy forum for Conservatives. The threat of socialism was perceived as strong and the area 'densely and toughly peopled, [its] low life... very low.'[13] Working there against vociferous opposition provided valuable grounding for women wishing to move into public life.

As Linda Walker has pointed out, entering public life via the Primrose League helped women to maintain an 'image of propriety and respectability'.[14] Nationally, articles in *The Primrose League Gazette* emphasised 'the difference... between the truly feminine influence of the Dames... and the unattractive pressure exerted by the ladies of the Liberal and Radical societies', while in Liverpool, Alderman Forwood condemned Liberal women's penchant for public speaking, holding up the more discreet local Dames as models of ideal female politicians.[15] The 'lady orators' of the League attracted none of the negative publicity given to the 'female speakers' who preached women's rights above the sanctity of the Empire.[16] League women admitted to lifting successful ploys such as a campaigning Ladies' Van from the radical camp. However, they escaped public censure through ensuring that the rhetoric they dispensed from the van was measured and feminine. Liverpool members similarly refined their campaigning methodology. In 1902, women from the Waterloo habitation borrowed an idea from socialists and established a cycling corps which made three trips a week into the surrounding countryside. The women were careful to preach nothing but a vague 'devotion to the constitutional cause'.[17] Hence, although their appearance was 'always sufficient to cause curiosity' their work passed without public reproach.[18]

The Primrose League provided some opportunities for women to learn and practise public speaking skills.[19] Elsewhere, some habitations encour-

11 Campbell, *Iron Ladies*, p. 10.
12 *The Primrose League Gazette*, December 1900.
13 Waller, *Democracy and Sectarianism*, p. 64.
14 Walker, 'Party Political Women', p. 180.
15 *The Primrose League Gazette*, 24 December 1894; *Liverpool Review of Politics*, 20 January 1894.
16 See *Liverpool Review of Politics*, 16 November 1895, which mentions 'Conservative ladies' and 'Radical female canvassers'.
17 *Liverpool Review of Politics*, 2 December 1895.
18 *Liverpool Review of Politics*, 1 August 1902.
19 Walker, 'Party Political Women', p. 180.

aged women to use these at all levels, including the public meeting, more contentious than canvassing which merely extended women's philanthropic work of visiting.[20] There could be no equivocation around the public site of the political platform where feelings often ran high, and the speaker was as likely to be attacked for the challenge she was presenting to a woman's traditional role as for her politics.[21] Following Forwood's concerns, Liverpool women avoided the open platform but did address small, invited audiences. However, despite the League's consistent emphasis on a distinct female nature, women were not restricted to specific topics that might then be marginalised as women's issues, as happened within socialism. Mrs Thomas Brocklebank, who defected with her family from Liberalism over the Irish Question, was one of Liverpool's most prominent women League members. As Ruling Councillor of the Rodney habitation, she addressed her branch on 'Europe after the death of the German Empire', essentially an anti-Home Rule speech that made no special mention of women but offered support for government policy against the National League.[22] Through the Primrose League, Brocklebank could address mixed audiences on such themes, and share committee work with men. Like electioneering skills, such public opportunities were vital for women who were to seek greater public involvement in the near future.

Yet, despite these successes, the Primrose League in Liverpool came nowhere near to achieving the profile it enjoyed in other parts of England.[23] Although Conservatism dominated local politics, many of the League's local branches were short-lived; few survived into the twentieth century. Also, while women were welcomed within the League, they never outnumbered men, and Brocklebank alone achieved the position of Ruling Councillor. Most of the other Liverpool habitations were run by male executives.[24] By the early twentieth century, women did not even figure in reports of League meetings.[25]

Why was the League so marginal in a city that was so strongly Conservative in its politics? The reason lies in the particular character of Liverpool Conservatism. Much of the national success of the Primrose League has been attributed to the work done by the women from the dynastic

20 See Campbell, *Iron Ladies*, p. 22.
21 Walker, 'Party Political Women', p. 180.
22 *The Primrose League Gazette*, 15 September 1888.
23 Martin Pugh has estimated membership of the Bolton branch at around 6,000 in 1900. While he offers no later figures for Liverpool, his figure of just above 1,000 for Toxteth in 1891 and figures for Everton that show a drop from over 100 in 1886 to 30 in 1888 indicate a much lower level of recruitment. See Pugh, *The Tories and the People*, Appendix xiv, pp. 240–42; also *The Primrose League Gazette* which shows little presence beyond Waterloo by 1900.
24 Waterloo was a slight exception having parallel positions of Dame President and Lady Secretary ensuring some female input into its executive.
25 *The Liverpool Courier*, 5 December 1901.

Tory families. These were the same women who had frequently moved throughout the local community in philanthropic work, and were now able to mobilise their links and knowledge on behalf of the local party.[26] As Waller and others have shown, there was no real local Tory elite in Liverpool, the political dynasties of the local bourgeoisie being almost entirely Liberal in character.[27] So, although MP's wives like the Baroness de Worms worked hard for the League during their husbands' associations with the city, they established no local roots. Philanthropy and charity were similarly marginal to local Conservative politics, being largely under either Liberal or religious control. Hence many local Conservative women lacked those personal networks that proved so politically advantageous in other areas of the country. Small numbers of women tried to overcome this. Almost 40 came forward to join the Ladies' Grand Council at national level following a drawing room meeting organised by Lady Lathom in December 1891, but her attempt to follow this up with a local Ladies' Grand Council in April 1892 failed due to the tenuous position of the local League.[28] For most women, League membership remained an individual rather than a collective experience.

The success of local Conservatives in creating their own brand of popular working-class Toryism also worked against the Primrose League. This, while not directly antagonistic, was not immediately at ease with the League's determination to foster a 'bond of union and sympathy... between the various classes of the community'.[29] Liverpool's Conservatives were 'practised in stooping to conquer'. They felt no need to blur class distinctions, but preached a belief that 'working men accepted that a leisured and educated class should conduct Government'.[30] However, they simultaneously recognised that there had to be a political role provided for the working man, for fear that he would otherwise take himself and his vote elsewhere. As a result, local Conservatives had developed a Working Men's Conservative Association, which sustained 12 flourishing branches in Liverpool by 1872, and expanded each decade up to 1914.[31] With such an organisation already in place, there was no real need for the Primrose League. Reconstitution in Liverpool was well in hand. While this was good news for the party, it was less encouraging to Conservative women. The Working Men's Conservative Associations were aimed at voting men. Their very name excluded women, and they provided no female public political platforms or election experi-

---

26 This view was put by B. Campbell in 'Iron Ladies', a paper delivered at the National Museum of Labour History, Manchester, November 1993.

27 Waller, *Democracy and Sectarianism*, pp. 16–18.

28 *The Primrose League Gazette*, 16 April 1892.

29 Primrose League Ladies' EC Annual Report, 1886.

30 Waller, *Democracy and Sectarianism*, pp. 16–18. See also Pugh, *The Tories and the People*, p. 9.

31 Waller, *Democracy and Sectarianism*, pp. 16–18.

ence. It was not until the next century that Liverpool's Conservative women were able to unite as explicitly political *women* under the banner of party, in the ranks of the Conservative and Unionist Women's Franchise Association.

Liverpool's Women's Liberal Associations

For Liverpool women whose political sympathies lay with the Liberal Party, the route into party politics was much more clearly defined. Through the WLF they entered political life and learned not only to canvass and speak in public, but to stand for election themselves. Within a separate women's organisation they were guaranteed the chance to represent themselves, to control their own branches, sit on their own committees, and set their own agenda. There was no question of having to compete with men for space in the way that Conservative women were forced to do. Thus despite the prominence of the Conservative Party in the Town Hall, it was the WLF that enjoyed unprecedented success as a party political organisation for local women, although like the Primrose League it was ultimately constrained by aspects of local and national politics that were beyond its control.

The WLF formed in 1887, in an attempt to join together the several Women's Liberal Associations (WLAs) that had emerged throughout Britain in the 1880s.[32] Although the Liberal Party in Liverpool was not enjoying much electoral success at this time, it did boast the support of the city's radical elite, allowing Liberal women to locate their political work within the friendship and kinship networks that local Conservative women lacked. With such strong links already existing between women Liberals it is not surprising that Liverpool was among the first 26 associations to join the Federation.[33] Furthermore, while some local associations followed the example of the Primrose League and headed branches with well-known personalities without local ties, there were sufficient prominent Liberal families in Liverpool to render this unnecessary. Mrs Robert Durning Holt, who presided over Liverpool's first WLA, typifies this. Her Liberal credentials were impeccable, and connected her to national radical politics. Born Lawrencina Potter, she was a sister of Beatrice Webb.[34] Her husband Robert was a leading local Liberal who achieved the distinction of becoming the first

---

32 There is no published history of the Women's Liberal Federation to date. Although an important site of women's political activity in the Edwardian period, its role has yet to be evaluated fully. The most recent material on it, Walker's comparative 'Party Political Women', and Hirshfield's 'Fractured Faith', pp. 173–97, re-establish it as an important political group, but only touch on its scope and strength, while other historians mention it only in relation to suffrage.

33 WLF Annual Report, 1888.

34 For Mrs Holt see B. Caine, *Destined to be Wives: The Sisters of Beatrice Webb*, Oxford, Clarendon Press, 1986, especially pp. 87–89, 154–57, 174–75.

Lord Mayor of Liverpool in 1892.[35] Mrs Holt's broader philanthropic connections spanned temperance, district nursing and the campaign to establish a university in the city. She was ideally placed in terms of both personal and political contacts to become a figurehead for local Liberal women.

In 1891 Liverpool established a second WLA in West Derby. This was founded by Nessie Stewart-Brown, 'one of the most unselfish and untiring of Liverpool ladies', who was to become both synonymous with Liverpool Liberalism, and a key figure in the national WLF.[36] Like Mrs Holt, she came from a prominent Liberal family. Her father was Dr Edmund Knowles Muspratt, a successful chemical industrialist and the first pro-chancellor of Liverpool University, who had stood unsuccessfully as a Liberal parliamentary candidate in 1885. One of her brothers, Max, was a Liberal councillor and later an MP. Her mother and two of her sisters, Julia (Solly) and Stella (Permewan), were active WLF members. Stewart-Brown herself was involved in many local causes including the RSPCA, and the Liverpool Women's Suffrage Society (LWSS), and was partly responsible for moving the local WIC away from socialism. Leaders like Stewart-Brown helped to popularise the WLAs among the sisters, wives and daughters of many leading figures in Liverpool society. By 1893, there were six branches at West Derby, East Toxteth, Everton, Walton, West Toxteth and Waterloo as well as a branch at Birkenhead and a separate branch of the Women's National Liberal Association (WNLA). Each of these offered their members, most of whom were already active in many social and philanthropic causes, the opportunity to develop a party identity for their political work. They also offered the Liberal Party a willing group of fashionable, articulate and organised workers for its political cause.

In contrast to the Primrose League, which sought a broad approach, the WLF was overtly a *party* political body. Its principal objectives, laid down in 1889, opened with the promotion of Liberalism. Like the Primrose League it also prioritised political education but for party reasons, using it 'to raise an intelligent interest among women in political questions... [and] enlist their sympathies on the side of Liberal principles'.[37] The main topics that Liverpool WLAs chose to discuss in their early years confirm their status as party organisations. Women's issues did not predominate over party concerns, indeed they barely figured. Speakers addressed local issues such as housing and municipal politics, and also tackled Liberal foreign policy, Home Rule and the Transvaal crisis.

Yet alongside its political focus, the WLF also recognised its members as

35 A brief biography can be found in Waller, *Democracy and Sectarianism*, pp. 494–95. See also Caine, *Destined to be Wives*, pp. 68–70.
36 *Liverpool Review of Politics*, 13 March 1897.
37 WLF Annual Report, 1888.

'women' as well as 'women Liberals'. Members discovered that their separate organisation, which stemmed from women's exclusion from full Liberal
Party membership, could be positive. It allowed space for issues that may
otherwise have escaped party attention, particularly when dealing with legislation relating specifically to women or girls. The WLF would sometimes
work with other women's groups around these issues, such as in their 1893
campaign for women factory inspectors which was carried out with the cooperation of the Women's Trade Union League. This campaign also revealed
some of the conflicts that beset WLF members. The executive committee
felt that 'the large number of women and girls employed in mills and factories' could only be served adequately by women inspectors, who could
understand and relate to women's problems and their place in society.
However, as an auxiliary body, they had no power to effect change but could
only hope that 'Mr Asquith may soon be able to… effect… [this] important
reform'.[38] Despite the size of the WLF, women Liberals were fairly powerless politically and remained reliant on men to pass parliamentary legislation
for their benefit.

In the early years of the WLF, members shifted between their personal
priorities of gender and party. They also saw national successes for their party
which fostered a mood of optimism. In January 1893, at the National Liberal
Federation conference held in Liverpool, Stewart-Brown and other leading
WLF members were given the honour of seats on the platform in 'an
acknowledgement of the position of the Federation in the Liberal Party which
has not before been accorded'.[39] After seven years of auxiliary work, women
who had gained invaluable platform experience through the WLF were able
to put this into practice at a national party event. However, such arrangements only worked when Liberal men and Liberal women wanted the same
thing. When the women collectively opposed the men, they found themselves
facing difficult choices between the loyalties they felt to their party and to
their sex.

Liverpool WLAs participated in their parent body. All local associations
were encouraged to help determine national policy. Initially associations
could send one delegate per 100 members to the Federation's ruling body,
but this was reduced to one per 50 and then one per 25, allowing smaller
associations a national voice. Local associations set their own programme
and enjoyed the autonomy of selecting from a variable and voluntary
subscription rate (from 1d to 3d), a move aimed at broadening participation.
County-based unions, formed in the late 1880s, furthered decentralisation.
(Liverpool was part of West Lancashire and West Cheshire.)[40] Furthermore,
while there is some merit in Walker's claims that it was the London base of

38 WLF Annual Report, 1893.
39 WLF Annual Report, 1893.
40 WLF Annual Reports 1892, 1893. Walker, 'Party Political Women', pp. 168–69.

the National Council that brought WLF policies to the attention of Liberal MPs, close study of the Liverpool associations indicate that this process was often begun in the local branches.[41] Members diligently followed the national progress of 'their' resolutions via delegates who reported back at regular intervals. Local associations devoted much time to examining the agenda of national meetings, and recommending actions for their delegates. Their official status within the Party was vital in facilitating this type of direct contact.

In their relations with the national WLF a degree of autonomy appeared essential to Liverpool's women Liberals. Indeed, in December 1898, when the National Council discussed a motion moved by Eva McClaren in which the hope was expressed that affiliated WLA members would refrain 'from taking part in parliamentary by-elections when the EC and the local WLA have both decided not to take action', the Wavertree association sent in a protest resolution. Stewart-Brown, who attended the National Council as a member of the National Executive Committee but was a Wavertree member, moved an amendment on the grounds that this interfered with national WLF policy on freedom of individual action.[42] Her choice to support her association rather than the NEC in this matter does not signify a pattern of deliberate dissent. Generally, Liverpool WLAs were happy to support the policy of their national organisation. What this does display, however, is their ability to disagree, and to voice disagreement publicly when they deemed it necessary.

The WLAs formed in Liverpool during a time of local Liberal resurgence which saw the party competing for an expanding working-class vote. A Liverpool Liberal Federal Council was established in 1889, behind a radical manifesto that declared itself 'for the people, for the poor'.[43] Increasing gains in municipal elections culminated, in 1892, with the victory of the first Liberal council the city had seen for 50 years. Liberal radicalism extended in its approach to women, and placed WLAs at the centre of developments in municipal politics. As with the Primrose League, certain boundaries had to be stretched. Elections gave rise to some particularly difficult debates. While some women were keen to participate in all election work, including taking to the public platform, others preferred to remain away from public view.[44] However, the determination of women who braved electioneering, and the credit this received from leading Liberals such as Richard Meade-King who acclaimed 'the work done by the WLA... with his return at the head of the poll', challenged those who sought to restrict women's role. By

41 Walker, 'Party Political Women', p. 170.

42 *Women's Liberal Federation News*, December 1898.

43 For further discussion of this see Waller, *Democracy and Sectarianism*, chapter 7.

44 Although Stewart-Brown publicly condemned women's hesitancy in January 1892, a Birkenhead by-election two years later still saw them behind the scenes 'tracing removals and doing clerical work'. *Liverpool Review of Politics*, 16 January 1892; *Women's Liberal Federation News*, October 1894.

the municipal elections of 1895, they were a recognised organising force:

> On polling day they furnished in every ward a most active contingent of
> workers. Mrs Egerton Stewart-Brown spoke night after night for various
> candidates, and the Liberal women issued a leaflet calling upon the women
> voters to support the Reform candidates... Although the results were disas-
> trous... it is gratifying to know that the women voters polled in some wards
> in larger numbers than the men, and that so far as can be judged the majority
> of them did not vote for the Tory Party.[45]

Even more contentious was the question of whether women ought to run
as candidates themselves. Again, most of the controversy surrounded the
idea of an actual election. In 1893, Col. Morrison, a well-known public figure,
proposed that Mrs Georgina Hubback ought to be appointed as a Poor Law
Guardian. Hubback was the widow of a Liberal Alderman, which made her
an ideal candidate in that she could be presented as merely continuing her
husband's work, maintaining a familial presence rather than undertaking an
independent path. Even so, there was strong opposition on the Board, with
one particularly irate Guardian insensitively suggesting that 'a lady coming
on... would in all probability be an unmarried lady with the hope that she
would soon be married'.[46] Although the Liberal Guardians remained firm,
the thought of an election bothered them to the extent that one gentleman
offered to resign so that a woman might be co-opted. This solution was vigor-
ously opposed by Lydia Booth, the Liberal president of the local branch of
the Society for the Return of Women Guardians, who explained that women
Liberals 'would only have women elected in the proper way'.[47] In West
Derby, Jane Calderwood sidestepped the party squabbling and was elected
as an independent candidate, although she received much support from local
Liberals.[48]

Calderwood's electoral success (along with Miss Johnson who was heavily
backed by Liberals in Garston) made all political parties reassess their opinions of women fighting elections and in 1894 the Liberal, Unionist and
Nationalist parties all ran female Guardian candidates.[49] The Liberal establishment was particularly keen to support women in this work, provided that
they remained within particular spheres as the *Liverpool Review of Politics*
explained:

> [Women] also have been, in some cases, elected to [School Boards, and
> other public bodies], and have discharged the functions associated with
> such with gentleness, intelligence and tact. On the School Board, the Select

45 *Women's Liberal Federation News*, December 1895.
46 *The Liver*, April 1893.
47 *The Liver*, April 1893.
48 *Liverpool Review of Politics*, 15 April 1893.
49 *Liverpool Daily Post*, 4 December 1894; 8 December 1894.

Vestry and various local Boards of Guardians, we have seen the beneficent influences exercised by [the] ladies... There are duties in respect to these organisations that women perform with much more tenderness and tact than can be expected of men. Ladies obtain the confidence of women and children, and among them make their influence felt for personal and public good.[50]

So local Liberal men made space for women within the public political arena provided that they dealt with 'women's issues'. There was also a certain 'trade-off' from male candidates who promised priority for women's issues in return for a willing body of workers at election time. Candidates would declare themselves 'converted to the principle of women's suffrage' as a result of the work women had done for their campaigns.[51] Such promises were easy to give, especially in a municipal contest, where the candidate, even if successful, would not be in a position to alter parliamentary legislation. However, none of this support was sustained when WLA members attempted to push beyond what their male party colleagues found acceptable. In 1898, three Wallasey women, Miss A. Hoyle, Mrs M. Jones and Miss Bessie Shilston, stood as council candidates. Shilston was active in the WLA locally and nationally but the three collectively eschewed any party banner and appealed for votes on the grounds of their sex.[52]

Their gender-based campaign was badly defeated, with the Liberal press being especially vitriolic. Confronted with the idea of women spilling out from the Boards of Guardians, where their 'practical knowledge of house-keeping' was considered an asset, to the council chamber, the *Liverpool Review of Politics* raged:

> While women, – nobly planned to warm, to comfort and command, – may be of most beneficent service as representatives of the Poor Law System to women and children, petticoats and street paving are strangely incongruous. In other words, a lady may do duty as a Poor Law guardian and be a useful woman to the community, but she would be lost if deliberating with men about gas, water, sewerage and other public works... neither in municipal administration nor in the conduct of the affairs of local... district councils is the feminine element countenanced.[53]

So, while Liberal men were becoming aware of women's political abilities through seeing them at work in public life, most still remained convinced of

50 *Liverpool Review of Politics*, 26 March 1898. This paper, initially published under the title of the *Liberal Review of Politics*, was edited by William Rathbone, who possibly wrote this anonymous leading article. As a publication its sympathies were wholly with progressive Liberalism.

51 *Liverpool Review of Politics*, November 1893.

52 *Liverpool Review of Politics*, 9 April 1898.

53 *Liverpool Review of Politics*, 9 April 1898.

the need to contain them within the confines of what they saw as their fit space, that part of the public sphere that bore the closest relation to the domestic. However, many Liberal women suspected any approach to politics that rested on gender rather than party. They found little common ground with Conservative women, despite making similar claims about the need for feminine influence in politics. In the local elections of 1895, women from both groups used leaflets and the local press to attack one another.[54] WLF members were becoming increasingly keen to push further into public life, but only wished to do so as Liberals.

Such tensions were bound to come to a head. Within the WLF, both locally and nationally, it was the issue of suffrage that forced women to make hard decisions as to whether they considered themselves to be women or Liberals first. It became increasingly apparent that they could not be both, as the question of parliamentary suffrage was one on which all women involved in politics had to take a position, even if it was one of self-consciously having no position (the line taken by the Primrose League). Liverpool's women Liberals were drawn into the suffrage controversy through Stewart-Brown who was central in determining the national Federation's suffrage policy. She was a committed suffragist, deeply involved in local constitutional campaigns. However, as a Liberal she was also concerned with the effect that suffrage had already had on the WLF. In 1890, adding the vote to its aims had split the Federation, with between 50 and 60 local associations leaving to form the WNLA.[55] Stewart-Brown was also worried about local unity. Abercromby WLA, Liverpool's first branch, opposed the new aim but remained within the Federation. When a pro-suffrage meeting was held in Liverpool the following year under the name of the local Women's Liberal Federal Council, Abercromby members publicly disassociated themselves, and affiliated their branch to the WNLA.[56] Although Abercromby members still joined WLA branches to work in local elections, the issue of suffrage prevented full unity.

Mindful of the strength of feeling among some women Liberals against turning the WLF into a pro-suffrage organisation, Stewart-Brown was nervous of attempts to make suffrage a 'test question'. Supporters of this idea aimed to prevent the WLF from working for any candidate who opposed women's suffrage. In 1896, Stewart-Brown defined what was to become WLF policy in her motion declaring that no association could dictate to others their stance towards individual Liberal candidates. Declaring herself a progressive, she explained:

> There are a great many Liberals who have not yet made up their minds on the question of suffrage, and if we force this test upon them we shall alienate

54 *Liverpool Review of Politics*, 16 November 1895.
55 For more details of this, see Hirshfield, 'Fractured Faith'.
56 *Liverpool Review of Politics*, 6 April 1892.

them entirely, whereas sometimes by working for a really good candidate we are able to convert him... *It is measures, not men that we work for.*[57]

In 1896 this position was easy to support. In Liverpool, Stewart-Brown had seen men converted to suffrage as a result of WLA electioneering. This was not her only justification for her beliefs. The Liberals' heavy defeat in the local elections of 1895 ran deep with activists, and made any attack on their own party painfully difficult. During the heated debate, Stewart-Brown admitted that although he was an exception, she would still have worked willingly for Sir Naylor-Leyland, the Southport candidate who had declared that he would rather enfranchise the donkey boys on the sands than the women active in his campaign. For several years she remained willing to work for anti-suffrage MPs to further the Liberal cause, an attitude that left her more and more isolated upon the EC and its suffrage committee, on which she sat from May 1895. In 1898, when called on to defend her position, she again warned against 'adopting a menacing attitude towards the Liberal Party'.[58] As motions about the 'Test Question' became an annual event, her need to resist the danger of alienating Liberal MPs remained prominent.

Stewart-Brown was equally opposed to local calls for test questions. In 1898 her views were challenged when Sir Naylor-Leyland again stood at Southport. She called a meeting to discuss WLA tactics, and

> urged the members to work for Sir Naylor-Leyland and said that at this momentous crisis no whole-hearted Liberal could stand aside, even when the candidate did not yet see the necessity for women's suffrage.[59]

Fifty-five women promised to help, and Sir Naylor-Leyland was elected. Defending this nationally in 1899 she declared:

> We are proud to feel that we are an important party organisation. It is that we love Liberalism more, not women's suffrage less that we oppose tests... The time has not yet come... to withhold support from those candidates who do not as yet feel that they can support women's suffrage.[60]

Although she was a passionate suffragist, she realised that this was a far more contentious issue for some male Liberals than Home Rule or Welsh disestablishmentarianism, both of which were approved as test questions in the same debate. Stewart-Brown's insistence at prioritising Liberalism over suffrage in this manner was to have serious organisational repercussions for the Liverpool WLAs before the First World War.

So, by 1905, although the Conservative Party was back in firm control of

57 WLF Annual Report, 1896.
58 WLF Annual Report, 1898.
59 *Women's Liberal Federation News*, August 1898.
60 WLF Annual Report, 1899.

the city council in Liverpool, it provided little in the way of openings for women wishing to enter the public arena through the world of party politics. The Primrose League was proud of the fact that it was the first national organisation to recognise the important role that women could play in political life, albeit one that was strictly demarcated, but it was marginalised by organisations dedicated to bringing Tory values to the working men of Liverpool. Of the two parties that held municipal power between 1890 and 1905, it was the Liberal Party which offered most to women. While its thinking was still heavily influenced by the ideology of separate spheres, it trained them as canvassers, gave them space as public speakers, and even selected them as candidates for certain offices. However, by 1900, these were no longer the only two parties that sought to capture the popular votes within the city. From 1892, there was a flowering of the socialist movement in Liverpool. New political parties and pressure groups evolved that welcomed women as members rather than auxiliary affiliates. It is in this direction that we must now look in order to assess fully what political parties had to offer women at this time.

Women and Socialism

On 16 April 1898, *The Clarion* carried a large advertisement for a soiree and dance organised by 'Liverpool Women Socialists'. The proceeds (one shilling and sixpence for a single ticket, and two and six for a double) were to go towards the building of a socialist hall in the city, and the advertisement closed with the promise, in large bold type, that 'The Women Socialists of Liverpool mean to Build a Hall'. This was the first time that a group of local women had identified themselves publicly in this way, but local *Clarion* readers would need no introduction to the five women whose names made up the list of ticket sellers. They had previously linked themselves with many political causes including Fabianism, the ILP and the WIC. Their public affirmation of themselves as 'socialist' rather than as members of particular organisations reveals much about the political culture in which their public activity was situated.

Many of the forms of socialism that have been identified nationally, from ethical through to economistic, flourished on Merseyside during the 1890s.[61] Local branches of the FS, SDF, ILP and a short-lived Labour Church reflected national diversity, while myriad smaller, non-aligned societies offered further choice. The SDF, FS and ILP often worked jointly together. Relations were not idyllic. The ILP was concerned about the overtly

---

61 For more information on these divisions and differences between the two types see Gordon, *Women and the Labour Movement in Scotland*, pp. 261–63; S. Yeo, 'A New Life: The Religion of Socialism in Britain, 1883–1896', *History Workshop Journal*, 4, Autumn 1977, pp. 5–56.

confrontational politics of the older organisation whose members could not 'keep their tempers' in political debate while the SDF was irritated by the emphasis that the ILP placed on ethical socialism.[62] Yet overall they were fraternal, even at election time, and many smaller socialist societies owed much to this cooperation.[63] The socialists of pre-First World War Liverpool also managed to avoid contact with religious sectarianism.[64] Most left this behind upon joining socialist parties, explicitly so in the case of those who were 'expelled from the Orange Lodges because they had joined the ILP'.[65]

The SDF, strong throughout Lancashire, formed one of its earliest branches in Liverpool in 1882. In June 1892 this was joined by the Liverpool FS, which recruited over 100 members in its first year.[66] Although the national FS had strong links to Liberalism, it encouraged the formation of local societies that were quite autonomous.[67] The Liverpool FS became one of the most significant of these. Edward Pease, the society's early historian, claimed that the branch's success lay in its unique relationship with the ILP. While the two societies worked closely together and shared many key personnel, they also retained distinct and separate identities with the FS concentrating heavily on publication of educational tracts.[68] This space allowed both groups to flourish whereas in other areas the ILP frequently eclipsed Fabianism. Liverpool was the only early local FS to survive into the twentieth century.[69] Its continued separation from the ILP also had special significance for women Fabians, as will be made clear.[70]

The ILP, which arguably predominated among local socialist organisations, formed its first Liverpool branches in 1893, the year of its national foundation. Recent trends in socialist historiography have moved beyond national and electoral perspectives, uncovering, in Eleanor Gordon's words,

62 *The Liverpool Labour Chronicle*, January 1895; Liverpool Report, *Justice*, 13 June 1896.
63 Nationally, Karen Hunt has also noted that the SDF failed to adhere to its sectarian stereotype. See Hunt, *Equivocal Feminists*, esp. pp. 7–15. F. Bealey and H. Pelling, *Labour and Politics 1900–1906*, London, Macmillan, 1958, p. 167, note East Liverpool as one of the prime supporters of reaffilliating the SDF to the Labour Representation Committee after its departure in 1901. See also John Shannon's report on electoral cooperation between the SDF, ILP, FS and Trades Council, Liverpool Trades Council Minutes, TRA/2/129, Liverpool Record Office. For smaller socialist societies see, for example, *The Clarion*, 27 October 1904 which outlines how the combined efforts of the SDF and ILP recruited 37 members to Walton Socialist Society in its first three months.
64 For a discussion of how sectarianism and politics functioned in later years see Whittingham-Jones, *The Pedigree of Liverpool Politics*.
65 *The Clarion*, Liverpool Local Report, 23 March 1895.
66 *Fabian News*, March 1893.
67 See M. Cole, *The History of Fabian Socialism*, London, Heinemann, 1961, p. 37; E. R. Pease, *The History of the Fabian Society*, London, A. C. Fifield, 1916, p. 102.
68 Pease, *History of the Fabian Society*, p. 103.
69 *Fabian News*, June 1901. See also Pease, *History of the Fabian Society*, pp. 102–03.
70 See also 'Grey Quill', 'The Liverpool Fabian Society'.

the 'flourishing and vigorous existence' of local socialist cultures far beyond those suggested by the national profile of pre-First World War socialist parties.[71] This approach has been particularly helpful in studies of the ILP where repeated focus on the 'determinedly provincial' branches has reinterpreted these as the real power base of the party.[72] Another key factor in the success of the ILP in its first decade was its characteristic eclecticism which embraced a variety of different political positions.[73] This was certainly the case in Liverpool where early recruits included the feminist 'New Women' Eleanor Keeling and Alice Morrissey, the wealthy Fabian intellectual John Edwards and trade union firebrand James Sexton. Also involved were members of earlier socialist groups including Jeannie Mole and Robert Manson, a local writer and artist whose 'Pezzers Society' formed a direct link back to Liverpool's mid-nineteenth-century radical coffee house culture.[74]

The many facets of socialism embraced by the ILP, combined with its willingness to work with other socialists, fostered a local socialist culture that was both varied and imaginative. Political meetings were held throughout the city, often several each day during summer weekends.[75] As well as general propagandising, there were more focused meetings of Socialist Sunday Schools for children and a Labour Church for more ethically minded socialists.[76] Many of these took place in the 'Ark', a building behind Kensington Co-Op. *The Liverpool Labour Chronicle* (1894–99), a joint monthly publication from the ILP and the FS, kept members up to date. This socialism may have been local, but it was hardly parochial. International links were also important. From 1880 to the First World War national and international leaders, including Wilhelm Liebknecht, appeared in the city.[77] Local socialists similarly had an international voice, sending delegates to congresses of

---

71 Gordon, *Women and the Labour Movement in Scotland*, p. 261.

72 R. E. Dowse, *Left in the Centre: The Independent Labour Party 1893–1940*, London, Longmans, 1966, p. 4. See also D. James, 'Researching the history of the ILP', in D. James, T. Jowitt and K. Laybourn, eds, *The Centennial History of the Independent Labour Party*, Halifax, Ryburn Academic Publishing, 1992, p. 339.

73 Dowse, *Left in the Centre*, pp. 6–7.

74 See Hamling, *A Short History of the Liverpool Trades Council*, p. 31; R. T. Manson, *Wayward Fancies of R. T. Manson*, Liverpool, Lyceum Press, 1907. For earlier coffee house culture see T. Joff, *Coffee House Babble*, Liverpool, privately printed, n.d.

75 *The Clarion* local reports columns provide a good source for frequency of meetings.

76 For the Labour Church see *The Labour Prophet*, March 1895. Details of the Sunday Schools can be found in *The Labour Prophet* and also in Anon., *Robert Weare of Bristol, Liverpool and Wallasey: An Appreciation and Four of his Essays*, Manchester, C.W.S. publishers, n.d. (1920?), pp. 38–39. I am grateful to Jon Lawrence for drawing my attention to this pamphlet.

77 Liebknecht's meeting showed that the links between local and international politics could go both ways, when he focused much of his speech around a recent socialist obstruction case in the city. See *Liverpool Daily Post*, 2 June 1896.

the Second International (1889–1914), who diligently reported back on the proceedings.[78]

Leisure time, an increasingly important concern for socialists, was also amply provided for with, among other things, a drama group, cycling club, choir, glee club, brass band and ramblers' group.[79] Less organised leisure was also offered via club nights at the Ark or through informal coffee shops. By the early twentieth century socialists had migrated from the temperance coffee houses that they had unofficially adopted to Robert Manson's Clarion Café where John Bruce-Glasier would sometimes drop in to lunch with the 'host of socialists assemble[d]'.[80] When viewing such activities from today's perspective, it is important to remember that opting to participate in socialist recreation meant more than finding an alternative to a night doing nothing. Clubs and societies of all types flourished in Liverpool at this time alongside numerous coffee houses, public houses and music halls. Choosing socialist recreational activities demonstrated participants' conscious effort to create a new, alternative culture, a reflection of the almost religious fervour that characterised their political beliefs.

The variety of active political participation offered to socialists roughly followed the Fabian desire to 'educate, agitate, organise'. Agitational work was characterised by particularly active forms of public propaganda; street corner meetings, large demonstrations and public meetings with noted national and international speakers. Education underpinned a vigorous programme of classes for adults and children alongside smaller meetings to interested non-socialist organisations. Organisation covered campaigns for council seats and other elected bodies, which provided more opportunities for political experience.

Equal membership and the breadth of work available appeared to offer women ample chances to become involved in the public political sphere through socialism. Yet despite impressive national pronouncements on equality, very few local socialist women achieved political prominence on Merseyside. Those who did managed to do so by carefully selecting their spheres of work, and ensuring that these remained, generally, within 'acceptable' areas (as did the women of the WLF).[81] Furthermore, the general lack

---

78 For example, following his attendance at the Amsterdam Congress of the Second International, where he represented the Walton Socialist Society, Frank H. Edwards reported back on proceedings in *The Clarion*, 27 October 1904. Other Liverpool delegates may be found listed in reprinted facsimile congress proceedings, *Histoire de la Deuxieme Internationale*, Minkoff Reprints, Geneva, 1980.

79 For a general discussion on British socialism and leisure in this period see Waters, *British Socialists and the Politics of Popular Culture*.

80 Joff, *Coffee House Babble*; John Bruce Glasier, diary, 5 October 1902, Glasier Papers 1.2, Liverpool University.

81 For details of the ILP's official stance towards women see Hannam, 'Women and the ILP', p. 205. For the SDF, see Hunt, *Equivocal Feminists*, especially Chapter 2.

of a separate organisational space for local socialist women before the First World War forced women into constant direct competition with men for all political work, without a separate base from which they could organise autonomously.[82] Few women socialists managed to attain office within their own organisations, and none was championed as a candidate for institutions such as the School Board, which had long been considered a 'natural' outlet for female political talent by other political parties.[83]

Socialist Activities by Liverpool Women

The reasons for this are complex and difficult to disentangle. There was certainly no overt misogyny from local socialist men. The small group of women frequently cited as central to the spread of socialism in Britain were familiar and welcome speakers on Merseyside. *The Liverpool Labour Chronicle* and the local reports in *The Clarion* and *The Labour Leader* all revealed the enthusiasm that greeted Katherine St John Conway, Enid Stacy, Caroline Martyn and Margaret and Rachel McMillan on their numerous local visits. John Edwards, a leading member of the FS and the ILP, went so far as to claim that much of the spirit that animated local socialism was 'attributable to [these]... women who have become prominent speakers at our meetings'.[84] Many local socialist men had wives who were also active in the movement, encouraged and supported by their husbands. Joseph Edwards and Eleanor Keeling, who married in 1895, developed a model socialist marriage with Edwards, who saw 'a close relation... between the social emancipation of women and the economic deliverance of men', supporting Eleanor, his 'true twin-spirit', in causes from dress reform to her insistence on retaining her maiden name.[85] John Wolfe Tone Morrissey, Liverpool's first elected socialist, and his wife Alice enjoyed an equally public partnership. John Edwards' first wife, although in poor health, was described as being 'in full sympathy with the movement' while his second wife regularly appeared on public platforms.[86]

---

82 S. Davies, 'Class, Religion and Gender: The Liverpool Labour Party and Women 1918–1939', in J. Belchem, ed., *Popular Politics Riot and Labour*, pp. 217–46, looks to the 1920s as a key period for women's separate organisations. However, there were earlier attempts such as local branches of the Women's Labour League, but not prior to 1906. An early edition of *The Labour Chronicle* in September 1894 also mentions a local women's branch of the ILP, but no further traces of this have been uncovered.

83 For socialist attitudes to the School Board see G. Fidler, 'The Liverpool Labour Movement and the School Board: An Aspect of Education and the Working Class', *History of Education*, vol. XXIV, 1979, pp. 43–61. For socialist women in Guardian elections see note 95.

84 *The Liverpool Labour Chronicle*, August 1895.

85 *The Liver*, 20 January 1894; letter from Moira Addison to Joseph Edwards, 15 February 1894, Joseph Edwards Papers, Liverpool Record Office.

86 *The Liverpool Labour Chronicle and Trades Union Reporter*, March 1901.

Not all local socialist men shared this vision of unity. Less assured was James Sexton, the dockers' leader who wrote many of Liverpool's local reports for *The Clarion*. Sexton was a keen promoter of women's unions but Keeling condemned his condescending attitude towards equality beyond the workplace.[87] Much of this was revealed in his language. Sexton often struggled for words to define women engaged in public work. Writing in praise of two local socialists, he declared, 'To comrades Mr and Mrs Brown. I "looks towards them". *Mrs Brown is a Man and a Brother*.'[88] A month later, he wrote of a demonstration by the unemployed that 'the women were the best men'.[89] Words flowed more easily when he described less contentious female activities. 'The skilful touch of the ladies – bless 'em' decorated halls for large demonstrations. 'Ladies' also provided refreshments at big events such as May Day rallies, despite the insistence of the hall fundraisers that they would call themselves 'women'.[90] Less overt, but still noticeable, is the language of the local Fabian and ILP newspaper *The Liverpool Labour Chronicle*, which persisted in referring to women as 'Miss', 'Mrs' or 'women comrades' whereas men were often simply 'comrade' (never 'men comrades').[91] These linguistics were not simply the manner of the day. The national socialist press did call Liverpool women 'comrade'.[92] Joseph Edwards demonstrated contemporary local awareness of gendered language when he explained in *The Liver* that he would use 'man to include hereafter men and women'.[93] Possibly such words might have reflected clumsy attempts at chivalry. There were some concerns among socialists about having mixed leisure environments, an innovative concept to many early recruits; one anonymous correspondent to *The Liver* raised the point that certain ILP members demonstrated a lack of 'decency or manners' towards women and children at their meetings by continually smoking throughout the proceedings.[94] Such attitudes were perhaps not intended to diminish women, but could still have the effect of restricting their public work.

Furthermore, socialist women had fewer opportunities than men to represent their parties in the later nineteenth century. Prior to 1907 women were ineligible to stand for election as local councillors. They could become Poor

---

87 Woman's Column, *The Clarion*, 23 March 1895.

88 *The Clarion*, 9 February 1895, my italics.

89 *The Clarion*, 16 March 1895.

90 *The Clarion*, 11 May 1895.

91 The importance of language in delineating gender relations within socialism has been discussed by K. Hunt in 'Fractured Universality: The Language of British Socialism Before the First World War', in J. Belchem and N. Kirk, eds, *Languages of Labour*, Aldershot, Ashgate, 1997, especially pp. 67–68.

92 See, for example, the report of 'Comrades Isabella Turner and John Morrissey' speaking at Park Street, *The Labour Leader*, 6 June 1896.

93 Joseph Edwards, 'Fabian Opportunities', *The Liver*, 9 December 1893.

94 *The Liver*, 25 November 1893

Law Guardians and School Board members and these elections were some-times contested by socialists in Liverpool. However, campaigns cost money, and although the local FS devoted its seventh tract to the subject of 'Women Voters and Municipal Elections' with a blank printed line to permit the inser-tion of candidates' names, there was little enthusiasm in its own branch to risk the novelty of a female candidate.[95]

Nevertheless, some local women did propagandise alongside men in particularly public fashion. A local cause célèbre between 1895 and 1896 saw several prosecutions brought against socialists for obstruction while holding public meetings.[96] One such case in Park Street, Toxteth, involved John Morrissey, and a woman socialist, Elizabeth (or Isabella) Turner, whose arrest and subsequent trial caused great excitement in the local press.[97] Trial reports portray Turner as intelligent, eloquent and spirited, willing to argue with the magistrate and equating her obstruction to that of a recent royal visit.[98] Although she was only active within her own branch and not on district committees, her case shows that, at an extremely local level, socialism gave women opportunities to speak in public in conditions that were as far removed as possible from the safe confines of the private sphere. This was further exemplified when, as part of the reverberations of this case, local meetings of the SDF were violently broken up. A report of the ensuing fight in *Justice* singled out 'our Anarchist friend Miss Sinnett [who] deserves all our praise for the plucky way she stood by through all the struggle'.[99]

The Clarion Van also offered opportunities for public work to some local women socialists. This van, which began its work providing soup for the unemployed during the particularly difficult winter of 1895, was turned into a touring propaganda van on the initiative of *Clarion* columnist Julia Dawson.[100] Although men and women participated in the tours, a banner running the full length of the van proclaimed it the 'Clarion Women's Van'.[101] Mrs Dean, who had delivered soup 'from within the bowels' of the van while

95 There are a few examples, such as Mary Ellen Morrisey, Poor Law Guardian candidate in Walton North in April 1905, but, as with their male counterparts, they were unsuccessful in their attempts to be elected as socialists.

96 See J. W. T. Morrissey in *The Clarion*, 20 June 1896.

97 See *Liverpool Daily Post*, 5 June 1896. While the *Liverpool Daily Post* report gives her name as 'Elizabeth', *The Labour Leader* calls her 'Isabella'. I discuss this case and its significance in much more detail in 'The Battle of the Boulevards'.

98 For the report of her trial see *Liverpool Daily Post*, 5 June 1896.

99 *Justice*, 7 November 1896.

100 Details of the soup van can be found in J. Braddock and B. Braddock, *The Braddocks*, London, Macdonald, 1963, pp. 5–6; *The Liverpool Labour Chronicle*, February 1895; *The Clarion*, 26 January 1895. For information on the motivation behind its transformation, see *The Clarion*, 29 February 1896. A useful summary is also given in D. Pye, *Fellowship is Life: The National Clarion Cycling Club 1895–1995*, Bolton, Clarion Publishing, 1995, Chapter 6, 'Women, cycling and the Clarion Vans'.

101 See photograph, *The Labour Annual*, 1897, p. 184.

male socialists addressed the unemployed crowds, was one of many local women who found that working as a 'vanner' allowed her to perform as a public speaker, albeit away from her own city.[102]

One public space that socialist women did manage to claim was in the pages of the socialist press where designated women's columns were beginning to make an impact.[103] One of the first of these, which appeared nationally in *The Clarion*, was initiated by Eleanor Keeling as a place where 'we women may settle down to a cosy gossip about our own affairs'.[104] Keeling's metaphorical assumption that her venture represented a physical space was further emphasised by her insistence that it was 'not a woman's article... [nor] a woman's letter... [but] a woman's *Column*'.[105]

In her first column, Keeling offered further thoughts on gendered language by declaring her readers 'sisters' rather than 'brethren'.[106] She too frequently struggled to find appropriate words, especially when searching for a title for herself following her refusal to alter her name after marriage, but her suggestion of the revival of 'mistress' as a title for 'grown women' proved unpopular.[107] National circulation did not prevent Keeling injecting much local material into her column. She publicised initiatives such as her work with women's unions which contributed to a sense of a broader women's socialism fostered by the column.[108] When Julia Dawson took over the enterprise in October 1895 she retained the feeling of female comradeship. Frequent mentions of individual women by name, not all of them national figures, along with small details and anecdotes combined to provide a suggestion of familiarity among the readership.[109] Under Dawson's editorship, the 'Woman's Letter' (she altered Keeling's chosen name) became an important forum for developing and promoting ideological positions around issues with particular relevance to women.[110]

102 *The Liverpool Labour Chronicle*, February 1895.
103 For an overview of women's columns in the socialist press see K. Hunt and J. Hannam, 'Propagandising as Socialist Women: The Case of the Women's Columns in British Socialist Newspapers 1884–1914', in B. Taithe and T. Thornton, eds, *Propaganda: Political Rhetoric and Identity 1300–2000*, Stroud, Sutton, 1999, pp. 167–82.
104 *The Clarion*, 9 February 1895.
105 *The Clarion*, 9 February 1895, my italics.
106 *The Clarion*, 9 February 1895.
107 *The Clarion*, 13 April 1895.
108 *The Clarion*, 2 March 1895.
109 Julia Dawson's residence at Wallasey meant that not all of the local flavour was lost, and Merseyside women continued to figure without introduction in her column. See, for example, her remarks on Jeannie Mole's illness, *The Clarion*, 19 December 1896.
110 L. Barrow and I. Bullock, *Democratic Ideas and the British Labour Movement 1880–1914*, Cambridge, Cambridge University Press, 1996, p. 157. For a discussion of the origins and importance of the parallel 'Matrons and Maidens' column in *The Labour Leader* see Hannam, 'Women and the ILP', p. 209.

The Liverpool Labour Chronicle also ran a 'Woman's Page' from October 1895. Edited by Jeannie Mole, it followed a similar pattern to the *Clarion* column, combining general articles with items intended to impart particular information about specific campaigns. Like the *Clarion* column, it was devoted to women's issues, although Mole never discussed its purpose in the way in which Keeling had done. These pages' separate status added to the impression that there were issues of specific importance to socialist women that were not being sufficiently addressed within the broader labour movement. Mole's column was particularly noticeable in this, especially with her emphasis on housework, which promoted discussion of the issue within a politicised forum, although it did little to challenge contemporary views on the sexual division of labour.[111] Women's columns undoubtedly faced the same accusation of 'ghettoising' their readership as did the promoters of separate women's sections.[112] Yet they were never above self-parody, as revealed by Keeling's expressions of mock horror when she 'descended' to publishing recipes.[113] Furthermore, they provided a space within which women could define their own political concerns, even if these stemmed from a politics rooted in the ideology of separate spheres.

Admitting to some belief in particular female qualities allowed local socialist women to carve out distinct niches in areas that were less contentious than the world of public politics. Motherhood, childcare and the education of children were seen as particular female concerns. While socialism theoretically refuted this, in practice many socialist men were happy to leave such issues to women. Nationally, education represented an area where socialist women were able to take a space that was allocated to them as 'suitable' and to transform it into something far more public.[114]

Merseyside women developed a similar approach towards the socialist education of children. Keeling took a leading part in this work. She had undertaken some formal teacher training which she was keen to put into service for socialism, believing that working with children would have more far-reaching effects than efforts towards adult or self-education.[115] In 1894 she published a series of outline addresses for children aimed at explaining socialism to the very young through metaphors of birds and animals.[116] She may well have drawn on these when with 'Sister Lena' [Mrs Wade] she

---

111 Particular examples include 'Housewives and Queens', *The Labour Chronicle*, December 1895; 'A Cry from the Kitchen', *The Labour Chronicle*, September 1897; 'Thrifty Housewives', *The Labour Chronicle*, October 1895.

112 Examples include the letter from Elsie Harker to *The Labour Leader* which complains of all 'reactionary sex distinctions', *The Labour Leader*, 11 April 1896.

113 *The Clarion*, 16 March 1895.

114 See, for example, Steedman, *Childhood, Culture and Class in Britain*.

115 Fidler, 'The Work of Joseph Edwards and Eleanor Keeling', pp. 293–379.

116 *The Labour Prophet*, October 1894.

assisted Robert Weare in Liverpool's first socialist Sunday School attached to West Derby ILP.[117] This venture soon attracted over 200 children, including many sons and daughters of socialist activists.

To spread the message of socialism beyond the children of the converted, a new organisation was required. *Clarion* editor Robert Blatchford had begun such an initiative in 1893 in the form of the Cinderella Clubs. These demonstrations of practical socialism at work were intended to provide a place where children from the slums 'could dance and play and have dolls and fairy tales'.[118] Their priority was feeding and entertainment, although socialist rhetoric underpinned their work. This work was described in detail in supplements to *The Labour Prophet* and also in Dawson's Woman's Column, the latter emphasising a femininised view of Cinderella work despite the participation of men. In November 1893 Keeling began preparatory work for Cinderellas in Liverpool.[119] The first one opened in Eldon Street in December.[120] At the second Cinderella, which opened in Faulkner Street in December 1896, 100 children were fed, with crowds more waiting to gain admission.[121] Eldon Street Cinderella was run by men and women, a situation that says more about the lack of prominent local women than about a direct attempt to exclude them. Jeannie Mole was to officially open the first one, but withdrew through illness at the last minute to be replaced by John Edwards. However, while men mainly did the organisational work needed on the day, women had a different attitude towards Cinderella. They saw it as an ideal opportunity to reach and recruit other women and tried to get the mothers of the children involved, first through helping with the food on the day, then later through sewing circles which came to be associated with the Cinderellas.[122]

Despite its association with motherhood, Cinderella work was not an easy option for women. Clubs faced an overt hostility from other community groups who felt that socialists and the poor were best kept apart. Some Christians feared that the excitement of the Friday night entertainments drew poor children away from more pious activities. When one Liverpool Cinderella temporarily withdrew from its premises due to difficulties with safety in the building, a local clergyman, Canon Hobson, crowed to his parishioners:

117 For the socialist Sunday School see Anon., *Robert Weare – an Appreciation*; 'Sister Lena'
       [Mrs Wade], 'The Children's Corner', *The Liverpool Labour Chronicle*, from August 1895.
118 *The Labour Prophet*, June 1893.
119 *The Liver*, 18 November 1893.
120 *The Porcupine*, 6 January 1894; *The Labour Prophet*, January 1894.
121 *The Clarion*, 2 January 1897.
122 See *The Clarion* Women's Column, 23 January 1897; 18 December 1897.

I am thankful to inform you that the Socialists have withdrawn from the parish where for some time they have been catering for our poor children... this is an answer to prayer and effort for some months to get back our dear little ones who were thus drawn from our school.[123]

'I don't object to Socialists feeding... the children in my Parish so long as they don't attempt to imbue [them] with Socialist ideals', he explained to *The Porcupine*.[124] Other problems could come from the children themselves. They could be difficult to handle, 'ill-clad, shivering little mortals with... quick wit and playful tricks'.[125] Few socialists possessed the talent of Robert Weare who 'could hold two hundred [children] enthralled, silent as mice' with his storytelling skills.[126] Sometimes men had to be placed on the door to prevent mobs of children from invading the clubrooms. Although women never explicitly complained, Mrs Dean, a stalwart of the Faulkner Street Cinderella, revealed much of their anxieties when she remarked that 'a pleasing factor of the work... [was] the improved cleanliness and behaviour of the children' over time.[127]

While Conservative participation was limited on Merseyside, both the Liberal and socialist parties offered women increasing opportunities for public political activity. Socialist women were offered equal membership and theoretically equal space. However, in practice, this often led to their losing out in direct competition with men and their demands being marginalised. Liberal women by contrast enjoyed less parity within their actual party, but developed a thriving auxiliary organisation. Here they found more political space and learned valuable organisational and orational skills but remained reliant on men for more public opportunities such as election work, which was not frequently granted. In addition to this, all parties placed particular restrictions on the women who could participate in the opportunities for public life that they provided, in that they obviously were open only to women of a particular political belief. In many instances the Liverpool material indicates that these political beliefs were often as much a matter of class and family networks as of personal choice, especially in the case of Liberalism.

Until 1905 this was not particularly problematic. It was unlikely that women with personal political affiliations would alter these lightly. Conservative women, for example, did not rush to join the WLAs, despite sharing the class background of many Liberal women, when the Primrose League failed to offer them wide political experience. However, as a large

123 *The Clarion*, 29 December 1900.
124 Cited by Julia Dawson, *The Clarion*, Women's Column, 19 January 1901.
125 Anon., *Robert Weare – an appreciation*, p. 40.
126 Anon., *Robert Weare – an appreciation*, p. 40.
127 *The Clarion*, 13 November 1897.

suffrage movement emerged on Merseyside, political parties faced a more severe challenge to their organisational practices towards women. Through its many organisations the suffrage movement appealed to all women, regardless of class or political affiliation. Increasingly, women who began their political activities through local political parties found their loyalties divided as suffrage took up more of their time.

CHAPTER FOUR

The Liverpool Women's Suffrage Society

By the turn of the century, women's parliamentary enfranchisement had
become a ubiquitous issue. It was one that all politically active women had
to face, regardless of their personal party affiliation. In local government and
within trade unions women had implemented parliamentary legislation
devised by men, or patiently lobbied the men who were able to alter it. Beyond
the municipal arena they had campaigned and canvassed to elect men to
parliament. The increasing prominence of suffrage campaigns threw into
stark relief many of the circles that loyal party women were trying to square.
These campaigns questioned women's very presence in the parliament-
centred world of party politics, forcing all organisations to declare their
position. Therefore, while the detailed responses of existing political organisations to the growing suffrage movement will be reviewed later, here the
suffrage organisations themselves must take centre stage, as they did in their
day.

The suffrage movement with its flamboyant actions and associated spectacle has attracted much historical attention, with many volumes now
devoted to chronicling the policies of the two largest suffrage organisations,
the Women's Social and Political Union (WSPU) and the National Union
of Women's Suffrage Societies (NUWSS).[1] However, in writing the history
of the suffrage movement on Merseyside, I have tried to move away from
constructing a narrative that simply concentrates on the more spectacular
actions that women undertook to achieve the franchise.[2] Although some fairly
sensational events will be mentioned, my concern is more with presenting
the suffrage organisations as *political* organisations whose agenda placed the
franchise alongside wider explorations of women's political roles. The
geographical boundaries of my study allow space for a broad range of organisations to be considered simultaneously. The purpose of this is twofold.

1   See, for example, L. Parker Hume, *The National Union of Women's Suffrage Societies
    1897–1914*, New York, Garland, 1982; A. Rosen, *Rise Up Women! The Militant Campaign
    of the Women's Social and Political Union 1903–14*, London, Routledge & Kegan Paul,
    1974.
2   For example, M. McKenzie, *Shoulder to Shoulder*, New York, Vintage Books, 1988; M.
    Ramelson, *Petticoat Rebellion: A Century of Struggle for Women's Rights*, London, Lawrence
    & Wishart, 1972.

First, within a single locality it is possible to interpret the success of the different approaches of individual organisations to politicising women by comparing the levels of access that each succeeded in providing members to the public political sphere. Second, close examination of how particular organisations function on the ground and are experienced by individual members can further our understanding of them as national political bodies. Calls for women's suffrage had permeated Victorian radical circles since the days of Chartistism.[3] The first suffrage petition, with 1,499 signatures, was presented to Parliament by John Stuart Mill in 1866. The first dedicated suffrage group, the London National Society for Women's Suffrage, formed the following year. This was followed by provincial groups in Manchester and Edinburgh, Bristol and Birmingham. These were not as parochial as their names imply, but recruited from a wide area; early members of the Manchester National Society came from Cambridge, Hertfordshire, York, the Isle of Wight and London itself.[4]

Although the early societies favoured discreet campaigns of petitioning, quiet individual lobbying and occasional public meetings, they were not wholly conservative in politics or outlook. The Manchester National Society in particular attracted a group of strongly radical campaigners including the insurgent feminist Elizabeth Wolstoneholme Elmy, and the leftward-leaning lawyer Dr Richard Pankhurst. Josephine Butler, who (helped by Elmy) was horrifying genteel society with her outspoken campaigns against the Contagious Diseases Acts, was also involved.[5] The first signs of suffrage agitation on Merseyside demonstrated close ties of personnel and politics to the radical Manchester circle. Josephine Butler collected 285 signatures for the suffrage petition that William Rathbone presented to the House on behalf of Liverpool residents in June 1869. In 1870 a further petition was presented with 498 signatures.[6] The following year Butler helped to form the first local organisation, the Liverpool National Society for Promoting Women's Suffrage. Members included her husband George, philanthropic campaigner, Miss Ellen Bibby, and Andrew Leighton, a Liberal who was in favour of women's rights.[7]

The Liverpool Society was joined by another in Birkenhead. Between 1870 and 1880 both held a small number of public meetings, in keeping with the national campaign.[8] Suffrage was not yet considered as a separate polit-

---

3 For more details see Holton, *Suffrage Days*.
4 *Women's Suffrage Journal*, 1 March 1870.
5 For details about the Butlers' position in Liverpool society see D. Wainwright, *Liverpool Gentlemen: A History of Liverpool College, an Independent Day School from 1840*, London, Faber & Faber, 1960, pp. 139–41.
6 Manchester National Women's Suffrage Society Second and Third Annual Reports, 1869 and 1870.
7 *Women's Suffrage Journal*, 1 March 1870.
8 The *Women's Suffrage Journal* between these years describes four such events.

ical cause. It remained one of many issues concerning the radical middle-class elite of Liverpool and similar Victorian metropolises. Members of prominent Liberal dynasties such as the Reas, the Holts and the Meade-Kings, who were later to involve themselves in the WLF, all attended suffrage meetings.[9] Local politicians including George Melly threw their weight behind suffragists in parliamentary debates.[10] There were also close links to the temperance movement, another cause dear to the heart of Liberal women. Suffrage was debated at local branches of the British Women's Temperance Association (BWTA) in Liverpool and Birkenhead. The support of such experienced campaigners undoubtedly helped to promote suffrage, although it could be limiting. Pressures on their time from other political commitments sometimes drew them away from suffrage work.

While the parliamentary vote remained elusive, local government proved an easier target. Jacob Bright's amendment to the 1869 Municipal Corporations Franchise Act enfranchised women ratepayers in certain districts. The number of Liverpool women entitled to vote totalled 8,398. Local suffragists marked this with a women's meeting in Hope Hall at which the vote was discussed within the broader framework of the duties surrounding citizenship and the responsibilities attached to the vote. Lydia Becker, the Manchester-based editor of the *Women's Suffrage Journal*, was the main speaker. Her address concentrated on the potential of women's suffrage to alter the current concerns of Parliament. There were many things, she argued, that 'were overlooked... [while] the things that were attended to were... solely in the interests of men' prioritising colonial wars over 'parks... well-built houses, and proper sanitary regulations'.[11] Her belief in the possibility of feminising the public sphere through a gender-based alliance of women did not ignore the competing concerns of party politics. She also recognised that 'among women... there were honest differences of opinion... [with] some women who would give a Liberal vote and others who would give a Conservative vote from equally pure political principles'.[12] How women might select between their conflicting loyalties remained uncertain.

The political parties that Lydia Becker chose as examples also demonstrated the beginnings of a shift in the composition of local suffrage groups. The 1869 Franchise Act retained a property qualification, but within its constraints attempts had been made to attract a broad audience with 'the milliner's apprentice' joining 'the merchant's wife... [and] women celebrated for their philanthropic work'.[13] Yet limits remained. It was not credible that

9 *Women's Suffrage Journal*, 1 May 1873.
10 See letter from Lydia Becker to George Melly, 11 May 1870, Melly Papers, 920 MEL/21/4030, Liverpool Record Office (LRO).
11 *Women's Suffrage Journal*, 1 November 1880.
12 *Women's Suffrage Journal*, 1 November 1880.
13 *Women's Suffrage Journal*, 1 November 1880.

any of the meeting's participants might consider using their vote to help Home Rule or Protestant Reform candidates, both choices offered to Liverpool voters. Nor was radical Liberalism secure in its role as the political promoter of the women's cause. Votes meant party politics, and the local Conservative Party now began to take an interest in the question, recognising a need to safeguard its own ends.[14]

For the next thirty years, constitutional suffrage on Merseyside was to remain largely in the hands of women with connections to Liberal and Conservative politics, at the heart of local society. Its initial connection to the sexual radicalism of the Butlers diminished, as it became almost exclusively the property of the city's middle-class reformers, ladies 'on the fringes of county' as the daughter of one participant recalled.[15] Among the most influential of these were Nessie Stewart-Brown and Mrs Edith Bright, 'one of the coming women of Liverpool'.[16] Bright was active in a variety of religious and philanthropic women's causes including the Mothers' Union and the National Union of Women Workers (with Stewart-Brown). Like the Stewart-Browns, the Brights were committed Liberals and Edith Bright was also active in the WLF. As their public work increased, both women saw suffrage as essential both for their personal political work and as an effective means of removing some of the gender inequalities that they believed underpinned many social questions. 'The key to the solution of all other [reforms]' was Bright's opinion. [17] Both therefore increasingly made franchise reform the main focus of their public activity.[18] Stewart-Brown put her name to the 'declaration in Favour of Women's Suffrage' in *The Fortnightly Review* in 1889.[19] Bright, who had been involved with a suffrage organisation in Southport in the late 1880s, joined the Central Society for Women's Suffrage

---

14 For example, a special meeting to discuss suffrage called by the Council of Liverpool Constitutional Association, 10 June 1884, Conservative Party Papers, Acc 4913/2, LRO.

15 Interview with Mrs Paula Francombe, daughter of Jane Colquitt of Liverpool NUWSS, 1 December 1993. For a further discussion of the importance of continuity between mid-nineteenth and twentieth-century suffrage see Holton, *Suffrage Days*, p. 90; Rubinstein, *Before the Suffragettes*, p. 233.

16 S. Tooley, *Ladies of Liverpool*, no publisher, 1885, p. 168. For Edith Bright see also B. G. Orchard, *Liverpool's Legion of Honour*, Birkenhead, published by the author, 1893; also portrait and biography, *The Liverpool Weekly Mercury*, 7 July 1906. For Allan Haywood Bright see W. T. Pike, *A Dictionary of Edwardian Biography: Lancashire*, Edinburgh, Peter Bell, 1986 [1903]; Waller, *Democracy and Sectarianism*, pp. 480–81. For a clear idea of middle-class women's philanthropic networks, which includes Stewart-Brown, Bright and Booth, see Webster's three-part article 'What Women are Doing in Liverpool', *Womanhood*, vol. 3, no. 16, March 1900, pp. 279–81; vol. 6, no. 32, July 1901, pp. 103–7; vol. 6, no. 34, September 1901, pp. 273–76.

17 See 'Mrs Allan Bright', Tooley, *Ladies of Liverpool.*

18 Tooley, *Ladies of Liverpool*, p. 168.

19 *The Fortnightly Review*, vol. XLVI, July 1889, pp. 123–39.

in the early 1890s, and decided that the time was ripe for a local branch.[20] A meeting was arranged for 1894 with Millicent Fawcett as the main speaker, and at this the Liverpool Women's Suffrage Society (LWSS) was formed.[21] This was followed by a branch in Birkenhead in 1894.[22] Both societies affiliated to the NUWSS when it formed in 1897.

For these women, the step into public life was easy. They both enjoyed the support of their husbands, friends and families as they moved together from philanthropy through Liberalism and into the world of suffrage. This was vital, as even elite women were not above public criticism when their behaviour challenged gender conventions, as Stewart-Brown explained:

> The private lives of our advanced women will bear the utmost scrutiny... But if one of our advanced women spends the afternoon at a committee, having a useful object, and goes out again for a couple of hours to address a meeting in the evening, our critics at one raise the cry 'what dreadful neglect of the home'... One would really think that the greatest crime was for a woman to try to be useful.[23]

There was, however, strength in numbers, and close family and friendship networks cushioned them from attacks. Most of Liverpool's early NUWSS members already knew one another and were used to working together. Some had worked with Stewart-Brown in the RSPCA.[24] Lydia Booth who presided over early meetings of the society had worked in the WIC.[25] Mrs Rendall, wife of the principal of Liverpool's University College had also been in the WIC, and was known as one of local society's foremost hostesses.[26] These women from well-established local families were soon joined by a younger generation of professionals more recently arrived on Merseyside who were also identified with women's rights issues. Dr Alice Ker, one of Merseyside's earliest women doctors, was an early apprentice.

---

20 Tooley, *Ladies of Liverpool*, p. 169. It is impossible to say whether this was the Central Committee of the National Society for Women's Suffrage or the Central National Society for Women's Suffrage society so it is not possible to locate Bright's position in the split between these two groups. See Holton, *Suffrage Days*, pp. 74–75.

21 Tooley, *Ladies of Liverpool*, pp. 168–70; National Society for Women's Suffrage Occasional Papers, 20 March 1893.

22 *Liverpool Daily Post*, 27 July 1895.

23 Tooley, *Ladies of Liverpool*, p.174.

24 For example, Miss Dismore who became a familiar speaker at NUWSS meetings.

25 She was also president of the Liverpool branch of the Society for Returning Women as Poor Law Guardians. See *The Porcupine*, 8 April 1893. For further details of her political and philanthropic work see Tooley, *Ladies of Liverpool*; H. A. Whitting, *Alfred Booth: Some Memories, Letters and other Family Records Arranged by his Daughter Harriet Anna Whitting*, Liverpool, Henry Young & Sons, 1917; obituary, *Liverpool Daily Post*, 1 November 1923.

26 Tooley, *Ladies of Liverpool*. For a further examination of the links between old radical families and the British suffrage campaign see Vicinus, *Suffer and Be Still*, p. 248.

In 1907 when Frances Ivens became Liverpool's first honorary female consultant she too joined the society.[27] Elizabeth MacAdam, a social worker at the Victoria Settlement attached to the University was another important recruit. Eleanor Rathbone, who was later to become as synonymous with suffrage as her family were with respectability, social reform and civic leadership, also joined through this route.[28] Rathbone's experience typified the quandary that faced many young middle-class ladies when they came back to Liverpool in the 1890s having been among the first women to benefit from higher education.[29] They returned home with a taste of independence and public life, but found outlets elusive. For socialist women, the Clarion Soup Van and the Cinderella Clubs of Mill Street beckoned. For respectable ladies, the way was not as clear. Rathbone, for instance, sought public life with a 'faith in her capacity and [the] acceptance of [her] worth' common to all Rathbone women.[30] Her education convinced her that this could be a profession rather than the philanthropic dabbling of previous generations, yet she remained aware that 'her professional and industrial opportunities were narrowly limited by custom'.[31]

With so many well-known local figures, the platforms at NUWSS meetings resembled a 'who's who' of local society.[32] Before the First World War the 'Season' was still an important aspect of Liverpool life.[33] Constitutional suffrage now became part of this, as fashionable ladies like Miss Harmood-Banner 'the charming hostess of Ashfield Hall, Neston' rushed to lend their drawing rooms to suffragists.[34] For women who were 'apathetic' or required further education on the issues and demands of the LWSS these were consid-

---

27 For recognition of Alice Ker's position in local society see Orchard, *Liverpool's Legion of Honour*. For Miss Ivens see W. T. Pike, *Liverpool and Birkenhead in the 20th Century*, p. 218; also E. Crofton, *The Women of Royaumont, a Scottish Women's Hospital on the Western Front*, East Lothian, Tuckwell Press, 1997, p. 238.

28 She became so closely associated with Liverpool suffrage work that it has been erroneously claimed that she began the campaign. See E. Warhurst, *Liverpool Women Citizen's Association*, n.d. (1943?), LRO.

29 Eleanor Rathbone had attended Somerville College. Parallels can be found locally in the experiences of Jessie and Margaret Beavan, Edith Eskrigge and Maude Royden as well as the women mentioned in this chapter.

30 M. B. Simey, 'Eleanor Rathbone', *Social Science Quarterly*, vol. Xl, no. 3, 1966–67, pp. 109–11.

31 E. Rathbone, 'Changes in Public Life', in R. Strachey, ed., *Our Freedom and Its Results by Five Women*, London, Hogarth Press, 1936, p. 20.

32 This mirrors the pattern developed by local philanthropic organisations from the 1850s. See M. B. Simey, *Charitable Effort in Liverpool in the Nineteenth Century*, Liverpool, Liverpool University Press, 1951, chapter V, 'Feminine Philanthropy 1850–1870'. For parallels outside Liverpool see R. J. Morris, *Class, Sect and Party: The Making of the British Middle Class, Leeds 1820–1850*, Manchester, Manchester University Press, 1990, p. 204.

33 For a description of the Liverpool Season and its importance see Nott-Bower, *Fifty Two Years a Policeman*.

34 *The Liverpool Weekly Mercury*, 13 October 1906.

ered ideal.[35] They were also national NUWSS policy, although Mrs Fawcett was aware that they carried inherent dangers. She warned:

> From [their] very nature... addressing as they do a limited class and very limited numbers, it is impossible to rely on them alone for the spread of the movement.[36]

Liverpool members largely ignored this and continued to focus their campaign towards educating 'ladies' for the next twenty years. Public work was limited. Most meetings occurred in members' homes, advertised by word of mouth as the chance recruitment of Jane Colquitt in July 1902 shows. At the age of 17 she was waiting for her father outside a pilotage meeting when 'one of the pilot's wives said "You don't want to sit round here, I'm going to a more interesting meeting. I'll take you" and introduced her to the LWSS'.[37] Colquitt was impressed by its overwhelming respectability. This was also important to her family who approved of her suffrage work despite her young age on the grounds that they knew that 'she was with nice ladies'.[38] As Greater Lancashire became a hotbed of 'radical suffragism' with strong socialist links, Merseyside retained a very different character.[39] Here, the social and personal contacts of early NUWSS leaders raised its public profile, and brought some important recruits. However, their presence limited the branch, restricting its numbers and holding it back from broader recruitment and a wider-based and more varied model of public activity.[40]

Not all local suffragists approved of these tactics. Birkenhead Women's Suffrage Society was criticised shortly after its formation for its 'too quiet' methods. 'Modesty is excellent, but... associations for public objects... must make themselves known or fail' complained a correspondent to the *Liverpool Daily Post* in 1895.[41] Things did not improve. Almost a decade later 'Jeannette', who wrote the women's column in *The Porcupine*, agreed with one of her correspondents that suffrage meetings were 'badly advertised or not advertised at all'. She warned that this would constrain the campaign, as 'a meeting entirely composed of supporters will not push the movement forward'.[42] The formation of the Liverpool branch of the WSPU in 1905

35 See the opinion of Millicent Garret Fawcett in T. Stanton, ed., *The Woman Question in Europe*, New York, Source Book Press, 1970 [1884], p. 1; 'Mrs Allan Bright', Tooley, *Ladies of Liverpool*.
36 'Mrs Allan Bright', Tooley, *Ladies of Liverpool*.
37 Interview with Mrs Paula Francombe, 1 December 1993.
38 Interview with Mrs Paula Francombe, 1 December 1993.
39 Liddington and Norris, *One Hand Tied Behind Us*, *passim*.
40 For work on the relevance of women's networks within their political activities see especially L. Stanley with A. Morley, *The Life and Death of Emily Wilding Davison*, London, Women's Press, 1988. Specific details of the process by which women were recruited to the LWSS come from an interview with Mrs Paula Francombe, 1 December 1993.
41 *Liverpool Daily Post*, 25 July 1895.
42 *The Porcupine*, 4 March 1905. See also 25 August 1905

provided a more direct challenge to the tactics of constitutional suffragists. Although this drew some women away from the NUWSS, it also strengthened its commitment to discreet campaigns, as those who wished for something more forceful now had an alternative. Hence, the emergence of a direct rival gave the NUWSS on Merseyside a remarkable degree of tenacity. Although there is some evidence that nationally the NUWSS was persuaded into more spectacular public demonstrations by the flamboyance of the WSPU's monster parades, there is nothing on Merseyside to reflect this.

The local NUWSS was always more concerned with building centres of influence to advance its case than in developing a mass campaign. Its members were not interested in laying claim to Liverpool's public political spaces. By 1908 there were four local branches at Liverpool, Wallasey, Birkenhead and Liverpool University, but outdoor campaigns were only attempted at Wallasey during the summer. The few public meetings that local suffragists did organise were large, ticketed, showpiece affairs. Merseyside members of the NUWSS did not involve themselves in any public work that was considered 'radical' or 'unfeminine' such as chalking the pavements or carrying sandwich boards to advertise their cause. Impromptu street meetings were unheard of. Even *Common Cause*, the national newspaper of the NUWSS, was not sold on the streets. Sales were consequently so poor locally that a special effort had to be made to encourage members to subscribe.[43] Unlike in other districts throughout Britain, the NUWSS never appointed a paid organiser on Merseyside. The affluence of many of its supporters meant that this cannot have been a financial decision. More likely, there was no need for one: they did not really attempt high-profile public campaigns, and for the work that they did there were sufficient leisured ladies within their ranks who could devote long hours to suffrage activities.

The more public work that some local constitutional suffragists occasionally attempted was located slightly beyond the immediate area. In May 1910 several members went to Widnes to attempt to form an NUWSS branch there.[44] Jane Colquitt undertook much of her campaigning in the Greater Lancashire area.[45] This approach allowed the LWSS to retain its image of a society of gentle persuasion against the increasingly outrageous WSPU. Even when inaugurating new societies the methods of the LWSS owed more to social conventions than political practice. One member recalled:

> We had cards printed with space for the names of five persons, and gave them to as many new members as possible and asked them to fill them up.

43 *Common Cause*, 16 March 1911.
44 *Common Cause*, 5 May 1910.
45 Interview with Mrs Paula Francombe, 1 December 1993.

By this means, membership is rapidly increased, and the members have something to do at once for the new society.[46]

Although rapid integration of members is an essential part of retaining their enthusiasm, filling up a card with names did not provide women with much direct experience of public political activity. Compared with the possibilities for action provided by the WSPU and the ILP, the LWSS appeared tame. Members of other suffrage societies noticed the differences, and referred to the LWSS members as 'lady suffragists'.[47]

What the LWSS did offer its members was a sense of familiarity and an assurance of respectability. One area in which it excelled was the development and expansion of a tight organisational structure. In building this, women such as Stewart-Brown and Bright were able to draw on the political experiences that they had gained in the WLF but put them into practice in an organisation that was not forced to take any account of male-dominated politics. In 1910, a West Lancashire, West Cheshire and North Wales federation was formed. This spawned a formidable array of committees including one to monitor and coordinate press coverage. LWSS members were able to utilise the opportunities presented by such committees and to gain valuable experience and important political skills through this work.

A key priority for Merseyside NUWSS branches that partly explains their attitude towards much public work remained that of attracting people of influence to their cause. Eleanor Rathbone believed that petitions were best restricted to 'medical men, the clergy... JPs... the wives of leading men' and similar rather than 'the miscellaneous signatures of Dick, Tom and Harry'.[48] Suffragists also believed that they ought to take positions of influence themselves whenever possible. In October 1907 they fought a strong campaign in support of Miss Ellen Robinson's attempt to become Liverpool's first woman councillor.[49] Although she failed, the campaign received some sympathy in the local press which was capitalised on in October 1909 when Rathbone became the first woman to sit in the council chamber in Liverpool. This was a tremendous coup for local suffragists. Women had played a large part in Rathbone's campaign and had turned out to vote for her in large numbers. Furthermore, there was now a suffrage voice in an official tier of government, and Rathbone was able to use her position to bring a pro-suffrage resolution before the city council where it was overwhelmingly passed.[50]

---

46 *Common Cause*, 5 May 1910.
47 *The Vote*, 9 April 1910.
48 *The Common Cause*, 5 September 1911.
49 *The Liverpool Daily Post*, 26 October 1907. For Miss Robinson see also *The Friend*, 22 March 1912; and entry in H. Josephson, ed., *The Biographical Dictionary of Modern Peace Leaders*, Westport, Connecticut, Greenwood Press, 1984. I owe these references to Heloise Brown.
50 *The Common Cause*, 9 February 1911.

Important as Rathbone's election undoubtedly was, the responsibility of providing Liverpool's first woman councillor placed further constraints on the public profile of the LWSS. Rathbone herself had always been fiercely anti-militant, believing that militancy 'came within an inch of wrecking the suffrage movement, perhaps for a generation'.[51] In part this came from her belief in the importance and seriousness of public duty. Many of her writings against militancy were permeated with the sense that it was somehow a flippancy. But she also needed to distance herself from what she saw as the publicly unacceptable face of the suffrage movement, as she began to seek public office. Ties to the Liberal Party also hampered broader development of the LWSS. At first they gave the society prominence and an air of respectability. However, as the WSPU increased its attacks on the Liberal government, constitutional suffragists who still supported the Liberal Party were placed in a difficult position. Attacks on the government undermined their party political work, but support for an increasingly anti-suffrage Parliament made them appear less than wholehearted to other suffragists.[52] Furthermore, many non-Liberal LWSS activists such as Dr Alice Ker and Alice Morrissey, who might have provided a counterweight to this, had abandoned the LWSS for the WSPU. To retain a respectable image and avoid confrontation with the Liberal Party the LWSS leadership continued its tradition of low-profile lobbying for suffrage, but also began to develop work in other slightly less contentious directions, such as attempts to educate women into the political process in preparation for the vote.

The Women's Citizens Associations

In October 1911, Eleanor Rathbone and Nessie Stewart-Brown inaugurated a new society, the Municipal Women's Association, aimed at 'awakening... interest on the question of women's suffrage amongst women municipal voters'.[53] It was closely linked to building support for suffrage petitions among women who possessed the municipal vote. Although two branches were formed after the first meeting they undertook little activity and the initiative may well have floundered were it not for a dramatic change in national NUWSS policy the following spring. The decision of the National Executive to open an Election Fighting Fund (EFF) in support of Labour Party candidates recognised both the effectiveness of the WSPU's anti-government election policy and the pro-suffrage policy of the Labour Party.[54] It also spelt

51 *The Common Cause*, 9 February 1911, p.24.
52 *Liverpool Daily Post*, 2 March 1909.
53 The other organisers of this new initiative were Evelyn Deakin and Cecily Leadley-Brown, both members of the LWSS and the Conservative and Unionist Women's Franchise Society, Miss Chubb, and Jane Colquitt, who later became an active Liberal. See also *Common Cause*, 19 October 1911.
54 M. D. Stocks, *Eleanor Rathbone*, London, Victor Gollancz, 1949, p. 69.

the effective end of political independence for the NUWSS.[55] Although it was a triumph for socialist suffragists such as Selina Cooper who had worked for it in the NUWSS and the Labour Party, women who were maintaining links with other political groups felt particularly compromised.[56] The Liverpool branch, with its strong leanings towards Liberalism, was outraged, and responded with a resolution calling on the EC to prevent the EFF from operating 'in any constituency where the effect would be to put in a Unionist'.[57] On the EC, Rathbone proved a particularly strong ally for her society. She felt that the EFF threatened the feminist unity of the NUWSS as it would potentially put non-socialist women in opposition to other women. On a more personal level her work on the city council had made her increasingly anti-socialist. Along with many local politicians she was fearful of the potential threat to social order demonstrated in the 1911 Transport Strike and the municipal advances for socialism that followed this.[58] After the Liverpool resolution was rejected, Rathbone became the focal point of opposition to the EFF on the executive, and resigned over this issue in June 1914.[59]

Locally the Municipal Women's Association provided an ideal forum for constitutional suffragists who were uncomfortable with the EFF, and it is no coincidence that most of its leaders remained active Liberals or Conservatives. In 1913, it relaunched as the Liverpool Women Citizens' Association (LWCA), a body with four aims: to foster a sense of citizenship in women, to encourage self-education in civic and political questions; to encourage the election of women in areas where they were eligible to stand; and to secure, by law-abiding methods, the parliamentary vote.[60] The LWCA also retained a certain exclusivity – initial invitations were sent out to women voters or voters' wives, concentrating efforts on 'superior artisan or lower

---

55 See J. Liddington, *The Life and Times of a Respectable Rebel: Selina Cooper, 1864–1946*, London, Virago, 1984; also Holton, *Suffrage Days*, pp. 176–77; J. Alberti, *Eleanor Rathbone*, London, Sage, 1996, p. 26; Stocks, *Eleanor Rathbone*, pp. 69–71.

56 J. Vellacott, *From Liberal to Labour with Women's Suffrage: The Story of Catherine Marshall*, Montreal, McGill-Queen's University Press, 1993, pp. 165–69. Vellacott goes on to argue that most Liberal women were later persuaded to the scheme, which was demonstrably not the Liverpool case.

57 Vellacott, *Catherine Marshall*, p. 323.

58 For contemporary perceptions of the level of chaos surrounding the Transport Strike see M. Cole, 'Guild Socialism and the Labour Research Department', in A. Briggs and J. Saville, eds, *Essays in Labour History 1886–1923*, London, Macmillan, 1971, p. 266; H. Hikins, *Strike! 1911*, Liverpool, Toulouse Press, 1981; Taplin, *Near to Revolution*; P. Taaffe and T. Mulhearn, *Liverpool: A City that Dared to Fight*, London, Fortress Books, 1988, pp. 19–25. For electoral reactions see Waller, *Democracy and Sectarianism*, p. 261.

59 D. Rubinstein, *A New World for Women: The Life of Millicent Garret Fawcett*, New York, Harvester Wheatsheaf, 1991, pp. 194–96; Stocks, *Eleanor Rathbone*, p. 70. Rathbone returned to the EC within a year.

60 E. Rathbone, *A New Form of Suffrage Propaganda*, London, NUWSS pamphlet, n.d. (1913?), Fawcett Library.

middle-class wards'.[61] Rathbone believed that women like this would be crucial in persuading uncertain MPs of the benefits of suffrage by offering 'a mature and moderating influence' on 'irresponsible' young male electors. She and other local organisers repeatedly claimed that the Women's Citizens Associations (WCAs) (which were later adopted by the NUWSS as official policy, but with the Liverpool one always remaining one of the strongest) were not in contention with the NUWSS, but were complementary organisations. However, the reality in Liverpool is that they became, in effect, NUWSS branches, colonising what had previously been LWSS concerns, while avoiding the need to tackle the question of support for Labour which the NUWSS now proposed.[62]

The LWSS had successfully expanded political opportunities for Liverpool's middle-class women prior to 1911. Following the formation of the WCA, it extended its concern for educating women into citizenship into 'respectable' working-class wards, but still restricted its message to those it felt fit to hold citizenship. This attitude led to a rapid collapse after 1918, as enfranchised women previously bypassed by the LWSS channelled their energies in different directions. Furthermore, the leading lights in the LWSS, Nessie Stewart-Brown and Edith Bright, were loyal party women, and returned to this part of the political arena. The LWCA was rapidly marginalised, and largely depoliticised by the early 1920s.

Prior to the foundation of the WCA, the LWSS successfully expanded political opportunities for middle-class women through a muted campaign that offered them control of their political work without any need to compete with a male membership. They also achieved unprecedented success in local government via the election of Eleanor Rathbone, albeit on a platform that was not officially linked to that of the LWSS. This electoral success fed back into the WCAs, which placed great emphasis on the duties and responsibilities attendant on the franchise, and determined to educate women to exercise these properly.

Yet, despite these successes, the LWSS was often restrictive in the opportunities that it provided for its membership in certain key areas. Its determination to remain respectable ensured that it largely operated in a private or semi-private context in drawing-room meetings or before invited audiences. Much of its practice drew inspiration from the rhetoric of separate spheres which accepted distinct roles for men and women within the political arena based on gender differences. When a suffrage organisation emerged that was prepared to dispute the construction of these roles and challenge their expectations, the LWSS faced a serious challenge to its practice.

---

61 *Common Cause*, 30 June 1916.
62 The LWSS launched the WCA with a series of meetings in each of Liverpool's municipal wards in October 1911. Following this, although meetings continue on the Wirral, only 10 LWSS meetings are mentioned in *Common Cause* prior to the outbreak of war in August 1914.

CHAPTER FIVE

'A real live organisation': The Liverpool Women's Social and Political Union, 1905–14

Early interest in suffrage on Merseyside coincided with the growth of socialism. In April 1905, both collided at the annual general meeting of the LWSS when an argument about organisation developed. Although the society was attracting attention, it had made no effort to extend its committee or alter its working practices. Concerned with the limitations of this approach, two socialist supporters brought an amendment to the AGM suggesting that, instead of automatically re-electing the committee en bloc, there ought to be a ballot of members. Mr Buxton, the proposer, explained that wholesale re-election was

> calculated to deprive the members of any share whatever of representation on the committee... ninety per cent of the women who would be enfranchised by the Women's Enfranchisement Bill would be working women, and yet [they] had no representation on the committee...[1]

Mrs Alice Morrissey, seconding, had further criticisms of the society:

> She had been a member... for twelve months and had been very much disappointed in the work. She had thought the society would be a real live organisation and she would wish to take an active part in it. No headway would be made unless meetings were to be held in different parts of the town...[2]

Buxton, who refused to negotiate the point in private, added that he 'strongly resented the idea that the committee should be reserved to ladies of a particular class or clique'.[3]

Stung by a public attack from fellow suffragists, the leaders of the LWSS retaliated. Mr T. Patterson, from the Chair, felt that the difficulty faced by 'Miss Rathbone and the ladies... on the committee' was 'how to induce the

---

1 *Liverpool Daily Post*, 13 April 1906.
2 *Liverpool Daily Post*, 13 April 1906.
3 *Liverpool Daily Post*, 13 April 1906.

working women of Liverpool to take an interest in the movement' which the socialists denied. Eleanor Rathbone, who found the motion 'distinctly discourteous', remarked cuttingly that

> If the committee which had worked for the movement for many years before the lady and gentleman who brought forward the amendment entered the society… had been advised that there was a desire for a more democratic organisation, they would have been delighted to agree.[4]

The meeting rejected the amendment almost unanimously.

A decade earlier, dissenters might have attempted to reform the LWSS. Now there was an alternative that offered a very different approach to public work, the WSPU, a group formed by Manchester ILP women in October 1903. Its first members imported tactics such as street corner meetings, learned in the ILP, into their suffrage campaigns.[5] In October 1905 they transformed themselves into an explicitly militant society when the well-documented interruption by Christabel Pankhurst and Annie Kenney of a Liberal meeting in Manchester led to their arrest and imprisonment.[6]

The imprisonments precipitated a week of 'indignation' meetings in the North West, and brought unprecedented levels of publicity to the suffrage campaign.[7] The WSPU used similar tactics again in its political campaign around the 1906 general election. Its aims were twofold. Most obviously, suffragettes sought a public pledge on suffrage from the Liberal Party. On another level, their interruptions constituted a challenge to a gendered public sphere in which the parliamentary political platform remained stubbornly masculine. In mounting this challenge, WSPU members drew explicitly on a radical heritage dating back to Chartism.[8] Many of them had personal experience of socialist free speech agitation in the 1890s in which they had fought for a political space for socialist rhetoric.[9] There was nothing particularly innovative in the early campaign nor its methodology. What was unique was

---

4 *Liverpool Daily Post*, 13 April 1906.
5 For some details of ILP/WSPU links in the 1903–5 period see H. Mitchell, *The Hard Way Up*, London, Virago, 1987 [1968]. ILP women in the early WSPU leadership included Flora Drummond, Teresa Billington, Annie Kenney, Helen Harker, Rachel Scott and the Pankhursts themselves. See also K. Cowman, '"Incipient Toryism?" The Women's Social and Political Union and the Independent Labour Party, 1903–14', *History Workshop Journal* 53, Spring 2002, pp. 128–48.
6 For details see C. Pankhurst, *Unshackled: The Story of How We Won the Vote*, London, Cresset Library Reprints, 1987 [1959], pp. 62–63.
7 See Pankhurst, *The Suffragette Movement*, pp. 190–92.
8 See, for example, Christabel Pankhurst's claim that 'the suffragettes are the Chartists of the Twentieth Century', *Liverpool Daily Post*, 1 September 1906.
9 Emmeline Pankhurst was arrested at Boggart Hole Clough agitating for the ILP. See *The Labour Leader* and *The Clarion*, June and July 1896. In Liverpool, Alice Morrissey's husband was among a group of socialists arrested during similar protests. See Cowman, 'Battle of the Boulevards'.

the appropriation of such strategies by unchaperoned women. Contemporary newspapers were quick to realise this, and made much of 'the unladylike behaviour' associated with militancy.[10]

The difference between the WSPU, now distinguished as 'suffragettes', and other suffrage groups in Liverpool crystallised with the first local act of militancy in January 1906.[11] The new Prime Minister, Sir Henry Campbell-Bannerman, spoke to a crowded meeting of 6,000 Liberals in the Sun Hall. A fortnight earlier in London he had sidestepped attempts by suffragette hecklers to persuade him to commit himself on the issue of votes for women with a promise to deal with the subject 'at an early date'.[12] Reporting his promise, *The Labour Leader* anticipated further attacks, commenting that 'as Liverpool is a stronghold of the women's movement he will doubtless redeem this promise when he goes there on January 9'.[13] At the Sun Hall, suffragettes from Manchester and Liverpool subjected him to sustained interruption.[14] Their demands concentrated on working-class women's claim to the vote and were held aloft on banners and shouted from various sides of the public gallery. The hecklers (who identified themselves as working class) were met with physical violence (which one woman returned, delivering a sound slap to a steward) as they were ejected from the hall. 'A pitiful exhibition' was the *Birkenhead and Wirral Herald*'s summary of the events.[15]

Although such tactics outraged local constitutional suffragists (including Nessie Stewart-Brown whose father, Edmund Muspratt, had hosted the event), other groups of women approved of them.[16] Liverpool WSPU quickly recruited an active membership from the ILP. Miss M. Labouchere from the Liverpool branch was its first secretary and Mrs Helah Criddle from Wallasey ILP another early recruit.[17] Another group of women with strong

---

10 See M. Murphy, *Molly Murphy, Suffragette and Socialist*, University of Salford, Institute of Social Research, 1998, p. 9. See also Pankhurst, *My Own Story*, p. 49.

11 The term 'suffragette' was introduced by the *Daily Mail* in 1906.

12 *The Labour Leader*, 29 December 1905.

13 *The Labour Leader*, 29 December 1905.

14 *Liverpool Daily Post*, 10 January 1906; *The Liverpool Weekly Courier*, 13 January 1906. The exact composition of the deputation of nine women is difficult to reconstruct. Although Sylvia Pankhurst makes no mention of her own involvement, another local suffragette, Mrs A. C. Abraham, later indicated that Sylvia may have been present. Flora Drummond and Teresa Billington were there, along with Liverpool WSPU members presumably including Alice Morrissey and Miss Labouchere. Christabel Pankhurst was not among them, having made a showpiece journey from Manchester to attract police attention from those who were intending to demonstrate. See T. Billington Grieg, 'Untitled Fragment', in C. McPhee and A. Fitzgerald, eds, *The Non-Violent Militant: Selected Writings of Teresa Billington Grieg*, London, Routledge & Kegan Paul, 1987, p. 99; Pankhurst, *Unshackled*, pp. 58–59; Pankhurst, *The Suffragette*, pp. 49–50; Pankhurst, *The Suffragette Movement*, p. 195; Dorothy Foster Place (née Abraham), 'Autobiographical Notes', unpublished typescript, private collection, p. 14.

15 *The Birkenhead and Wirral Herald*, 13 January 1906.

16 *The Birkenhead and Wirral Herald*, 13 January 1906.

socialist sympathies came from Pembroke Chapel, a key location for radical and socialist activities before the First World War. These included Miss Ada Broughton who was to be one of the WSPU's most active local public speakers, Mrs Hattie Mahood and Mrs Emma Hillier, the first President of Liverpool WSPU.[18] The third circle to have a sustained input into Liverpool WSPU can be classified as 'Bohemian feminists', women who, like constitutional suffragists, held radical views on a number of social questions, but eschewed respectable, fashionable society in favour of their own social networks, often with strong socialist sympathies.[19] Artists formed a key section of this group, and the WSPU recruited many on Merseyside including the sculptress Ethel Frimstone (née Martin) and painters Mary Palethorpe, Constance Copeman and Jessica Walker.[20] As well as lending an air of flamboyant celebrity to the WSPU, such recruits had a practical use and designed local posters and banners. Alice Burton, an actress, found her stage training invaluable in public speaking for the WSPU.[21] Bohemian society also furnished Liverpool WSPU's most important early recruit, Patricia Woodlock, who was virtually a full-time (if unpaid) worker until the First World War.

The potent combination of socialist and bohemian feminism gave Liverpool suffragettes a unique focus on public work. They had no concerns about remaining within the conventions of respectability. In the WSPU they found an all-female organisation that gave them centre stage.[22] The strong socialist links of many founding members also led Liverpool WSPU to look to working-class women for its first constituency. Its first concerted local campaign in September 1906 was built around lunchtime gate meetings at factories with a female workforce, such as Copes' tobacco works and Crawford's biscuits.[23] Regular open-air meetings were quickly established at recognised socialist venues such as the Wellington Column and Islington

17 ILP Annual Report, 1906. For more details on the Labouchere family and their importance in local socialist circles, see Grey Quill, 'The Liverpool Fabian Society'.

18 For Pembroke Chapel see I. Sellers, 'Salute to Pembroke', and 'An Experiment in Humanism: Windsor Street Ethical Church, Liverpool, and its Founder, Rev. Harry Youlden', unpublished typescripts, Liverpool Record Office.

19 Sandra Holton has noted the importance of such women at national level. See Holton, Suffrage Days, chapter 7.

20 For Martin see R. F. Bisson, The Sandon Studios and the Arts, Liverpool, Parry Books, 1965, pp. 9–10, 73; also A. Bowers, J. Sharples and M. Shippobottom, eds, Charles Reilly and the Liverpool School of Architecture 1904–33, Liverpool, Liverpool University Press, 1996, pp. 11–12. Both works explicitly connect local art, bohemianism and radical socialism, and detail the involvement of figures such as Jim Larkin and Tom Mann.

21 See Cowman, 'Crossing the Great Divide', pp. 37–52.

22 Although the local WSPU welcomed the support of a small group of men, membership remained reserved for women. Consequently, of the more than 1,000 public activities that the suffrage press recorded by the WSPU on Merseyside between 1906 and 1914, only 70 featured male participants.

23 Women's Franchise, 5 September 1906.

Square. However, despite strong political links, the WSPU did not become a class-based organisation in any Marxist sense, nor did it recruit from the ILP alone. Rather, it attempted to promote an alliance of *all* women for its campaigns, arguing that gender was as important in promoting class identity as any economic factor, and that women in fact constituted a class. The popularity of the LWSS among upper-class women kept them away from the new organisation, but the WSPU did recruit numbers of teachers and nurses – women who might be classed as upper-working or lower-middle class. In achieving this, they succeeded where other campaigns had failed. The personal networks of local suffragettes drew groups of women into the WSPU who felt marginalised by constitutional suffrage, but ultimately it was the organisation's inclusiveness that proved the key to its success.

As well as constructing a visible presence on the streets of Liverpool, local WSPU members participated in national events. Liverpool's first suffragette prisoner was Alice Morrissey who was arrested with her husband after they interrupted a Liberal meeting at Belle Vue, Manchester in June 1906, and served a week in Strangeways Gaol.[24] The WSPU also took its membership beyond the local networks of the north west to participate in direct assaults on the heart of the political establishment in London. Increasingly, suffragettes made use of symbolic protests that emphasised women's exclusion from all aspects of politics. A series of raids on Parliament demonstrated the extent to which the House of Commons remained a male enclave. In 1907, the regular Women's Parliament, which comprised delegates from branches throughout the country and culminated in large marches on Westminster, was initiated at Caxton Hall.[25] Delegates' expenses were met by the WSPU.[26] Emma Hillier and Patricia Woodlock took part in one of the first raids on the House of Commons in December 1906. Several women entered the building where Hillier initiated the demonstration by climbing up on a bench to shout 'Votes for Women' until she was pulled down by the police. Woodlock refused to leave the House and clung firmly to the wall, needing two policemen to remove her. In court both women explained their motivation, claiming that local conditions had influenced their actions as suffragettes. Hillier spoke of the general condition of women before being overruled by the magistrate. Woodlock was more specific. 'I am from Lancashire', she explained. 'What else could I do, when I come from the North where there is such misery and poverty... Now if women had votes... ' Their militant actions were not wholly ignored in their speeches. Woodlock, who had lost her hat during the skirmish, provoked an outburst of laughter when she refused to pay her fine. 'I won't waste money. I will buy a new hat with it,'

---

24 For details see *The Labour Leader*, 29 June 1906, 6 July 1906; Mitchell, *The Hard Way Up*, pp. 142–46; Pankhurst, *The Suffragette*, pp. 87–88.

25 See Pankhurst, *The Suffragette*, pp. 138–41.

26 *Daily Express*, 22 March 1907.

she declared, her humour revealing a sense of pride and enjoyment in political work.[27]

Woodlock established a national reputation as a persistent offender the following year. She was arrested with Criddle in the 'wild scenes' and fierce battles with police that ended the first Women's Parliament in February 1907.[28] The following month, only weeks after her release, she participated in a parade of Lancashire working women. This time she was harshly treated by the police who recognised her, and by the magistrate who 'said that he would give everybody warning that if they were convicted in this manner on more than one occasion they would share the fate of the present prisoner'.[29] Woodlock again drew on her background and her wider political beliefs to explain her actions. 'I am proud to be a prisoner for the third time', she stated in the dock, adding that it was 'an honour... to go to prison for the cause of women not for [myself] but for poor, miserable, weak, downtrodden women'.[30]

The confidence of local women participating in national demonstrations had repercussions in their own area. A national profile helped further the WSPU's distinct political identity on Merseyside. By February 1909, the local branch was able to host 'the largest indoor meeting yet in Lancashire'.[31] A fortnight's building went into this, with intense organisational preparation, involving only women. Two parades were held in the city centre on the preceding Saturday, posters were displayed throughout the city, and special cards were printed and left in waiting rooms and at the landing stage. The emphasis on attracting women from all classes continued; Woodlock organised a series of smaller outdoor meetings including several at factory gates aimed at persuading working-class women to come to Sun Hall. At the meeting women stewarded, arranged the platform and made the speeches.

The success of the February meeting rested on vibrant local activity. Unlike the LWSS, the WSPU was constantly concerned with recruitment, and with remaining firmly in the public eye. In addition to regular street meetings, the branch held twice-weekly 'At Home' meetings in the Engineers' Rooms in Mount Pleasant where members and new sympathisers could meet together. As the branch grew, new ways of consolidating a membership were sought. A scheme to divide the city into areas grouped under local captains was attempted, but something more permanent was required.[32] To facilitate this, the branch opened a special fund, and in May 1909 Mary Phillips came

---

27 Details from *The Daily News*, 18, 19 December 1906; *Daily Mail*, 18, 19 December 1906; *Daily Express*, 18, 19 December 1906; *Liverpool Daily Post*, 19 December 1906; Pankhurst, *The Suffragette*, p. 132.

28 *Daily Mail*, 15 February 1907; *Daily Express*, 14 February 1907. Both accounts misspell Mrs Criddle's name, having her as Ella Briddle.

29 *Liverpool Weekly Post*, 23 March 1907.

30 *Daily Express*, 21 March 1907.

31 *Votes for Women*, 28 January 1909.

32 *Votes for Women*, 11 February 1909.

to Liverpool as a salaried local organiser for the WSPU, the first woman to hold such a post on Merseyside.[33]

The work of organisers has been somewhat neglected within histories of the WSPU where they appear as somewhat shadowy figures sent into provincial areas from London to ensure that the will of the Pankhursts was consistently imposed on branches.[34] There is also some evidence that local branches had little or no say in their choice of organiser.[35] Yet surprisingly little is known about the large group of women who drew salaries from the WSPU as organisers, effectively becoming the first women to make politics a career.[36] Those for whom details are available do not slot easily into any single category. The first organisers were early members such as Annie Kenney and Teresa Billington. As the Union grew, salaries enabled working-class women to become organisers. Mary Gawthorpe and her friend Dora Marsden both exchanged teachers' salaries for the two pounds per week available from the WSPU while Hannah Mitchell, a working-class housewife, recalled being 'really glad of the small salary the WSPU paid'.[37]

Organisers provided the main link between an area and the WSPU headquarters, although no formal mechanism of meetings existed to facilitate this. Letter and telephone were the main methods of communication, both allowing for a degree of interpretation.[38] Dissent was possible, but against this remained the fact that organisers did represent the official face of a large political organisation that preferred its membership to adhere to policy as much as any political party.

So did organisers aid the development of a female political culture, or did they simply 'police' dissent? Aside from Mary Phillips who was evidently merely laying some foundations, Liverpool had three paid WSPU organisers from 1909 to 1914, all very different individuals.[39] Comparing their tactics, it becomes clear that a solid core of members was far more important to an

---

33 The ILP had appointed a paid organiser for some months in 1899, but selected a man, Egerton P. Wake. See *The Liverpool Labour Chronicle*, December 1898.

34 See, for example, D. Mitchell, *The Fighting Pankhursts: A Study in Tenacity*, London, Jonathan Cape, 1967; Rowbotham, *Hidden from History*, pp. 77–89.

35 L. Leneman, *A Guid Cause: The Women's Movement in Scotland*, Aberdeen, Aberdeen University Press, 1991, pp. 72, 195–96.

36 Elizabeth Crawford notes 30 WSPU organisers in 1909, the figure increasing in subsequent years. See E. Crawford, *The Women's Suffrage Movement: A Reference Guide*, London, UCL Press, 1999, pp. 478–79.

37 Mitchell, *The Hard Way Up*, p. 167. For further teaching examples see H. Kean, *Deeds not Words*, London, Pluto Press, 1990, pp. 12–13.

38 See, for example, the exchanges between Emmeline Pethick-Lawrence and Dora Marsden, January 1909–December 1911, Marsden Papers, microfilm, University of York.

39 These were Miss Mary Phillips (May 1909–June 1909), Miss S. Ada Flatman (June 1909–December 1910), Miss Alice Davies (June 1910–September 1912) and Miss Helen Jollie (September 1912–August 1914) when the branches closed in line with national policy on the war.

area than an effective local organiser. Organisers succeeded in expanding suffrage work when following methods established in the local area, but attempts to impose alien methods of organisation were largely ignored by the local membership. Merseyside branches were not constantly in conflict with the national centre, but nevertheless initiated their own preferred methods of working, and quietly circumnavigated any policies that did not suit these.

The second local organiser, (Susan) Ada Flatman, was a woman of independent means who had converted to women's suffrage while touring in Australia. Liverpool was her second organisational position, following a difficult time at Aberdeen.[40] She had visited once in December 1908 to help with a particularly stormy protest against Lloyd George, when she made contacts who helped her to plunge straight into her new job. Her lodgings at 22 Mulgrave Street came to serve as an office for the WSPU, its first in the area.

The first large event to organise was Woodlock's release celebration. Her fifth arrest during a deputation of Lancashire working women to the Prime Minister had led to her fourth prison sentence of three months.[41] A strong local campaign of indignation at her sentence and the imprisonment of three other local women ensued, concentrating on the fact that, by refusing to receive women who were representing their region, the Prime Minister was delivering a snub to Lancashire. The campaign raised local sales of *Votes for Women* to 700 in five days.[42] Unfortunately, other street spectacles interfered with Woodlock's release. The large suffragette procession, which featured decorated carriages and a band, did not make the front pages of any of the local papers as it coincided with the beginnings of the Orange marching season. Always a site of trouble, this year the rioting began early. Catholic and Protestant women in the city centre 'fighting each other with knives, [with] a great many arrests made' proved more newsworthy than the large WSPU procession at which 'the police were a present force, but their services were not requisitioned'.[43]

To ensure continuous press attention, peaceful suffrage demonstrations would no longer suffice. Here, the importance of a paid organiser becomes clear. Flatman had inherited a good functioning network of suffragettes with an effective if informal leadership, and was able to add to this. Local suffragettes continued their public speaking after Flatman's arrival, but her lack of any work or family commitments outside the WSPU enabled her to participate in a larger number of events. St George's Plateau and the Wellington Column were now joined by a number of venues on the Wirral. While the LWSS remained ensconced in drawing rooms, the WSPU's colonisation of the public sphere proved a far more effective recruiting tactic; some presti-

40 Leneman, *A Guid Cause* p. 71.
41 See *Votes for Women*, 2 April 1909; *The Liverpool Courier*, 1 April 1909.
42 *Votes for Women*, 23 April 1909.
43 *Liverpool Daily Post*, 3 May 1909.

gious recruits including Dr Alice Ker were poached from the constitution-alists at this time.[44]

Regular public meetings and street sales of *Votes for Women* raised the WSPU's profile and attracted new members, but could not ensure a conti-nuity of publicity or support. For this different methods were needed. Flatman and her members determined to open a suffrage shop. Nationally, shops were an essential part of WSPU marketing.[45] They sold a variety of items: literature; badges, shawls, scarves and bags in the colours; Votes for Women tea and matching china; postcards of the leaders of the movement; even fundraising games with names like 'In and Out of Holloway' and 'Pankasquith'. Shops also helped in recruiting work. Situated in accessible areas, they actively encouraged local women to drop in and find out more about the Union. Their extended opening hours allowed local members to spend more time working together, building a sense of belonging to a team. Although other local shops were the subject of feature profiles in *Votes for Women*, the Liverpool shop was never publicised in this way. This is because in its opening, Flatman defied the wishes of the national WSPU leadership, showing that an organiser could act independently with the support of her branch.

The objections to Flatman's scheme came from the WSPU treasurer, Mrs Pethick-Lawrence, who was worried about its financial aspects. The Merseyside branches were in a good state of growth and were solvent, but not particularly affluent. They had not recruited many wealthy sympathisers and relied instead on a large number of small donations. Yet local suffra-gettes were confident that they could make the shop a success. To persuade Pethick-Lawrence, they arranged a public meeting featuring Mrs Pankhurst for September 1909 to cover the cost of starting the shop.[46] The treasurer then dropped her objections, convinced that such a meeting 'could go very far in paying a year's rent and fitting and decorating'.[47] However, she felt that the scheme ought to be left for a short time. A summer holiday campaign in the Isle of Man had already been arranged by Liverpool suffragettes, and it was 'impractical to enter into business arrangements which... call for the close supervision of a responsible organiser' at such a time.[48] Full of enthu-siasm for the new scheme, Flatman and her members ignored this directive.

44 See Alice Ker's diaries, 8 June 1909, Private Collection, also Lady Constance Lytton to Alice Ker, 13 November 1909, Autograph Letter Collection, Women's Library.

45 For more details see D. Atkinson, *The Purple, White and Green: Suffragettes in London, 1906–14*, London, Museum of London, 1992. I am grateful to Diane for wider discussions around this theme.

46 The meeting, which took advantage of Mrs Pankhurst's presence in Liverpool en route to the USA, eventually took place in October.

47 Emmeline Pethick-Lawrence to Ada Flatman, 28 July 1909. Correspondence of Ada Flatman, Museum of London Suffragette Fellowship Collection, MOL 50.82/1134.

48 Emmeline Pethick-Lawrence to Ada Flatman, 28 July 1909. Correspondence of Ada Flatman, Museum of London Suffragette Fellowship Collection, MOL 50.82/1134.

While Flatman ran the campaign in the Isle of Man, Woodlock, Miss Dunn from Wallasey and Miss Thompson fitted, decorated and stocked the shop, supporting their organiser in this minor act of defiance against Headquarters. Their faith paid off, as the shop recruited 50 members in its first month.[49]

Branch members staffed the shop on a rota basis, leaving Flatman free to continue organising. With the shop as a base, the WSPU was able to increase the public work that brought them local success. Weekly poster parades were now held advertising *Votes for Women*. The paper sales themselves became more of an event with sellers converging on the shop and then processing out together to their various pitches. Yet, in the middle of this success, Flatman attempted to alter the direction of her local campaign, with unfortunate results.

In her first year on Merseyside, Flatman had worked with the local branches, and found members willing to support her even in potentially difficult situations with Headquarters. Her problems during her next year show how organisers were often powerless in working against the wishes of their branches, even if they remained in step with Clements Inn. The National WSPU was increasingly basing its campaign on large, 'set-piece' demonstrations, drawing away from its early populist origins. In line with this in November 1909, Flatman publicly repeated an appeal that she had first made privately for 'ladies to open up their drawing rooms during the Winter'.[50] Her claim that this would avoid speakers having to stand in the cold ignored the long tradition of open-air meetings by local radicals and socialists within which the WSPU had centred its appeal. There was little likelihood that the 'large crowds' whom she felt needed to be kept warm would fit into a drawing room. Besides, the Engineers' Rooms still hosted indoor meetings. Flatman's true motivation was more likely a desire to alter the class base of the WSPU.

This intention emerged as the scheme floundered. Flatman's main obstacle was the fact that no ladies offered a drawing room. Meanwhile, local suffragettes (most of whom had no drawing room to offer) continued lively open-air work for the General Election of January 1910, including protest meetings outside Walton Gaol where suffragettes were being forcibly fed.[51] With the election over, Flatman again attempted to change her branches. The 'At Homes' in the Engineers' Rooms were cancelled to release members for the holiday campaign, but not resumed. The focus of work moved to the Wirral where Mrs Abraham, one of the few wealthy local recruits in the WSPU, was persuaded to lend a drawing room to complement a season of indoor meetings in cafés and tearooms.[52] Some of these developed an air of

49 *Votes for Women*, 19 November 1909.
50 *Votes for Women*, 26 November 1909.
51 Notably Constance Lytton, disguised as Jane Warton. See C. Lytton, *Prisons and Prisoners: Some Personal Experiences by Constance Lytton and Jane Warton, Spinster*, London, William Heinemann, 1914, pp. 242–45.

exclusivity, such as a large meeting with Mrs Pankhurst that concluded with a private reception, attendance restricted by ticket to invited members only. In Liverpool the shop facilitated more public work, hosting meetings and contributing to a large suffrage bazaar at Pembroke Chapel. Those suffragettes who had enthusiastically developed the outdoor campaigns such as Morrissey and Woodlock did not get into open conflict with their organiser, but were conspicuous by their absence at drawing-room meetings.[53]

Flatman's attempts to take the branch members away from their chosen tactics were effectively blocked by a lack of local enthusiasm. Flatman began to write to Clements Inn requesting a transfer.[54] A part-time organiser was sent in to assist her but no improvement in her personal feelings about her position followed, and she abruptly left the city in December 1910. Despite their disagreements on policy, her resignation left local suffragettes with problems. They had managed before the appointment of an organiser, but there were now four local branches leaving members with a much larger task. Furthermore, Flatman had persuaded Geraldine Lyster, the local secretary, to leave the city with her. Morrissey volunteered as temporary organiser and secretary. Mrs Avery, who had been active in the Union since loaning her car for the January 1910 election campaign, took over the important organisational position of *Votes for Women* secretary. Birkenhead, Wallasey and Liscard appointed their own secretaries and *Votes for Women* secretaries at the same time, as the lack of a full-time paid organiser caused problems in coordinating the work across the River Mersey. The branches on the Cheshire side continued to expand, with the Birkenhead *Votes for Women* sales reaching 100 per week.[55] The support given to the WSPU at this time by local members indicates a broad layer of active membership that is not reflected within the suffrage press. Although the names of these women are not awarded a place within any suffrage history, and in many instances do not survive, it was their efforts that consistently maintained an active suffrage presence within the district as much as those of the more prominent activists.

The clear signals that local suffragettes sent out about their preferred ways of working were ignored when the WSPU leadership selected Liverpool's next organiser, Miss Alice Davies. Davies was not anti-militant, and was

---

52 Mrs A. C. Abraham was a recruit from the LWSS who was to prove a vital force for the WSPU.
53 Patricia Woodlock and Alice Morrissey did not drop out of suffrage, or political work. Morrissey kept up her socialist work, and took over the running of the WSPU branch immediately on Flatman's abrupt departure, while Woodlock was arrested in London following the national demonstration of Black Friday, November 1910. Their lack of activity in the Liverpool branch becomes specific to an area, when located within this broader context.
54 Correspondence of Ada Flatman, Museum of London Suffragette Fellowship Collection, MOL 50.82/1134 details her requests, the first of which came in March.
55 *Votes for Women*, 10 March 1911.

imprisoned herself during her time in Liverpool for participating in the WSPU's mass window-smashing in London in the spring of 1912. Her problem, from the perspective of the local branch, was that she preferred these more flamboyant (often London-based) spectacles over the smaller but often more public forms of militancy. Liverpool hosted several large events during her tenure. Edith Craig visited to produce a version of 'The Pageant of Great Women' featuring local suffragettes. The branch also staged its own production of Cecily Hamilton's *How the Vote was Won*. Yet, while these allegorical stagings of women's civic demands brought in funds and were enjoyed by their audiences, their visibility was confined to the auditorium.[56] The successful and popular open-air meetings that had long typified the Liverpool suffrage campaign were largely dropped in favour of indoor meetings and social receptions. The 'At Homes' remained suspended. According to her advertisements in the suffrage press – the most reliable indicator of a branch's activity – Davies, with four functioning branches to help her, achieved a level of public activity between 1911 and 1912 only slightly higher than that of the first small branch between 1908 and 1909.[57] There was still room for individual suffragettes to negotiate around this, which many of them did. Unlike Flatman, Davies was happy to see branches organising meetings that did not feature her as speaker, and the Wirral branches in particular were able to continue some open-air meetings without her. Several of the more active public workers on Merseyside, including Avery, Ker and Woodlock, spent much of Alice Davies' time speaking at Wirral meetings, joined by early suffragettes such as Ada Broughton and Helah Criddle. They did not effectively sabotage the efforts of their organiser to alter the tactics of the branch, but developed their own strategies to overcome their differences, finding alternative areas in which their preferred methods could operate freely.

Davies' work did have some tangible, detrimental effects. The first casualty was the shop, which was abandoned in March 1911 and replaced by

---

56 For a useful discussion of The Pageant and similar spectacles, see L. Tickner, *The Spectacle of Women: Imagery of the Suffrage Campaign 1907–14*, London, Chatto & Windus, 1987, chapter 3, pp. 55–150; also B. Green, *Spectacular Confessions: Autobiography, Performative Activism and the Sites of Suffrage 1905–38*, London, Macmillan, 1997, pp. 75–78.

57 In her 15 months between June 1911 and September 1912, approximately 230 public events were organised or participated in by Merseyside WSPU branches, compared with 152 in the last 15 months before the appointment of a paid organiser, from February 1908 to May 1909. When these figures are considered in the light of the increasing national membership of the WSPU from 1909 to 1912, it can be seen that Davies was not mounting as effective a public campaign as she might have done. In the six months before her arrival, between January and June 1911, the branch members, without an organiser, arranged 50 events, a figure that compares well with the 203 events during the same months of 1910 when it is remembered that 87 of these were directly connected with the General Election.

'more convenient and central offices'.[58] Offices were taken in Renshaw Street, a continuation of Berry Street where the shop had been. They provided a meeting room and headquarters, but lacked the public profile, window frontage and accessibility of a shop. Existing financial figures for Liverpool WSPU demonstrate a massive drop in literature profit, from eighteen pounds, seventeen shillings and one penny in 1910/11, to nineteen shillings and ninepence 1911/12.[59] Local stalwarts reasserted themselves whenever they had the chance. In 1912 when Davies was in Holloway, Woodlock took over as temporary organiser and began 'addressing meetings at a great rate'.[60] Recruitment and growth, however, did suffer from the change in direction.

Davies was also less companionable with her branch members than Flatman had been. She moved the branch's summer holiday campaigns from the Isle of Man, which was a popular destination for Liverpool's more affluent working classes and had allowed the WSPU to continue to target a local audience.[61] Davies preferred the Lake District where she took no local members but joined with Vida Goldstein and Beatrice Harraden, well-known national figures in the WSPU. When she did work with her branch, she appeared almost surprised by their abilities. In the autumn of 1911 she attempted to link up with the LWSS and the Conservative and Unionist Women's Franchise Association (CUWFA) for a large suffrage meeting in the Sun Hall. The event brought little publicity for the WSPU; the *Conservative and Unionist Women's Franchise Review* gave them only a passing notice while *Common Cause* did not mention that they had been present. The snubbed suffragettes returned to hosting their own meetings, with a large gathering featuring Mrs Pankhurst in the Hardman Hall in February 1912. In one of her fullest local reports, Davies confessed that she 'would not have dared to attempt [the] meeting' had she 'not been able to rely... on a body of members who were willing to put in days of real hard labour'.[62] She then thanked several members by name. This was by no means the first large meeting that the Liverpool WSPU had organised. Others had been run by a similar team, Mrs Morrissey and Mrs Abraham particularly having a wealth of experience behind them. Davies' uncertainty in her ability to bring such an event off shows how the lack of public activity that she had pursued within the local branch had led to a crisis in confidence in its and her own organisational abilities. She did not believe that her public meeting could succeed because she had never seen the branch in action on this scale.

The differences between Davies and her branch were ultimately political

58 *Votes for Women*, 17 March 1911.
59 WSPU Annual Reports, 1910–11 and 1911–12.
60 Dr Alice Ker to Margaret Ker, 14 March 1912. Autograph Letter Collection, Women's Library.
61 See *The Liverpool Courier*, 20 August 1909.
62 *Votes for Women*, 9 February 1912.

and not personal. Many of her local members respected her even if they did not agree with her tactics. Ker, who had been particularly involved in keeping public work going on the Wirral between 1911 and 1912, was in Holloway with Davies and mentioned her affectionately in letters to her daughters.[63] On Davies' release, suffragettes held their first ever local garden party, providing her with a welcome much more in keeping with her taste than the large demonstrations that had met Woodlock and other Liverpool members on their release from jail. There was no serious parting of the ways between organiser and branch as occurred elsewhere.[64] Davies simply drifted away from the city, running a second Lake District campaign, and then taking a holiday from which she did not return, rather than abruptly disappearing.

In 1912, the national WSPU presented a very different picture from the organisation that had attracted socialist and bohemian feminists to a Liverpool branch in 1906. Many of its early leaders had altered their political perspectives. Annie Kenney and Christabel Pankhurst (the latter in exile in Paris) were working to counter their concerns that the movement was becoming too dominated by the working-class women of the East End of London.[65] Teresa Billington-Grieg had severed her WSPU connections and formed the Women's Freedom League (WFL) which Hannah Mitchell had joined. Many of these changes did not reflect the priorities of the more active Merseyside suffragettes. Fortuitously they were also not the priorities of the fourth local organiser, Miss Helen Jollie, who arrived in September 1912. Working with the local membership she revitalised the branch, recruited new members and regained a highly public space for suffragettes.

The period between 1912 and the WSPU's collapse at the outbreak of the First World War has been characterised as representing a 'descent into chaos'.[66] Violent militancy increased, and its scope widened to include private as well as public property. Arson and bombing were added to a selection of tactics intended to disrupt as much as possible. The pages of *The Suffragette*, the WSPU's new paper from October 1912, show that Liverpool was well to the fore in the new campaign, with almost as many instances of direct action as London. Suffragettes set fire to a school at Greenbank Drive next door to Eleanor Rathbone's home. They burned the altar and choir stalls at St Anne's Church.[67] They placed bombs in the Stock Exchange and the Palm House in Sefton Park and damaged numerous pillar boxes and attractions at the Liverpool exhibition. Far from driving support away from the Union, the local WSPU grew alongside this violence. There are two main

63 Alice Ker's prison letters, Autograph Letter Collection, Women's Library.
64 For details of such splits in Scotland, see Leneman, *A Guid Cause, passim.*
65 Pankhurst, *Unshackled, passim.*
66 S. A. Van Wingerden, *The Women's Suffrage Movement in Britain 1866–1928*, Basingstoke, Macmillan, 1999, pp. 136–50.
67 *Aigburth Parish Magazine*, 1 January 1914, p. 3, which comments that 'the sacrilegious outrage was perpetrated by suffragettes'.

reasons for this. First, the WSPU fitted in well with an important local political climate. The syndicalist-inspired transport strike of 1911, which
culminated in armed intervention by the Home Secretary, showed the willingness of large sections of the local population to engage in direct political
action.[68] The LWSS, which unlike its parent body was actually moving
further away from socialism, offered no outlet for this. Second, and more
importantly, there was the work of the WSPU itself. This provided a wide
range of actions from which militant suffragettes could select the most appropriate to them. Although violent militancy played an important role within
the Liverpool WSPU, it never completely replaced other tactics, but was situated within a broad range of militancy.

· Nevertheless, violent militancy did incur particular costs. Helen Jollie's
first innovation as an organiser was a fund to cover the legal costs of arrested
women and allow non-participants a role in direct action.[69] Each donor was
carefully listed in *The Suffragette*. This unusual tactic unwittingly revealed
the breadth of support for militant actions, as it showed that the Liverpool
fund came from numerous small donations.[70] While five amounts of ten
pounds or more indicate some level of approval among more affluent
Liverpolitans, most donations were for less than one pound, and most of
these for less than five shillings. Their wide base (they did not include the
regular membership subscriptions of well-established activists) demonstrates
that extreme militancy did not detract from support. At the height of the
arson campaign in Liverpool the WSPU collected fifty-three pounds, six
shillings and eight pence from the public in support of their self-denial
fundraising week.

Publicly donating money to an organisation involved in illegal activities
can be read in itself as one form of militancy for women concerned with
personal respectability. Nor was it without risk; increasingly the government
was attempting to prosecute anyone associated with the WSPU, including
the commercial printers that handled its material. For members more willing
to take action, arson was not the sole option. Militancy continued to involve
colonisation of a male public sphere by women. The first indication that the
local WSPU was to return wholeheartedly to the work it had done in this area
was the announcement that a new shop was to be opened.[71] From the shop,
Jollie initiated a wider variety of techniques than any previous local organiser. New paper sellers were encouraged in order to meet a target of 400 sales
per week. The weekly open-air meetings were reinstated. There were also
weekly poster parades of 15 or more suffragettes advertising their newspaper.
When Flora Drummond came to speak at large meetings in the city centre,

68 See, for instance, Taplin, *Near to Revolution*.
69 *The Suffragette*, 15 November 1912.
70 Approximately 164 individuals donated 376 separate amounts.
71 *The Suffragette*, 1 November 1912.

and in Co-Operative Hall, Garston, Jollie returned to the tried and trusted Liverpool methods of daily street meetings and poster parades to attract support. Wirral branches also rented advertising hoardings at mainline stations for WSPU posters and persuaded local shops and businesses to display them, raising the local profile of the Union and ensuring that the colours remained on public view. In this aspect, militancy does not appear to have deterred local businesses from linking in with the WSPU. Indeed, the sole example of public hostility during the entire militant period came when the council refused the loan of a local library for a lecture on 'Militant Methods'. The WSPU's Liverpool premises were never subjected to reprisal attacks as were those in other cities.[72]

Unlike previous organisers, who simply advertised events in *The Suffragette* or *Votes for Women,* Jollie used her local reports to consolidate and inspire new members. Each week she named recent recruits. She utilised three categories of membership: a paper seller was the first step, either street or door-to-door, then came formal membership (new paper sellers were frequently welcomed as new members a few weeks later); and finally the maiden speech when members were welcomed as new speakers. During her period as organiser, the average weekly paper street sales of *The Suffragette* reached about 300 copies, exceeding those reported under Flatman's leadership, when no attacks on property were occurring. The best sellers each week were always congratulated by name, with their totals ranging from about 50 to 75 papers. Members were always encouraged to take as active a part as they could. So, for example, when 17 women volunteered to make up part of a deputation of working women in January 1913 the finance columns report a flood of donations towards their expenses.[73]

Jollie appears to have brought a unique sparkle to the local suffrage campaign. Quite simply, she made it fun, and it was possibly this sense of the excitement of direct action that attracted new members. On several occasions she took her branch to the cinema or to the theatre for a new type of protest. The first time this occurred, in the Palais de Luxe Picture House, the audience was amazed to find that the intermission provided them with an on-the-spot view of suffragettes in action. One woman made a speech while others handed out leaflets about forcible feeding. Jollie reported that there were 'many remarks of sympathy and appreciation of the women's courage' and that the manager himself bought a paper, and apologised for any discourtesy the attendants may have shown the women during their ejection. Four dozen more copies of *The Suffragette* were sold on this occasion. Sometimes the protests were planned to reflect aspects of the performance. This interruption came after a film about the Statue of Liberty, when obvious

72 Leneman, *A Guid Cause*, p. 114. See also Crawford. *The Women's Suffrage Movement*, p. 633.
73 *The Suffragette*, January–February 1913.

parallels were drawn. The most furious occurred at the Liverpool Rep, when James Sexton's play *The Riot Act* was staged. The play was the first ever attempt to portray local working-class life on the stage, and attracted an atypical audience of working men. However, as the only female character in the play 'was disloyal, lied, had a past, and made open love to her employer – and was a suffragette', the WSPU singled it out for special attention.[74] Jollie and her members consistently interrupted the performance from the stalls until Sexton agreed to tone down his character.[75] Similarly, during the opera *The Dance of Death*, a song by French soldiers about fighting for freedom preceded an interval during which suffragettes addressed and leafleted the audience. This time they were so violently ejected that one woman in the audience donated five pounds in protest at what she had witnessed.[76]

Local suffragettes also challenged a different public sphere through participation in the national 'prayers for prisoners' initiative, interrupting church services to pray for suffragette hunger strikers.[77] In Liverpool they focused on the new Lady Chapel in the Anglican Cathedral, which was dedicated to famous Christian women including, ironically, one of Liverpool's first suffrage campaigners, Josephine Butler, which offered a perfect backdrop to militant spirituality.[78] The first protest in January 1914 ended with one suffragette unfurling a banner with the text 'I came not to send peace, but a sword.'[79] The sanctified location did not prevent the protestors from being knocked to the ground. The following week saw the peculiar spectacle of six policemen and a sergeant guarding the Lady Chapel in an unsuccessful attempt to keep women away from evensong. Such actions, along with the theatre and cinema protests, represented a type of militancy that did not include the risk of imprisonment, but was every bit as daring in that it laid its participants open to public ridicule and physical violence.[80]

During the same period, Jollie attempted to broaden the appeal of the Liverpool branch in other directions. Nationally, the WSPU leadership was becoming increasingly anti-male. In 1913, Christabel Pankhurst had begun the series of articles that were to make up *The Great Scourge and How to End It*. In these, she delivered a fierce attack on the sexual double standard, culminating in her new slogan, 'Votes for women and chastity for men'. Locally

74 G. Wyndham Goldie, *The Liverpool Repertory Theatre, 1911–1934*, Liverpool, Liverpool University Press, 1935, pp. 92–93.
75 *The Porcupine*, 14 March 1914.
76 *The Suffragette*, 6 February 1914.
77 Pankhurst, *The Suffragette Movement*, p. 510.
78 For a contemporary feminist appreciation of the Lady Chapel, see *The Vote*, 11 November 1909. I discuss the religious contexts of the Liverpool protests in "We intend to show what Our Lord has done for Women': The Liverpool Church League for Women's Suffrage, 1914–18', *Studies in Church History*, vol. 34, 1998, pp. 475–86.
79 *The Suffragette*, 23 January 1913; 30 January 1913.
80 *The Suffragette*, 27 February 1914; 6 March 1914.

there is no evidence for a 'sex-war'.[81] Rather, the opposite can be seen. In a move that cut directly across national trends, Jollie worked more closely with men than any other Liverpool organiser. David Jenkins, a local artist who designed propaganda banners for the WSPU and Lawrence Fenn from the Fabian Society became particularly noticeable supporters. However, men were still debarred from membership, which continued to differentiate the WSPU from other contemporary political groups and ensured that ultimate political control rested entirely with its female membership.

Jollie also widened the scope of WSPU meetings, moving from suffrage and feminism to include other political topics. She organised meetings on diverse themes, for example Dr Ker on 'The Medical Aspects of Women's Suffrage', the trade union activist Miss Hackey on 'The Position of Women in the Post Office' and Lawrence Fenn on 'Why I am a Socialist'. Political education was taken seriously, and a suffrage library developed from which members could borrow. This broadening also coincided with the LWSS's formal shift away from the Labour Party and helped the WSPU cement (or in some cases reaffirm) links with local socialists. The only time the LRC ever discussed suffrage was in 1913 when it passed a resolution condemning the treatment of Mrs Pankhurst under the Cat and Mouse Act. The resolution recognised that suffragettes were engaged in a political struggle, an important acknowledgement by any political party and one which the WSPU had long sought.[82] There was also some evidence that individual suffragettes were simultaneously moving towards socialism. Margaret Ker, for example, who was best known within the WSPU for her direct action firing pillar boxes, was introduced to the FS by Fenn.

These tactics and the move back to highly public activity reactivated some older WSPU members while a new generation could be seen holding street meetings and running the shop. This makes it possible to reinterpret militancy not as the logical conclusion to an increasingly marginalised and sectarian political campaign, but as a carefully planned political tactic that increased the appeal of the movement by allowing women excluded from the main political sphere as represented by Westminster to take part in their own forms of direct political action. The case of Liverpool WSPU demonstrates that even the more violent militant actions did not deter individual women from joining its ranks. Rather, the opportunity that the Union provided for local women to participate in a wide variety of militant actions, all involving a breaking of conventions, led to its becoming the largest women's organisation within the city. Again, a mixture of women participated, showing how the major key to Liverpool WSPU's success came in the ability of local activists to pitch a campaign at a level that would attract many different

81 See S. Kingsley Kent, *Sex and Suffrage in Britain 1860–1914*, London, Routledge, 1987, chapter 6.
82 Liverpool Labour Representation Committee Minute Book, 3 July 1913.

women through prioritising concerns about gender. Sometimes this borrowed methods familiar to the local socialist parties, except that within the WSPU women controlled *all* aspects of such campaigns. Other activities such as the theatre protests were unique to the WSPU and demonstrate its originality. As new methods were never allowed to supersede the WSPU's original tactics of street meetings, a level of continuity was achieved while innovative techniques simultaneously ensured that fresh layers of the population were constantly being exposed to suffrage propaganda.

While it is no longer helpful to examine the WSPU merely in terms of the actions and policies of its leadership, a local study does not provide an alternative view of the Liverpool WSPU as an 'island' untouched by the decisions of Clements Inn. The success of the local branch was tied in to the fortunes of the national organisation to a great extent; the position of organiser was nationally funded, for example, and ventures such as the shop, although later self-sufficient, relied on national funds to get them under way. Yet the Liverpool evidence reveals that these ties were not rigid. Extreme militancy provides the best evidence of this, for while Liverpool suffered some of the severest cases of arson attributed to suffragettes in England, such actions never eclipsed other forms of public activity, nor discouraged new members from joining the Union.

Liverpool WSPU offered local women their first opportunity to enter the public political arena as part of a large organisation that was open and amenable to all women regardless of their class, religious or party-political allegiances. In this, and in the total autonomy that it offered women within the confines of an organisation, it was unique within Merseyside politics. It cannot be disputed that the WSPU did succeed, between 1905 and 1914, in opening up the world of public political campaigning to more local women than any other organisation had managed to do, and that it was the only large body that allowed women complete autonomy in selecting and directing its policies and actions.

However, a close study of the WSPU raises some broader questions about the levels and nature of women's political involvement within the Merseyside region. This chapter has shown how important the WSPU was to local women before 1914. There is a paradox between this and the fact that the Liverpool WSPU ceased to function as an organisation in September 1914, when the National WSPU folded. At this point, the autonomy demonstrated by the local branch on previous occasions appears to have evaporated. Although a small branch of the United Suffragists did appear in Liverpool, run by some of the long-term WSPU activists such as Patricia Woodlock and Dr Alice Ker, it remained a small and fragmented group, never achieving anything approaching the success of the WSPU. Yet at the same time, the Women's Party, which the National WSPU became, also remained small in the city, its membership drawn from among women with no previous recorded connection to the WSPU. Although reasons for this will be

discussed later, it is important to stress at this stage that there was no significant continuity of activity by local WSPU members in either of these two
groups. For some reason, the largest and most successful women's political
organisation in the area collapsed in 1914. Whether this was due to a general
downturn in women's public political activity from the outbreak of the First
World War, or whether the disappearance of the WSPU was linked to a
simultaneous rise in a number of other organisations in the district will form
an important question for later chapters. Also, although the WSPU mobilised
women into public activity around its campaign, the extent to which it really
managed to open up new avenues of political involvement to Merseyside
women who remained in the area after the WSPU itself had vanished must
also be considered. An answer to this question can only be attempted when
the WSPU's campaign is located alongside other suffrage campaigns within
the city, and the input of all these political organisations re-examined in the
light of national events between 1914 and 1920.

CHAPTER SIX

Other Suffrage Organisations

Both the constitutional campaigns of the LWSS and the flamboyance of the WSPU demonstrate the richness of suffrage politics, as practised at a local level. They also emphasise that suffrage was not just a campaign for the vote but a catalyst that politicised Edwardian women and drew them into the public arena. There was a steady entry of women into public political life on Merseyside as the suffrage campaign progressed. Women directed their suffrage activity not only through the WSPU and LWSS but also into a myriad of smaller groups dedicated to the issue. Some of these formed from splits in the WSPU. Others emerged from larger political groups such as the Women's Liberal Suffrage Federation, providing a forum for suffrage work for those women who preferred their politics to be party based. A further group including the church societies often shared membership with larger suffrage organisations. By 1914, there were 53 national bodies in which writers, actresses, artists, Liberal women, Jewish women, and many more could proclaim their identity as suffragists.[1] While membership of some of these was dependent on external factors such as religious or political affiliation, others allowed for an overlap in membership which also demonstrates the vital importance of friendship networks in building local branches and breaking down barriers between organisations that appear impenetrable at leadership level.[2]

The presence of so many smaller groups suggests that it was suffrage that persuaded many previously apolitical women to leave the private sphere and adopt a public identity as political actors. It also highlights the necessity for further questioning the focus of suffrage historiography on the WSPU/NUWSS' militant/constitutionalist split.[3] The broader range of

1 *Votes for Women*, 6 February 1914.
2 For the importance of friendship in suffrage see K. Cowman and H. Brown, 'Exploring Suffrage Friendship', in H. Brown, A. Kaloski and R. Symes, eds, *Celebrating Women's Friendship Past, Present and Future*, York, Raw Nerve Press, 1999, pp. 121–54.
3 For example, Rosen, *Rise Up Women!*; Mitchell, *The Fighting Pankhursts*; A. Raeburn, *The Militant Suffragettes*, London, Michael Joseph, 1973; and R. Fulford, *Votes for Women*, London, Faber & Faber, 1957, are mainly concerned with the policies and tactics of the WSPU, while Liddington and Norris, *One Hand Tied Behind Us*; Strachey, *The Cause*; Hume, *The National Union of Women's Suffrage Societies*; and S. Stanley Holton, *Feminism and Democracy: Women's Suffrage and Reform Politics in Britain, 1900–1918*,

organisations attracted a membership that spanned this divide, and became important in their own right, making the division irrelevant. Organisations can be divided into two categories: 'oppositional' groups, which splintered from the WSPU, demanding both the vote and alternative methods of organising for it; and 'alternative' societies, which sought to expand sites of suffrage activity while allowing their members to retain allegiance to other suffrage organisations. One organisation has reluctantly been omitted: the Liverpool Men's League for Women's Suffrage (LMLWS).[4] This branch, which formed in 1908, gave great support to the NUWSS, the WFL and the WSPU.[5] Its members, many of whom were related to suffragettes, were also involved in bodies such as the Church League for Women's Suffrage which admitted men.[6] The League had no direct political affiliation and recruited both socialists and liberals locally. However, despite its undoubted contribution towards furthering the suffrage cause on Merseyside, its lack of female membership means that it does not sit comfortably within an account of women's politics.

The Women's Freedom League

The Women's Freedom League (WFL) formed in October 1907 when Teresa Billington-Grieg and some supporters left the WSPU amid accusations of undemocratic practices. They continued to support militancy, but sought a less autocratic experience of political activity than the WSPU.[7] Local branches formed throughout Britain. The Liverpool branch was launched at a large meeting at Picton Hall in January 1909, organised by Liverpool

Cambridge, Cambridge University Press, 1986, have more to say about the history of the NUWSS.

4 Two important reassessments of male involvement in the campaign are A. V. John and C. Eustance, eds, *The Men's Share: Masculinities, Male Support and Women's Suffrage in Britain, 1890–1920*, London, Routledge, 1997; and Holton, *Suffrage Days*, especially chapters 7 and 9.

5 *Women's Franchise*, 4 June 1908.

6 These included Mr Noel Frimstone, husband of Ethel Martin a long-standing WSPU member arrested for her part in the 1911 London window-smashing and Mr Bernard whose sister was also in the WSPU.

7 There is as yet no monograph devoted to the League. For details of its history see C. Eustance, '"Daring to be Free": The Evolution of Women's Political Identities in the Women's Freedom League 1907–1930', DPhil thesis, University of York, 1993. A synthesis of some of this work is available in C. Eustance, 'Meanings of Militancy: The Ideas and Practice of Political Resistance in the Women's Freedom League 1907–14', in J. Purvis and M. Joannou, eds, *The Women's Suffrage Movement: New Feminist Perspectives*, Manchester, Manchester University Press, 1998, pp. 51–64. See also H. Frances, '"Our Job is to be Free": The Sexual Politics of Four Edwardian Feminists from c. 1910–1935', DPhil thesis, University of York, 1996; H. Frances, 'Dare to be Free! The Women's Freedom League and its Legacy', in Purvis and Holton, eds, *Votes for Women*, pp. 181–202.

MLWS and featuring Teresa Billington-Grieg.[8] This meant that from January 1909 there were two militant suffrage societies organising in the city. National differences between the two groups are not difficult to reconstruct. However, less is known about how they operated adjacently in a smaller area. What did the experience of WFL membership offer to Merseyside women that was not already provided via the WSPU?

The most obvious point of difference was the physical location of the WFL branch. Although it was known as the Liverpool branch, it was situated north of the city in Waterloo, part of the neighbouring borough of Bootle. Subsequent local branches remained firmly rooted in the North End, in Aintree (formed in April 1912) and Anfield (June 1914). A brief attempt to spread across the water and form a branch in Liscard failed, leaving the WFL active in districts without WSPU branches.[9] Thus the League did not compete directly for membership with another militant society.

Although its branches were in the North End, the WFL did not remain there for all of its public work. In its first year members successfully competed for public political space in the city centre. Here, a slight difference in the focus of public activity can be discerned between the WFL and the WSPU. The League developed a distinctive political campaign between spring 1909 and the following winter. It developed a synthesis of militant and constitutional methods, confronting a selected audience but with a very public and direct methodology. Targeted petitions were aimed at 'influential businessmen, officials on the stock exchange and the cotton exchange, shipping people, editors of newspapers'.[10] These were consolidated with a vigorous campaign of public meetings at Exchange Flags, in the heart of the business district.[11]

Like the WSPU, the WFL also relied on salaried organisers to build and recruit. Miss Broadhurst (MA) and Miss Margaret Milne Farquharson (MA) were sent to Liverpool by the League. Both always mentioned their educational qualifications when speaking or writing on behalf of the League, reflecting the importance it placed on education. League members also highlighted their femininity, proudly repeating reports from *The Liverpool Courier* of WFL meetings, where

> the hats and gowns of the guests were as charming almost as the wearers. The atmosphere was as feminine as it was strenuous... No one can look at this evolutionary movement and say that the finest, most attractive women stand outside it.[12]

8 *Women's Franchise*, 28 January 1909.
9 *Women's Freedom League News*, October 1909.
10 *Women's Franchise*, 13 May 1909.
11 Exchange Flags was also favoured by the WSPU, but they appear to have taken the idea from the WFL in this instance.
12 Extracts from *The Liverpool Courier*, quoted in *Women's Franchise*, 20 May 1909.

The Liverpool WFL mixed the respectability of the LWSS with the militancy of the WSPU. This, and the more respectable form of public campaign it created, which relied on the organisers rather than local women speakers, attracted women who disliked the formality of constitutional campaigns but feared the violence of the WSPU.[13] Large numbers of teachers joined the branch.[14] However, this is not to say that WFL members were as unwilling to engage in the rougher side of public activity as the LWSS. Indeed, they were quick to acknowledge that their work in the general election campaign of January 1910 had resulted in women being 'rushed up side streets and knocked about', but that they were 'making great headway... in spite' of such treatment.[15] Although they eschewed the more violent direct actions of the Liverpool WSPU, League members were keen to support some militancy, once 'noting [the] certain apathy with which suffrage was discussed by the general public, owing to the temporary cessation of militant methods'.[16] Even in the more restricted locations of their street meetings, they faced public ridicule. Farquharson assured her supporters that

> [at] a meeting... held on the Exchange Flags... as [I] touched on the many injustices to women, the indomitable spirit of the women in the movement, and the lack of manhood in the men of the country when they allowed women to be so inhumanly treated as they were now in prison, the jeer dying from their faces was succeeded by expressions of interest.[17]

However, the jeer still had to be faced. Thus the WFL members' experience of public political activity was only slightly different from that offered by the more numerous WSPU branches, probably explaining why the later organisation was never able to compete with the WSPU directly. Locally, from the summer of 1910, the League retreated increasingly from public campaigns into branch meetings.

On party politics, the WFL differed from the WSPU and the LWSS. As its membership was not largely recruited from women already in political organisations, it possessed no unofficial party identity. Neither did it model its campaigns on those of individual parties, but attempted to appeal to all three. Initial meetings were aimed at the Liberal Party, which, although not in control of the city council, represented a strand of bourgeois radicalism.[18]

13 An identical pattern has been noted in Scotland. See Leneman, *A Guid Cause*, p. 115.
14 In the local reports column of *The Vote*, 26 October 1912, it was reported that a local branch meeting was well attended despite the teachers' half-term holiday, indicating that a large percentage of the membership was drawn from this constituency.
15 *The Vote*, 22 January 1910.
16 *The Vote*, 26 March 1910.
17 *Women's Franchise*, 14 October 1909.
18 See, for example, report of meeting with the Birkenhead Liberal Federation, *Women's Franchise*, 6 May 1909; report of campaign around National Liberal Federation Conference, *Women's Franchise*, 1 July 1909; report of President of local Liberal Federation at Mrs Despard's Waterloo meeting, *The Vote*, 16 March 1912.

Local Conservatives approved of its anti-government (and therefore Liberal) stance and were well disposed towards the League, which received sympathetic reports in the pro-Conservative *Liverpool Courier*.[19] And from November 1912, the League began to forge links with the local ILP, through the person of John Edwards, who spoke at several meetings for them while simultaneously promoting suffrage through Kensington ILP.[20] Unlike the broad-based WSPU, the League drew its membership largely from the lower middle-class of Waterloo and its surrounding areas. Although it was more aware than the LWSS of the issue of class within its campaigns, it concentrated more on courting a working-class audience than on recruiting a working-class membership. Its work in Scotland Road, for example, was deemed worthwhile because the 'populous working-class neighbourhood [had] a voting power which we can turn to our advantage on future occasions'.[21]

Must we conclude that the WFL did not offer Liverpool women anything significantly different from the WSPU? On one level, this is clearly the case. WSPU members sometimes spoke at WFL meetings where they were made very welcome. When Miss Marks of the WSPU spoke to Aintree WFL in 1913, she was introduced as 'one of the pioneers of the militant movement in Liverpool' with no distinction drawn between the two organisations.[22] It was largely this lack of distinction that restricted the size of local WFL branches, a factor that in turn limited its work. In January 1910 its general election campaign was every bit as imaginative as that of the WSPU, involving public meetings, and the unique tactic of midnight gatherings to reach the tram drivers as they changed shifts.[23] But it was concentrated only in Walton constituency, while both the WSPU and the NUWSS campaigned across the city. After January 1909, Farquharson and Broadhurst were removed, leaving the branch without organisers. (Farquharson had earlier requested a fund to raise the 500 guineas a year necessary to fund an organiser and headquarters, but the amount was obviously not forthcoming.)[24] A full-time salaried organiser had had a significant impact on the levels of WSPU activity. Without one, the Liverpool WFL branch could not sustain the required level of activity to expand significantly. Also, recruits would not flock to the League if it had nothing distinctive to offer. Attempts to build the branch, reported in *The Vote*, repeatedly show a membership spread too thinly, with frequent repeated appeals for paper sellers and helpers. Public

---

19 See extracts in *Women's Franchise*, 20 May 1909.
20 *The Vote*, 30 November 1912; 30 May 1913; 27 November 1913; 14 May 1914.
21 *Women's Freedom League News*, 21 October 1909.
22 *The Vote*, 13 June 1913.
23 *The Vote*, 22 January 1910.
24 The League did have the services of Miss Muriel Matters and Miss Violet Tillard on Merseyside from January to April 1910, but this was accidental, due to the fact that they were both sailing to Australia from Liverpool, and were combining this international suffrage campaign with a smaller one in the port.

meetings resulted in financial deficit, something never incurred by the NUWSS or WSPU.[25] The existence of flourishing branches in areas where they represented the sole suffrage activity underlines the fact that much militant suffrage activity was really located in individual contacts and feminist friendships rather than stark differences in national policy.[26]

The suffrage campaign in Liverpool became more fluid as it progressed, and sustained many groups with interorganisational membership by 1914. The WFL stood to benefit from this development, as the suffrage campaign broadened into one that facilitated exploration of a wealth of simultaneous priorities such as religion, work and equal pay. It attempted a relaunch in May 1914, when a large central Liverpool branch formed which would work with smaller new groups in the suburbs.[27] The first of these new groups was established in Anfield in June 1914. While the outbreak of war prevented this new initiative from fully realising its potential, it did not stifle it completely. The contribution of the members of the WFL to providing a political space for Liverpool women between 1914 and 1918 was by no means insignificant, and will be returned to later.

The Votes for Women Fellowship

Chronologically, the second 'oppositional' suffrage organisation to form local branches was the Votes for Women Fellowship (VFWF). Although the impetus for its formation came from the expulsion of Frederick and Emmeline Pethick-Lawrence from the WSPU in 1912, it was not 'oppositional' to the same degree as the WFL. However, both its existence and the nature of its activities reveal much about the importance of the issue of feminist friendship within suffrage campaigns, and the ability of friendship at a local level to transcend splits among the national leadership. While the VFWF appears here among the 'oppositional' suffrage organisations, its small shared membership with the WSPU could place it just as comfortably among the later 'alternative' ones.

Following their expulsion, the Pethick-Lawrences retained control over the Women's Press and its publications, including *Votes for Women* which they had edited since 1907.[28] The retention of the paper, inseparable, in the eyes of the public, from the WSPU and its campaigns, provided them with

25 *The Vote*, 26 March 1910.

26 Stanley with Morley, *The Life and Death of Emily Wilding Davison, passim.* See also Holton, *Suffrage Days.*

27 *The Vote*, 22 May 1914.

28 The details of the split, occasioned by the Pethick-Lawrences' objection to Christabel's movement towards a guerilla war type of militancy, have been chronicled adequately elsewhere. For more details see Rosen, *Rise Up Women!*, chapter 14; Stanley with Morley, *The Life and Death of Emily Wilding Davison, passim*; E. Pethick-Lawrence, *My Part in a Changing World*, London, Victor Gollancz, 1938, *passim*; F. Pethick-Lawrence, *Fate Has Been Kind*, London, Hutchinson, 1942, chapter 10.

a valuable mouthpiece through which they could have organised their supporters into a dissenting body. However, they had no interest in establishing an alternative court to Clements Inn. For both, the unity of the suffrage campaign transcended personal and sectarian concerns. Emmeline later remembered:

> Many people appealed to me to start a new suffrage organization. I considered the matter carefully and came to the conclusion that the ground was covered already.[29]

Her husband agreed:

> Our disagreement with the new militancy had been sufficiently expressed once and for all by our extrusion from the WSPU. There was no need to restate it. Our quarrel was with the government, and not with our fellow suffragists.[30]

Their actions have been presented as further evidence of the totality of the Pankhursts' leadership which met no opposition.[31] Yet this was no more an example of a weak and cowed membership than it was the result of a veneer of unity imposed over a mass of discontent. One important by-product of the parting between the Pethick-Lawrences and the Pankhursts was that it forced the WSPU membership to examine the actions of their leadership. The outcast couple had been at the heart of the 'inner circle'. Frederick himself was acutely aware of this, pointing out that their departure

> forced the women of the rank and file into a fresh exercise of their own judgement... Once inside the ranks, women [had come] under the influence of the combined judgement of ourselves and the Pankhursts... When the partnership at the top was dissolved, not only had they to decide at the time whether (as *Punch* put it) they were 'Peths or Panks', but, as fresh developments occurred, they had constantly to consider their position, and use their independent judgement. In this way, they took a further step in their self-emancipation.[32]

For many suffragettes who were concerned over the episode, leaving the Union was not in question. But their choice to remain within the ranks of an organisation that they had been instrumental in creating, and whose direct militant policies they applauded, did not reflect a blind acceptance of the Pankhursts' opinion in all things.[33] Liz Stanley and Ann Morley have

29 Pethick-Lawrence, *My Part in a Changing World*, p. 286.
30 Pethick-Lawrence, *Fate Has Been Kind*, p. 101.
31 Rosen, *Rise Up Women!* p. 177.
32 Pethick-Lawrence, *Fate has Been Kind*, p. 101.
33 As I have illustrated in Chapter 5, supporting the more violent militant actions did not always lead to individuals participating in them. It was the constant variety of militant actions offered by the WSPU, coupled with the freedom given to individual women to decide how far their support and participation would go, that held the key to their success.

attempted to recreate how the WSPU actually worked at branch level and concluded that

> Any large scale organisation which exists on both a national and a local level – where local groups are active and involve large numbers of people – is complex and its activities are not easily summarised. Moreover, this is only to deal with the *formal* organisation. Cross-cutting this, at both levels, will be informal connections between people made on the basis of friendship, political analysis, social interests… This is true of the WSPU, but what has most often happened is that vast generalisations have been made about the WSPU from… the formal pronouncements of the leadership.[34]

The story of the Liverpool VFWF exemplifies this. The organisation provided members with continued contact with the views and leadership of the Pethick-Lawrences but also united members of individual suffrage organisations in a way that was impossible within existing organisations that distinguished them as 'militants', 'non-militants' or 'Pankhurst supporters' rather than simply 'suffrage campaigners'.[35]

The VFWF could do this because it was never really a formal organisation although it supported individual members, subscribers and branches. Rather, it was conceived as a network to enable *Votes for Women* readers to continue their association with the paper after it ceased to represent the WSPU. Immediately after her expulsion Mrs Pethick-Lawrence appealed to her readership:

> [We] as co-editors of the paper have entered into fellowship with you, and are one with you in your bond of common purpose. It is our desire that this relationship shall be continued, strengthened and extended.[36]

This would not be achieved without effort. Not only had *Votes for Women* lost the support of the WSPU, but Mrs Pethick-Lawrence was now able to reveal that it had been making substantial losses for some time. To keep it alive was of vital importance, as it not only signified suffrage to the many who saw it on sale each week, and perhaps occasionally bought it, but also it represented a continuity of participation in the movement for these occasional supporters. Earlier suffrage papers, such as *Women's Franchise* and *Women and Progress*, had vanished when *Votes for Women*, which enjoyed organisational backing, appeared. How *Votes for Women* would survive as a non-aligned journal against the challenge of *The Suffragette* remained to be seen.

The VFWF's first aim was to keep the newspaper afloat. This was crucial

---

34 Stanley with Morley, *The Life and Death of Emily Wilding Davison*, p. 175.
35 They had, after all, made frequent visits to Liverpool as speakers, and were well known to several members of the local leadership such as Patricia Woodlock and Alice Ker.
36 *Votes for Women*, 1 November 1912.

to its later development, as it meant that support for (or later membership of) the Fellowship did not imply secession from the WSPU or other suffrage organisations. Indeed, Emmeline Pethick-Lawrence was insistent that the Fellowship was 'not a suffrage society', but aimed to boost existing suffrage work and facilitate contacts between a number of different suffrage societies.[37]

The Liverpool Fellowship centred around the art studio of Miss Mary Palethorpe, a WSPU member who with her sister Fanny had assured her militant credentials in Holloway following her part in the 1912 mass window-smashing in London. Her studio appeared in the first list of VFWF branches published in *Votes for Women* in February 1913. From January 1914, it hosted regular Fellowship meetings on Thursday afternoons. Members were not easily identified as a group of dissidents opposed to the WSPU's national policy. Many had maintained their long involvement with the WSPU. Mary Palethorpe designed the Liverpool WSPU's official Christmas card in December 1913.[38] Patricia Woodlock spoke at public and private Fellowship meetings in 1914 while still very much active in the WSPU. Dr Alice Ker was also attached to both organisations and recorded visits to Miss Palethorpe's studio in her diaries along with regular trips to the WSPU shop.[39] Some, such as Mrs Imlack, had only been associated with the WSPU since 1914, and yet simultaneously identified themselves with the earlier suffrage paper. Others were willing to use the talents they had discovered through *Votes for Women* in its support, such as Mrs Abraham, previously lauded by the WSPU for achieving the highest national sale of its paper.[40]

Fellowship meetings consisted of 'a reading from literature with bearing on the women's movement, followed by a discussion' rather than dedicated speeches aimed at recruiting new members. This reflects Mrs Pethick-Lawrence's insistence that nationally the VFWF represented 'a rallying ground for all suffragists, men and women, "militant", "spiritually militant", "tax-resisting", and "constitutional" who mean business' rather than an attempt to build an alternative society with a distinct and separate identity.[41] However, the local Fellowship meetings, both by their location and through their emphasis on literary discussion rather than political action, also proved

---

37 *Votes for Women*, 9 May 1913.
38 There is a problem of identification here, as the sisters are sometimes identified as 'Miss Fanny' or 'Miss Mary Palethorpe', sometimes 'Miss F' or 'Miss M. Palethorpe', but often just 'Miss Palethorpe'. As the artist, it is likely that it was Mary who gave her studio for Fellowship meetings. However, both Miss Fanny Palethorpe and Miss Palethorpe appear in the same list of women who had donated money to the Fellowship in October 1913. The second Miss Palethorpe here must be Mary, indicating that both sisters continued to support *Votes for Women*.
39 Dr Alice Ker, diary, 3 April 1913; 24 January 1914.
40 *Votes for Women*, 11 July 1913.
41 *Votes for Women*, 30 January 1914; 9 May 1913.

attractive to the Bohemian circle and the Liverpool Fellowship did attract new recruits. As an umbrella organisation it united militants and constitutionalists, despite *Votes for Women*'s continued support for militant actions.[42] Its greatest coup was securing Miss Kate Riley for a meeting in 1914. Riley was a very active Liberal in Southport, and involved in Southport NUWSS, but had never appeared on a suffrage platform in Liverpool before. The VFWF also allowed male supporters some room, and members of the local Men's League were familiar faces at studio meetings.[43]

Although the VFWF did not provide organised opposition to the WSPU, it became more than a loose coalition. By September 1914 it was in a position to employ some local organisers, who acted as facilitators between the many coexisting suffrage organisations, bringing individuals together, while also continuing to support the paper. Miss Phyllis Lovell, a Southport WSPU supporter, became its Liverpool organiser in May 1914 and organised several Fellowship meetings before the outbreak of war.[44] It is impossible to speculate about the length of time that the VFWF could have sustained this pattern of public activity. Over the summer of 1914, it held weekly open-air meetings on Waterloo sands, and campaigned with its cycling corps, which visited local villages. Meanwhile, the WSPU matched its level of meetings, while fighting a vigorous campaign to combat the Home Office threat to newsagents who continued to stock *The Suffragette*, and seeking novel ways of presentation, including a boating parade for Suffragette Week. Cooperation was achieved by the determination of supporters, many of whom were simultaneously engaged in WSPU work, to retain an active voice in the suffrage campaign for *Votes for Women*. Bearing in mind the histories of previous non-aligned suffrage papers, and the increasing competition, from *The Suffragette*, and other additions to the suffrage media, *Votes for Women* could not sustain this indefinitely.

Ultimately, the VFWF was about offering supplementary activity rather than attempting to find a new direction for the suffrage campaign. When groups appeared that bridged the approaches of the VFWF and the two main national societies, it was decided that *Votes for Women* might again represent an organisation. In August 1914, it became the official organ of the United Suffragists. How this decision affected the Liverpool Fellowship will be considered at the end of this chapter.

42 Other organisations mentioned in this chapter, the 'alternative' sites, also do this, but only because an alternative focus is prioritised.
43 Alice Ker makes particular mention of Mr David Jenkins, a local artist who designed a banner for the WSPU. See Ker, diary, 3 May 1912.
44 For Phyllis Lovell's suffrage activities see *The Birkenhead News*, 21 August 1915.

The Church League for Women's Suffrage

A more consistently alternative location for suffrage activity which did not imply opposition to a larger organisation could be found within those suffrage societies that linked to existent bodies. The Church League for Women's Suffrage (CLWS), which formed nationally in December 1909, was an organisation that added an extra dimension to the suffrage campaign. It was non-party and welcomed both militants and constitutionalists as members, but restricted membership to practising Anglicans, making it sectarian in religious but not in political terms.[45]

From its founding, the organisation, which was open to men and women, drew heavily on the rhetoric of separate spheres. Many churchmen used the issue of suffrage to promote their personal views on women's space and role within the church. There was nothing new about the association of these views with the suffrage campaign. As early as 1895, the Central Society for Women's Suffrage attempted to 'remove a fear still to be found in some quarters that the women's suffrage movement is not consistent with the religious aspect of women's work and duty'.[46] Some of the rhetoric of ministers in the CLWS could have been lifted directly from the prescriptive literature around the separate spheres of men and women abundant in the mid-nineteenth century. They stressed women's 'special' or 'superior' qualities, which meant that

> Women have a greater initial facility for worship than men... [and] will raise worship to a new place in the life of the whole church by teaching men to revere something which women most easily do.[47]

They also expanded the theological belief that women had an important role to play within the church, not identical to men's role, but of equal importance with 'no question of superiority or inferiority'.[48] The more radical women in the CLWS applauded this. For them, Christianity did not equate with passivity and they were keen to affirm that, despite advances in society,

> it remained for Christianity to fully declare that the accident of sex is nothing, and that in the Christian Commonwealth there is 'neither male nor female'.[49]

45 For more details of the national CLWS see B. Heeney, *The Women's Movement in the Church of England, 1850–1930*, Oxford, Oxford University Press, 1988. The Liverpool branch is discussed and contextualised in greater detail in Cowman, 'We intend to show what Our Lord has done for Women', pp. 475–87.

46 Anon., *Women's Suffrage: Opinions of Leaders of Religious Thought*, London, Central Society for Women's Suffrage, 1895.

47 Rev. W. Temple, MA, *The Religious Aspect of the Women's Movement*, London, The Collegium, 1912.

48 Rev. J. A. Kempthorne, *Speech to the Queen's Hall*, London, The Collegium, 1912.

49 Rev. G. Williams, *Women's Rights: A Sermon*, Glasgow, Candlish Memorial U. F. Church, 1914.

The CLWS represented more than simply a way for Anglicans to demonstrate their support for women's suffrage. Christianity had long played an important part in suffrage politics, especially among the most militant of its adherents.[50] In Liverpool, too, there were strong links between radical nonconformity and suffrage. Many of these centred around Pembroke Chapel where suffragettes Emma Hillier, Ada Broughton and Hattie Mahood were active members, and occasionally organised WSPU meetings in the Chapel.[51] Nonconformity also gave constitutional suffragists a voice in the Unitarian congregations of Hope Street and Ullet Road.[52] However, it was not until January 1913 that a local branch of the CLWS was formed, allowing Anglicans a chance simultaneously to declare themselves suffragists.[53] Locally as nationally, the CLWS recruited both militants and constitutionalists, as the intermingling of the single issue of the vote with broader concerns about spirituality allowed the issue of militancy to become less relevant. Women who joined the CLWS were claiming a public identity that proclaimed that their Anglicanism was as important to them as their suffrage.

This dualism allowed the local branch to serve as a suffrage melting pot where militants and constitutionalists could work side by side. As it formed at a time when hostilities between the two camps were augmenting, it provided an important space where supporters of both sides could meet and work together. Indeed, at one stage, the Southport CLWS, forerunner of the Liverpool branch, had regular paper sales of the *Church League for Women's Suffrage Monthly Paper*, *Votes for Women* and *Common Cause*.[54] National concern over the high proportion of WSPU members in the CLWS had echoes in Liverpool.[55] An early attempt was made to bar 'militants on active service' from membership of the Liverpool CLWS which the majority of the branch opposed. The first president and secretary resigned after the deci-

50 For example, Emily Wilding Davison, *Votes for Women*, 3 September 1909. Further discussion of the uses that militants made of religious rhetoric can be found in M. Vicinus, 'Male space and women's bodies in the suffragette movement' in her *Independent Women*, London, Virago, 1985.

51 Pembroke Chapel Minute Book 1891–1905, Regents Park College Oxford. For further details see Sellers, 'Salute to Pembroke'; also L. Smith, *Religion and the Rise of Labour*, Keele, Keele University Press, 1993, pp. 145–53.

52 H. D. Roberts, *Hope Street Church Liverpool and the Allied Nonconformity*, Liverpool, Liverpool Booksellers Company, 1909, lists the Meade-Kings, Miss E. C. Greene, Miss H. Johnson and the Misses J. and E. McConnell, all also associated with the LWSS, as subscribers to the church bicentenary fund.

53 *Church League for Women's Suffrage Monthly Paper*, January 1913. Pembroke Chapel was the main site for pulpit radicalism in Liverpool. For more details see Sellers, 'Salute to Pembroke'.

54 *Church League for Women's Suffrage Monthly Paper*, August 1912.

55 *The Standard*, 25 September 1913, cited in Heeney, *The Women's Movement in the Church of England*, p.112.

sion, but the rest of the membership remained in place.[56] The activists of Liverpool CLWS were predominantly WSPU members, but this did not deter constitutionalists from involvement.[57] At the AGM in January 1914 the constitutional suffragist Cecily Leadley-Brown proposed that 'the CLWS merits the support of all Church Suffragists', accurately reflecting the situation in the ranks of the local branch.[58] This denial of all difference, gender or policy-based, was outlined at the local League's inaugural meeting when Rev. J. Coop preached on Mark 1.31:

> In Christ Jesus there was 'neither male nor female'... the Church League intended to show those outside what our Lord had done for women when 'he took her by the hand and lifted her up'.[59]

The belief that common faith transcended policy differences between political organisations united individuals from opposing suffrage societies on Merseyside. In 1914 Eleanor Rathbone, the most anti-militant of local suffragists who was always concerned with scoring an advantage over the WSPU, chaired a CLWS meeting with WSPU supporter Mr Bernard as speaker. Neither party appeared to feel compromised.[60]

The CLWS never sought a mass membership or a high-profile campaign. Its main aim, nationally and locally, was promoting suffrage within the Anglican Church. Liverpool members had opportunities to share faith as suffragists, during special church services where the spiritual dimension of the movement was discussed. Members also attended public meetings and sold literature. At its own public meetings the CLWS explored different dimensions of the suffrage campaign. These were not as numerous as those of other suffrage organisations, but were no less popular. The first one drew over 300 people to Church House to hear the Bishop of Hull declare:

> There is not a parish in Liverpool... the work of which would not collapse if there were no women workers, and it is little short of a scandal that in our church councils women who do the lion's share of the church's work should not have the privilege of a vote.[61]

---

56 Church League for Women's Suffrage Fourth Annual Report, 1913.

57 An analysis of the Liverpool members named in the *Monthly Paper* shows that of the 19 who had been associated with other local suffrage groups nine had WSPU links, while six were NUWSS supporters, and four were involved with the WFL.

58 *Church League for Women's Suffrage Monthly Paper*, March 1914.

59 *Church League for Women's Suffrage Monthly Paper*, January 1913.

60 'The recent developments of militant policy and the... reaction in public opinion to which they have led make it more important than ever that the constitutional and conciliatory methods of the National Union should be kept prominently before public attention.' E. Rathbone, 'The Methods of Conciliation', *Common Cause*, 5 September 1911.

61 *Votes for Women*, 18 April 1913.

He was supported by Cecily Leadley-Brown who 'gave splendid arguments and reasons for women having the vote'.[62] Similar events came to characterise the local campaign.

The rise in local CLWS activity coincided with an increase in public expressions of spirituality by the WSPU. Local suffragettes had taken up the national 'prayers for prisoners' initiative, when church services were interrupted by women praying for hunger strikers, and were centring their attention on the new Lady Chapel in the Anglican Cathedral. The protests did not impress the local church authorities, and a WSPU deputation to the Bishop of Liverpool in April 1913 was told that rather than being willing to intervene on the subject of forcible feeding, he 'declined to lift a finger to help... until... the women desisted from brawling in the churches'.[63] In the midst of this conflict the local CLWS allowed suffragists space to practise their faith without renouncing their political beliefs.

The CLWS was not a radical association. It steered its membership away from issues such as the ordination of women, many of its most ardent supporters concurring with the view that 'the priesthood... is debarred to women... that is a permanent prohibition'.[64] Even Maude Royden admitted that her personal support for women priests was 'extreme' and warned her fellow League member Ursula Roberts to be very wary of this subject.[65] For some local women, therefore, it failed to provide the spiritual space they sought. This they attempted to create for themselves through the establishment of a Women's Church in Wallasey. The church, which met in the Liscard Concert Hall, held both mixed-sex and women-only services, and was aimed at helping women who, finding the Church 'like a cage... [had] come away in sheer disgust at the attitude of the clergy towards the things which to [them] are dearer than life'.[66] The inaugural services were held by Rev. Hatty Baker, 'one of the pioneer women preachers in the Congregational Church' and a co-pastor in Plymouth. She was instrumental in founding the Free Church League for Women's Suffrage, although this group was never represented on Merseyside.[67] As well as providing a space for women to run services, the Women's Church attempted to move away from a wholly masculine presentation of God, and explore His feminine

62 *Church League for Women's Suffrage Monthly Paper*, March 1913.
63 *Church League for Women's Suffrage Monthly Paper*, April 1914.
64 Rev. M. Bell, *The Church and Women's Suffrage: Sermon Before the Inaugural Meeting of the Church League for Women's Suffrage*, London, Church League for Women's Suffrage Pamphlet no. 1, 1909.
65 See S. Fletcher, *Maude Royden: A Life*, Oxford, Blackwell, 1989, pp. 143–44.
66 Miss Hoy, letter to *The Wallasey and Wirral Chronicle*, 14 March 1914.
67 For biographical details of Rev. Baker see *Free Church Suffrage Times*, January 1917.
68 For more detail on the Wallasey Women's Church see letter from Miss Amy Brand, *The Wallasey and Wirral Chronicle*, 24 January 1914. Also, reports in *Votes for Women* and *The Suffragette* during March 1914. For a brief discussion of how the church was received

aspects.[68] Women would 'preach the sermons, offer the prayers, provide the music and take the collection; the whole administration [was] to be in [their] hands'.[69] The Church attracted some suffrage support. Alice Ker, who had more or less given up Anglicanism in favour of Theosophy by this time, attended.[70] Its treasurer was Miss Hoy, an executive member of Wallasey WSPU, and it received publicity in *The Suffragette* and *Votes for Women*. However, it appears to have folded during the First World War, and it is likely that while it provided an important focus for some Christian feminists, the majority felt more comfortable within the boundaries of established religion. The CLWS itself continued meeting throughout the war, and to press its demand for suffrage when it could, although 'pressure of other duties' on its members, some of whom enlisted, blunted its effectiveness.[71]

The Catholic Women's Suffrage Society

While suffrage organisations were adept at avoiding the religious sectarianism that permeated other areas of local political life, the success of the CLWS demonstrated the need of some activists to bring their religious affiliation into their suffrage work.[72] This dual identity carried special significance for Catholic women who were also combatting anti-Catholic prejudice.[73] One of the earliest provincial branches of the Catholic Women's Suffrage Society (CWSS) formed in Liverpool in 1912.[74] The society, which admitted both men and women to its ranks, and linked their common struggle for the vote with wider struggles for Catholic emancipation, continued throughout the war years, expanding its membership in a way unique within local suffrage politics.[75]

in radical freethinking circles, see E. Royle, *Radicals, Secularists and Republicans*, Manchester, Manchester University Press, 1980, p. 248.

69 *The Free Church Suffrage Times*, April 1914.

70 Alice Ker diary, 29 March 1914.

71 *Church League for Women's Suffrage Monthly Paper*, May 1916. Arthur Allerton, founder of the Liverpool Men's League and treasurer of the CLWS, enlisted at the beginning of the war and was awarded the military cross in December 1917. The war also deprived the CLWS of women members. Nurse Lupton of the WSPU and CLWS was reported 'on active service' in December 1914.

72 For details of links between religion and politics on Merseyside, see Waller, *Democracy and Sectarianism*; J. Bohstedt, 'More than One Working Class: Protestant and Catholic Riots in Edwardian Liverpool', in J. Belchem, ed., *Popular Politics, Riot and Labour*, pp. 173–216; Neal, *Sectarian Violence*.

73 F. M. Mason, 'The Newer Eve: The Catholic Women's Suffrage Society in England, 1911–1923', *Catholic Historical Review*, vol. 72, pt 4, October 1986, pp. 620–38.

74 For the broader history of the CWSS, see L. de Alberti, 'History of the Catholic Women's Suffrage Society', *Catholic Citizen*, vol. XIV, no. 9, 15 October 1928, pp.77–81.

75 See J. Clayton, *Votes for Women – the Appeal to Catholics*, London, CWSS pamphlet, n.d., which claims that 'Catholic men and women are striving to get votes for women as they strove in earlier days for better government and for Catholic emancipation.'

Despite the peculiarities of local sectarianism, and the success which the CWSS achieved among working-class Catholics, it was not simply another social organisation linked to a church, taking its alliances from the politics of the local neighbourhood.[76] Rather, it further demonstrated the adaptability of grass roots Edwardian feminism in a era when its leaderships have been portrayed as rigid and unbending. It was founded by Miss Florence Barry, the educated daughter of Persian immigrant Zacharie Balthazar Bahri, and his Austrian wife, Frances Jane Shroder. The family lived in Birkenhead, where Florence's father was a merchant, and her mother an ardent charity worker.[77] Florence, active in the WSPU, was initially unconvinced 'that there was either a need or a scope for a purely Catholic women's organisation'.[78] It is uncertain what made her change her mind, but these early doubts indicate that it was suffrage rather than sectarianism that motivated her.

Early Annual Reports show that like the CLWS, the Liverpool CWSS attracted support from both suffragists and suffragettes. Patricia Woodlock appears as a subscriber as does Jane Colquitt, the Catholic suffragist who 'adored the Bible and Bible stories'.[79] With the publication of *The Catholic Suffragist*, activity becomes far easier to trace. Here, the CWSS uniquely combined war work and suffrage up to 1918. The branch engaged in different types of welfare work. However, although one of the last local suffrage organisations to form, its suffrage war work during the war displayed a degree of tenacity that other organisations were unable to match. While other similar organisations had suspended suffrage work in favour of relief work, the CWSS continued to proclaim itself 'suffragist', retaining this word in its paper until after enfranchisement. Locally, it determined that it would not only do war work, but

> help to keep the suffrage flag flying that we may be powerful to get wrongs realised when peace is restored.[80]

Although both of the religious suffrage societies could be seen as emphasising differences between individual suffrage campaigners, they also brought unity to the local campaign. Their holistic approach joined suffragists and suffragettes together, providing them with common ground at a time when local divisions over militancy were at their height. Yet they also

---

76 For a discussion of the strength of social organisations based on neighbourhood politics between rival churches see Bohstedt, 'More than One Working Class', pp. 206–7.
77 N. Stewart Parnell, *The Way of Florence Barry, 1885–1965*, London, St Joan's Alliance, 1973.
78 Parnell, *The Way of Florence Barry*, p. 8.
79 CWSS Annual Report, 1912–13, Fawcett Library; Interview with Mrs Paula Francombe, daughter of Jane Colquitt, 1 December 1993.
80 *The Catholic Suffragist*, February 1915.

recognised that Anglican and Catholic suffrage campaigners formed distinct groups, and allowed them to devise a separate identity from those provided by larger suffrage societies. For women already linked to an organisation, this added an extra dimension to their campaigning work. For others, the CLWS and CWSS provided the opportunity to proclaim publicly their adherence to the suffrage cause without having to embroil themselves in the machinations of suffrage politics.

The Conservative and Unionist Women's Franchise Association

The final 'alternative' organisation with significant local presence is the Conservative and Unionist Women's Franchise Association (CUWFA). This provided an alternative site for suffrage activity, restricting its membership to women active in the Conservative Party, and allowing its members to declare publicly their dual allegiances as suffrage activists and Conservatives. Again, it coexisted with other suffrage organisations, and sometimes shared members. It was formed nationally in 1908 by the Countess of Selbourne in reaction to attempts at organisation by anti-suffragists within the party, and recruited prominent women such as Betty Balfour who left the Primrose League for its ranks after her local MP voted against the franchise extension.[81] However, while opposing individual Tories in cases such as this, CUWFA members retained their Conservatism and did not attempt to orchestrate a suspension of party activity, remaining pledged not to oppose any Unionist candidates in elections, while agreeing not to work for any candidate who did not support suffrage. Initially, the organisation was London based, but it formed national branches from 1909. Within Liverpool, it provided a vital space for those Conservative women who did not find the Primrose League a receptive centre. Its wider affiliation also provided women with political training and experience in the arena of party politics.

Liverpool was an early centre of CUWFA activity. When the *Conservative and Unionist Women's Franchise Review* began publication in November 1910, the local branch provided one of eight local reports, establishing it as an early centre of activity.[82] It was headed by Miss Evelyn Deakin, who was also a LWSS activist. The CUWFA was not overtly opposed to militancy, and claimed to be open to all Conservative women who wished for the parliamentary vote. However, where its Liverpool members also belonged to another suffrage organisation this was usually the LWSS. While the WSPU was not hostile to the CUWFA, joint membership was very difficult. During

---

81 See Campbell, 'Iron Ladies', p. 42, which erroneously refers to the Conservative and Unionist Women's Suffrage Organisation.

82 *Conservative and Unionist Women's Franchise Review*, November 1910. The report indicates that the branch was recent.

the lifetime of the Liverpool CUWFA branch, the local Conservative Party was in the ascendancy, and controlled the city council. Frequently positioning their organisation as respectable in the face of the city's growing radicalism, the women of the CUWFA were unlikely to participate in actions that would give local Liberals or their press an opportunity to condemn their party. A few Conservative women such as Miss Canning did join the WSPU and participate in low-level militancies such as public paper sales, but generally Conservative women avoided the Union, which was further tainted by its socialist connections. The CUWFA comprised women who, although seeking suffrage, were primarily united by their common political beliefs, and prioritised the issue of party politics over other concerns.

The experience of membership of the CUWFA did not differ significantly from that of the LWSS. Although the CUWFA was a campaigning organisation, it held no outdoor meetings at all on Merseyside, but spread its message through 'At Homes' in the large drawing rooms of its members, or at indoor public meetings. The sale of literature played an important part in its campaign, showing that, like the other organisations in this chapter, it was conscious of its message as representing something significantly different from the focus of other suffrage organisations. The main difference for members derived from the prioritisation of party political concerns. Women who joined the CUWFA and wore its colours of pale blue, white and gold were Conservative Suffragists, and were claiming a public identity for themselves as such. Often, their Conservatism appears more important than suffragism. The vote itself, for example, is frequently claimed not as a means of raising the status of women, but as a tool to perpetuate Conservatism against the threat of socialism.[83] Women were by nature Conservatives, it was argued, and therefore the vote was the best way of safeguarding against a socialist government. It is doubtful that a woman such as Evelyn Deakin, who also worked closely with the WLF via the LWSS, could have seriously believed this, but the argument demonstrates a degree of political expediency among Conservative women.[84]

The existence of a separate organisation that was Conservative before it was suffragist also allowed suffrage arguments to be discussed in wider circles. Not all of Liverpool's Conservative women were suffragists. Evelyn Deakin appears to have been pleasantly surprised when addressing a meeting of the Sefton Park Women's Conservative Association that 'although no resolution was put... it was quite obvious that a large majority of those present

83 See G. Samuel, 'Women's Franchise: A Safeguard Against Socialism', *Conservative and Unionist Women's Franchise Review*, Issue 3, May 1910.
84 It is also worth reminding ourselves that this argument did carry some weight at the time, being frequently cited by socialist men as a reason to campaign against extending the franchise to women on the same grounds as it was available to men.

were in sympathy with the movement'.[85] The label 'Conservative' also allowed privileged access to fellow party members over other non-party suffrage groups, especially to MPs. The Merseyside branches took full advantage of this, waiting regularly on local Conservative MPs. As part of their campaign around the Conciliation Bill, they helped with the local LWSS petition in Arthur Bonar-Law's constituency, whereby Deakin and her colleagues persuaded 'thirty eight out of the fifty members of the executive committee of the local Conservative Association, including the Chairman, Vice-Chairman, Hon Secretary, Hon Treasurer and the Chairmen of thirteen out of the fifteen wards' to sign in support of the Bill.[86] The branch saw this 'political work as being of the utmost importance in view of the present momentous session', and also brought their powers of persuasion to bear upon Rigby Swift, MP for St Helens, who was 'much impressed with a memorial presented to him, signed by a large number of his most influential supporters'.[87] Similar work was also carried out in the city council, when necessary. The LWSS campaign to have a suffrage resolution passed at this forum relied very heavily on the CUWFA to contact members of the ruling group.[88]

However, political affiliation also restricted the association. The prominent position of the local Conservative Party discouraged the CUWFA from participating in militancy. When they met with opposition, they quietly withdrew rather than attempting to fight their corner. In February 1914, when the CUWFA organised a block attendance at an anti-suffrage debate in Birkenhead, they griped in the *Review* that

> No verbal question being allowed, all questions had to be written with the result that many remained unanswered. The resolution against the enfranchisement of women was put to the meeting by the Chairman who declared it carried, and although many members of the audience asked for a 'count' this was refused.[89]

Members of more overtly militant societies would have demanded answers to their questions at this stage rather than let such an opportunity go by. CUWFA members feared bringing their party into disrepute by 'unfitting' public conduct. Even in their relationships with Conservative 'antis' they were keen to avoid the risk of schism. When the highly pro-suffrage MP

---

85 *Conservative and Unionist Women's Franchise Review*, Issue 11, April–June 1912. Unfortunately this is the only mention I have found anywhere for separate Conservative Women's Associations on Merseyside.

86 *Conservative and Unionist Women's Franchise Review*, Issue 11, April–June 1912.

87 *Conservative and Unionist Women's Franchise Review*, Issue 11, April–June 1912.

88 *Conservative and Unionist Women's Franchise Review*, Issue 7, April 1911. The resolution, moved by Eleanor Rathbone, was passed successfully by 44 votes to 19.

89 *Conservative and Unionist Women's Franchise Review*, Issue 19, April–June 1914.

Edward Marshall Hall was replaced by J. S. Rankin in East Toxteth, the CUWFA deputation that attempted to gain his support for their cause reported 'regret that he does not see his way clear to support the movement' but dropped the issue. Conservative women were not about to break rank with their party over the suffrage issue, nor was it their policy to attempt to influence the selection of candidates so that only pro-suffrage MPs were put forward for election.

For the women of the CUWFA, party politics remained the priority they chose over other possible allegiances. Most of them were middle class, but it was not this factor that united them. Indeed, they made repeated attempts to spread their message to women from different class backgrounds, notably through the work they did among the local Union of Women Workers.[90] In this, they tried to reach women across class divides as Conservatives rather than as women. Although membership of the CUWFA was limited to women, they took advantage of the pioneering work done by Alderman Forwood in establishing working-class Conservatism as a force in Liverpool in the previous century, securing invitations to speak to Liverpool's WMCAs.[91] Here again party politics rather than class or gender provided the unifying bond. The presence of a CUWFA branch that coexisted successfully with the LWSS, despite an overlap in methods and membership, serves as further testimony to the variety of political positions that composed the suffrage campaign in Liverpool, and to the political choices available to women who chose to fight publicly for the vote.

The United Suffragists

The final suffrage organisation to emerge on Merseyside was the United Suffragists (US). Much of its activity occurred during the war years, and will be dealt with later. However, for its later role to be understood fully it is necessary to devote some time to an explanation of its origins. Its existence has been glossed over until recently by historians who preferred to present the Pankhursts' conversion to nationalism and support for the war as total.[92] Occasional mentions highlight its small size and the lack of public activity it engaged in, presenting it as the work of an unrepresentative group of dissi-

---

90 The National Union of Women Workers received good coverage within the *Review*; see, for example, the article by Lady Laura Riding, Issue 15, April-June 1913. For local details, see Chapter 2.

91 See Waller, *Democracy and Sectarianism*, for details of local working-class Conservatism.

92 For instance, D. Mitchell, *Women on the Warpath: The Story of the Women of the First World War*, London, Jonathan Cape, 1966, mentions only the Independent WSPU. The only published account of the US to date is my own essay '"A Party Between Revolution and Peaceful Persuasion": A Fresh Look at the United Suffragists', in Purvis and Joannou, eds, *The Women's Suffrage Movement*, pp. 77–88.

dents seeking to create another, less militant, opposition to the WSPU.[93] The confusion around its aims is extended to its origins which are variously placed between 1912 and June 1914.[94] Part of this is due to historical accident. The US actually formed in February 1914, six months before the outbreak of the First World War.[95] The effect of the war on women forms a central part of the 'conclusion' of many suffrage histories. War work has been the main focus of British women's history between 1914 and 1918, and the US slotted in as a brief postscript.[96]

At its formation, supporters of the US had both the intent and the potential to develop an important new direction in suffrage politics. It was open to men and women 'irrespective of membership of any other society, militant or non-militant'.[97] The US was inspired by the success of the umbrella tactics of the VFWF, recognising that they were essential if the WSPU was not to be dismembered by an increasingly authoritarian state response to militancy. While Emmeline Pethick-Lawrence was keen to point out that she and her husband 'had foreseen that the adoption of more drastic militant policy [would force] the WSPU into underground channels' she did not condemn the tactics outright.[98] Instead, she explained that the US was essential as an aid to such tactics, as well as necessary for those constitutionalists who felt increasingly marginalised by their chosen methods of campaigning:

> Now, it is absolutely essential to the welfare of the whole movement that as the militant section is driven underground there should arise a strong intermediate party, occupying a position between the revolutionary section and the party of peaceful persuasion – an intermediate party determined of front, strong of action, politically militant and ready if need be to challenge oppression – yet with a stable organisation that remains above ground and intact for constitutional agitation.[99]

The US was therefore an 'intermediate suffrage party' intended to pursue similar work to the VFWF, but on a larger, and more coordinated scale.

---

93 See, for example, B. Harrison, *Prudent Revolutionaries: Portraits of British Feminists Between the Wars*, Oxford, Oxford University Press, 1987, p. 228, and Rosen, *Rise up Women!*, p. 224.

94 Harrison, *Prudent Revolutionaries*, p. 251. Stanley with Morley, *The Life and Death of Emily Wilding Davison*, p. 83.

95 *Votes for Women*, 6 February 1914.

96 For example, H. L. Smith, *The British Women's Suffrage Campaign 1866–1928*, London, Longmans, 1998, chapter 5. For examples of histories that concentrate on work done by women during the war see A. Marwick, *Women at War*, London, Fontana, 1977; Mitchell, *Women on the Warpath*; G. Braybon, *Women Workers and the First World War*, London, Routledge, 1989; A. Woollacott, *On Her Their Lives Depend: Munition Workers in the Great War*, Berkeley, California University Press, 1994.

97 *Votes for Women*, 6 February 1914.

98 *Votes for Women*, 10 July 1914.

99 *Votes for Women*, 10 July 1914.

However, it also sought to recruit 'those suffragists… who have not hitherto joined any suffrage society', believing that there were large numbers of people in this position who were 'ineffective' in contributing to the cause due to their isolation.[100] There were certainly many more of these than one might suspect. Both the religious societies and the WSPU were still recruiting new members locally in 1914. Nationally the US attracted some unexpected supporters including Phyllis and Audrey Coleridge, daughters of the judge who had sentenced Mrs Pankhurst and the Pethick-Lawrences in their conspiracy trial.[101]

Some local areas formed US branches immediately, but in Liverpool the VFWF continued to meet. In April 1914 Dr Helena Jones visited the city and held a series of meetings in the name of the US, but no local branch formed as a result. However, the VFWF did begin a vigorous campaign of open-air public meetings in the summer of 1914, and appears to have been developing stronger political aims than simply sharing fellowship and building a feminist paper, as a result of the US campaign nationally. The key to the survival of the Liverpool VFWF lay in its fluid interpretation of the divisions between local societies, and its ability to allow individuals to bridge them. Often individual contacts and feminist friendships facilitated this, but these were helped by a political perspective that raised the vote as a common aim above divisions based on tactics or affiliations of class or politics. However, the US does not appear to have been needed in the district.[102]

A change in the national circumstances of the US between April and August 1914 altered this. There was increasing concern that a coalition organisation could not continue. It was decided to pass *Votes for Women* over to the US to become its official mouthpiece. This was to be mutually beneficial – *Votes* was struggling without an organisational focus. Emmeline Pethick-Lawrence, who remained as editor, simultaneously agreed that 'the British section of the Votes for Women Fellowship will… become merged [into the US]… to strengthen the great middle party of suffragists that is growing up to occupy the wide field that separates the revolutionary party from the party of pure propaganda'.[103]

The paper was handed over in August 1914. The decision was taken some months earlier, at a time when nobody could have foreseen that the chosen month would be a significant date in suffrage history for another reason altogether, that of the outbreak of war. The dislocating effect of war on the many suffrage societies cannot be underestimated. One Scottish Freedom League member noted that 'The WSPU… left all their organisers unpaid, several

100 *Votes for Women*, 10 July 1914.
101 Pethick-Lawrence, *My Part in a Changing World*, p. 303.
102 For a discussion of the problems that the US faced in forging a distinct identity in the provinces see Cowman, 'A Party Between Revolution and Peaceful Persuasion'.
103 *Votes for Women*, 14 August 1914.

applied to me for help to get them to their various homes.'[104] Added to this, the problematic nature of communications during wartime made any new initiative difficult to sustain. It was not until March 1915 that a Liverpool US branch formed, by which time the face of local suffrage politics had changed beyond recognition.

★ ★ ★

These three chapters on suffrage have attempted to reinterpret individual organisations as key locations for women's political activity prior to the First World War. While some spectacular individual actions have been included, many more have been omitted in favour of a consideration of the organisational policies of individual groups. The point here has been to uncover the local practices of suffrage organisations, particularly in relation to their attempts to recruit and retain a membership, in order to assess their effectiveness at drawing their membership into the arena of public politics. Sometimes the effect could be quite subdued, as in organisations such as the LWSS which drew heavily on the ideology of separate spheres and concentrated on providing special space for women within mainstream politics where their 'superior influence' could be exercised to greatest effect. Here, women were still allotted a particular space within organisations that was seen as 'female' aside from the 'male' mainstream. Yet even this could be extremely radical in certain contexts, such as in religious suffrage groups, or in the work of the CUWFA which succeeded in providing space for Conservative women, something that the Primrose League had failed to do on Merseyside. On other occasions, the politicising effect of suffrage organisations was quite apparent, most obviously within the WSPU. This organisation removed the novel quality of women's public campaigning from the local political environment. From 1905 to 1914, women bedecked in WSPU colours became a familiar sight on Merseyside streets, addressing crowds, selling papers, and devising and utilising increasingly original methods to keep themselves in the public eye.

Collectively, the suffrage organisations drew unprecedented numbers of women into the public political sphere. Many of these women were new to any form of political activity. Others had previous experience within political parties or trade unions. For them, the suffrage years represented a period of time when they increased their public activity for new organisations while attempting to retain loyalty to earlier ones. Working within suffrage groups where women took all major positions and policy decisions showed clearly the inadequacies of other political organisations in this direction. Before allowing the war to interrupt the narrative, we should now return to an exam-

104 Eunice Murray, quoted in Leneman, *A Guid Cause*, p. 209.

ination of some of the solutions attempted by women whose political loyalties were divided by their suffrage activism through a detailed examination of their work within the Liberal and socialist parties during this time.

CHAPTER SEVEN

Later Party Political Activity, 1905–14

The campaign for parliamentary suffrage provided local Conservative women with the organisational base that the Primrose League had failed to deliver. It also had far-reaching effects on the local political development of the Liberal and socialist parties. For women who continued to work within parties there were difficult and painful choices between their personal wish for the vote, the official attitudes of their parties towards the question, and the perceived political opportunities that their parties continued to offer them. The WLF eventually split over the Liberal government's repeated attempts to avoid the issue in Parliament, while socialist women attracted to the WSPU found themselves forced either to prioritise their allegiance to men from their own class within their party, or to follow the WSPU's directive to stop party work until the vote was won. Or at least that was the national picture. Locally, it is possible to discern occasions when individual women circumnavigated these choices, buoyed up by support networks of close friendships and political camaraderie. Their actions demonstrate that political activism is rarely as simple as studies of national movements would have us believe.

Liberal Party Women

Local Liberal women were in a very difficult position in 1905. The election of a Liberal government should have given them cause for celebration, but many of them were committed suffragists and the government was somewhat reticent on this question. Furthermore, the local party was in decline following a series of municipal defeats.[1] Conseqeuently members had to be very careful in any criticism of government policy for fear of being left open to accusations of furthering the local Liberal demise.

By 1905 the WLF had local branches at Wavertree, West Toxteth, East Toxteth and Birkenhead. Kirkdale and Walton had folded but had been replaced at Waterloo and West Derby in 1906, making a total of six branches which remained until the First World War.[2] Membership of these provided

---

1 Waller, *Democracy and Sectarianism*, p. 230.
2 Before 1914 there was also an intermittent branch at Wallasey, and two new branches, which formed from a split in the WLF.

women with direct political experience and they continued their successful work as Liberals on the Boards of Guardians. However, this often resulted in the WLF losing some of its best workers. In January 1905, for example, Miss Japp resigned the Chair of East Toxteth WLF 'to the great regret of all, [due to] pressure of work' as a Guardian.[3] Losing a branch member to local government meant more work for the remaining members, but local Liberal women were extremely proud of their achievements in this direction. They also developed a feminised version of politics through the public presentation, at WLF meetings, of very personal gifts to one another in recognition of public work. These presents, which included a bag, purse, cheque and flowers to Poor Law Guardian Mrs Ellis, a dressing bag to Mrs Stewart-Brown and a 'handsome silver teapot, hotwater jug and basket of flowers' to Miss Biggs, contrasted starkly with the conduct of male Guardians who made no public mention of one another's work except if one of them died in office.[4]

Feminised practices brought comfort to many women Guardians who were often belittled by men on the Boards. They also reflected a continued belief in distinct female qualities which Liberal women employed in the campaign to elect women to municipal bodies following the removal of their legal disqualifications in 1907. Stewart-Brown, at the heart of this as in other debates concerning women's involvement, called on all Lancashire and Cheshire Women's Liberal Associations (WLAs) to prioritise the selection of women candidates 'in view of the need of their help in administering the laws specifically affecting women and children'.[5] The local press was similarly supportive, drawing attention to particular areas such as 'the appointment of female sanitary inspectors... the inspection of lodging houses... and of unsanitary property' as 'branches of municipal work which called for some supervision on the part of women'.[6] This was a marked improvement on the coverage of the previous decade which claimed that women would be lost 'deliberating with men about gas, water, sewerage and other public works'.[7] Women were becoming accepted as councillors working in certain areas, but there was still resistance to viewing them as genderless politicians. The long local tradition of municipal duty among leading families furnished a ready contingent of women to undertake these public tasks but, while comparisons were drawn between housekeeping and local government finance, areas such as the local budget were still considered outside the province of women. Stewart-Brown, who argued in favour

3   *Women's Liberal Federation News*, January 1905.
4   *Women's Liberal Federation News*, November 1910; April 1912; *Women's National Liberal Association Quarterly Leaflet*, March 1911.
5   *Women's Liberal Federation News*, November 1907.
6   *Liverpool Daily Post*, undated press cutting from miscellaneous cuttings relating to the 1910 municipal elections, Town Clerk's cuttings books, LRO.
7   *Liverpool Review of Politics*, 9 April 1898.

of distinct female qualities, did attempt to reconceptualise the issue by explaining that women's new municipal role demonstrated that Liberalism was important to feminism, and not vice versa. As a suffragist, she had pressured the government for more municipal votes for women.[8] Now she took more pride as a Liberal in the decision of 'her' government to permit female municipal candidates.[9] Furthermore, she believed that

> Every step in advance which had been made to improve the condition of women had... been made by the Liberal Party. Conservative legislation had retarded their powers which had now been regained and enlarged under the Liberal government.[10]

Despite this, and surprisingly considering how willing the local Liberal Party was to stand women candidates in Guardians' elections and use their organisational talents to further their own political ambitions, few women were actually selected as municipal candidates. Those who were selected found themselves placed in Tory wards against stiff political opposition. Miss Ellen Robinson and Miss Georgina Crosfield, experienced political women with impeccable philanthropic credentials, were allotted West Derby where both failed.[11]

Experiences like this drew other women away from the strongly pro-party line of Stewart-Brown. While the WLAs had been quite cautious about attempts to elect women as women in the nineteenth century, members now began to question this publicly. Mrs Allan Bright, always a loyal Liberal, went so far as to express her hope

> that some women would stand independently of Party Politics so that they could specifically look after the interests of women and children.[12]

Independent women who laid claim to these priorities could count on WLA support. When Eleanor Rathbone first stood as a city council candidate in 1910, Liberal women were so prominent in her campaign that the Conservative *Liverpool Courier* queried:

> if elected, will she remain a party to herself, or will she be officially counted among the Liberals? How is it that in the list of Liberal meetings sent [to us] Miss Rathbone's meetings are included? This significant recognition... is not consistent with [her] posing as an independent candidate.[13]

8 See her resolution at Waterloo AGM; *Women's Liberal Federation News*, October 1906.
9 Hollis, *Ladies Elect*, p. 392.
10 Stewart-Brown to Wallasey WLA, 12 November 1907. *Women's Liberal Federation News*, December 1907.
11 Georgina Crosfield was one of Liverpool's first female Poor Law Guardians. Ellen Robinson was also a Guardian but had achieved national recognition for her work as a Quaker pacifist. See Obituary, *The Friend*, 22 March 1912.
12 *Women's Liberal Federation News*, January 1908.
13 *The Liverpool Courier*, 28 October 1910.

The paper had a point. Miss Japp, Liberal member on the Board of Guardians and a former Liberal Mayoress, was Rathbone's committee secretary. Yet, despite close family and friendship ties with many local WLAs, it would be stretching the point to describe Rathbone as a Liberal. On the matter of suffrage she was well in advance of official WLA policy, having decided as early as 1905 to urge 'all women workers to refuse to work for candidates who would not support the enfranchisement of women'.[14] Much of her identification with the WLA came through the work that she and WLA activists such as Stewart-Brown and Bright performed together in the local NUWSS. This, and the increasing conviction of many WLA members to ensure 'that the interests of women should be directly represented by someone of their own sex', account for her strong support from Merseyside branches.[15]

Liberal Women and the Suffrage Issue

Although local WLA members were now more willing to consider an approach to political campaigns that was based on gender rather than on party, they remained, above all, party activists in their work within the associations. In the decade before the First World War their loyalty to party was to be stretched to its limit over the question of suffrage. As the Liberal Party remained in government, this question came to dominate the WLF both nationally and locally. The high level of joint membership between the WLAs and the NUWSS made it extremely prominent on Merseyside. Stewart-Brown's involvement in determining much of the national WLF policy on suffrage gave further emphasis to the issue. Clare Hirshfield has argued that elsewhere Liberal women were forced to put party loyalty before suffrage in this period.[16] However, despite the added problems of local Liberal decline, the close links between Liberalism and constitutional suffrage in Liverpool often led local Liberal women to take different positions, even tentatively, finally working against their own party.

Initially Liverpool WLA members believed that just as their MPs had supported their calls for protective legislation for women in the nineteenth century, the new Liberal government would be favourably responsive to pressure from within its own party. In February 1905, West Toxteth branch declared that

> the committee firmly believes that the return of Liberalism means the securing of religious and personal liberty, a series of reforms for the benefit of the working-classes, and *above all the extension of the franchise to women.*[17]

14 Eleanor Rathbone to Wavertree WLA, *Women's Liberal Federation News*, March 1905.
15 E. Rathbone, election address for 1910 campaign, Rathbone Papers, X1V.3.3, Liverpool University Library.
16 Hirshfield, 'Fractured Faith', pp. 173–97.
17 Mrs Ellis to West Toxteth AGM, 23 February 1905. *Women's Liberal Federation News*, March 1905, my italics.

Stewart-Brown who led this branch was especially keen not to slacken the attacks on anti-suffrage MPs and warned other Liberal women that

> they must not allow the government to go out of office before they had dealt with women's suffrage.[18]

The national executive was equally vigilant. In November 1906 it had opened a special suffrage fund and initiated a scheme for suffrage work through the Federation in response to the popularity of the WSPU. While Lady Carlisle wanted the Federation 'to be disassociated in the public mind from those misguided zealots (militants)', other members could not fail to notice that the WSPU did appear to be doing something while their own government did less and less.[19] Although they remained publicly silent, local Liberal women were severely embarrassed by the scenes that greeted Campbell-Bannerman at the Sun Hall in January 1906 which have been previously described. He had pre-empted this first outbreak of suffrage militancy in Liverpool by refusing to answer suffrage questions the previous month but promising 'to deal with the question on an early date'. Both *The Labour Leader* and the WSPU made good political capital from this, using the Sun Hall – his next public meeting – to push the issue.[20] WLA members must privately have queried whether their Prime Minister could have prevented it by answering the question for which he must have been prepared. There was extra embarrassment for Stewart-Brown who was on the platform at the meeting. From there she watched the scene with indignation, fuelled, in all probability, by her inability to draw attention to the tactical differences that existed between herself and the interrupters.[21]

Such scenes forced the WLF to tighten suffrage policy, with Stewart-Brown's presence on the national executive drawing local women into these debates. Some executive members concurred with Eva McLaren that the WSPU was effecting a 'revolution' in attitudes towards women's suffrage.[22] Stewart-Brown was more sceptical, and felt that the WSPU was ruining all that she had worked for within her party. In November 1907, she seconded an EC resolution which condemned both the present disturbances at political meetings, and the subsequent banning from them of Liberal women. Although this was lost (and an amendment condemning the banning of *all* women passed), Stewart-Brown's original motion underlined from where the main part of her opposition originated. As a loyal party woman, she was progressing slowly through Liberal ranks. She had shared platforms with leading Liberals, and was the first woman elected to Liverpool Liberal Federal Council. The more that militancy became directed against the

18 *Women's Liberal Federation News*, January 1907.
19 Women's Liberal Federation Annual Report, 1906.
20 *The Labour Leader*, 29 December 1905; Parkhurst, *The Suffragette*, p. 50
21 *The Porcupine*, 13 January 1906.
22 Eva McLaren, quoted in Hirshfield, 'Fractured Faith', p. 180.

Liberal Party, through interruptions of meetings and the WSPU election pledge to 'keep the Liberal out', the more marginalised women would become within that party. So great was the extent to which Stewart-Brown prioritised party loyalties over those of gender that hers remained a voice of dissent when the WLA finally made suffrage a test question in 1908, holding to her belief that a Liberal woman should work for a selected party candidate, no matter what his views on the vote.[23]

Stewart-Brown was quite isolated in her position. The opposite argument, put publicly by Mrs Allan Bright, was that the Labour Party would prove more reliable on suffrage, so possibly deserved women's support.[24] Yet amazingly the local WLAs managed to stave off any direct conflict around this issue. As the NUWSS developed on Merseyside, there was an increasing overlap of membership between it and the WLF, especially at managerial level. Of the 12 official branch positions in Liverpool WLAs in 1909, a third were filled by women who were also active in the NUWSS. Such overlaps meant that, despite frequent assertions that the Federation was not simply a suffrage organisation, it was increasingly becoming one. Indeed, by 1910, the Liverpool WLAs appear to have discussed little else but suffrage. The *Federation News* for this period notes the subject arising time after time, in many different guises. At Wavertree in June 1910, Mrs Solly (Stewart-Brown's sister, resident in South Africa) told the branch that she 'regretted that the franchise had not been extended to the natives under the new government [in South Africa], although Cape Colony, as a whole was favourable to the step'.[25] Miss E. C. Greene discussed suffrage when giving the vote of thanks to Rathbone at East Toxteth in October 1910. John Lea, parliamentary candidate for East Toxteth, informed the branch there that the ward 'would have been won for the Liberals [in January] if women could vote', and, by November, Wavertree WLA passed a resolution 'pledging the association to try to assist in securing parliamentary candidates... who should be in favour of Women's Suffrage.'[26] Such moves were bound to broaden the outlook of the Associations beyond party political issues. As suffrage increasingly dominated WLA meetings, the local branches helped to organise a large suffrage demonstration at St George's Hall in July 1910, joined by the ILP, the CUWFA and the NUWSS, and Mrs Edwards, Socialist and Fabian, gave her 'Spiritual Side of the Women's Movement' lecture to East Toxteth Branch in December 1910. Through concentrating on raising the profile locally of constitutional suffrage demands, on which all WLA members were agreed, the organisation managed temporarily to avoid the larger question of where their party stood on this question.

23 Women's Liberal Federation Annual Report, 1908.
24 *The Clarion*, 1 June 1906.
25 *Women's Liberal Federation News*, August 1910.
26 All details of meetings from *Women's Liberal Federation News*, January–December 1910.

Such solutions could not last indefinitely, especially when the broader concerns of the Liberal Party made demands on its women auxiliaries. At the second general election of 1910, Miss Greene, secretary of East Toxteth WLA, had 'begged suffragists to consider before they stood aside from Liberal work, not withstanding the bitter feeling roused by the non-passing of the Conciliation Bill'.[27] Finally, in November 1911, Stewart-Brown gave the first public indication that she was losing patience. At a meeting at Wavertree Town Hall called to acknowledge the 16 years' service she had given the WLF, she offered no contradiction when Mrs Charles Morrison 'said she was tired of working for Liberals when Liberals would do nothing for women, and she would no longer work for any political party until justice was done to women'.[28] Mrs Morrison did not resign; she went on to stand as a candidate in the Guardians' election the following March; but her public declaration served as a warning that even the most loyal women had tired of equivocating between their personal stance on suffrage and the official stance of the party whose name their association bore.

Stewart-Brown continued to oppose militancy at every possible opportunity, while supporting all measures to get Liberal MPs to vote for suffrage amendments. In January 1912, she used her position on the Liverpool Liberal Federal Council to move a motion supporting Lloyd George's attempts to bring a women's suffrage amendment to the Manhood Suffrage Bill. When this failed, she continued to view the militant alternative as 'the deplorable tactics of an extreme but small section of woman suffragists and [hope] that Liberal women would not on that account be any less active in furthering the Cause by constitutionalist means'.[29] Other local women were less patient. Mrs Jones warned Waterloo WLA that 'if some [suffrage] amendment is not incorporated... large numbers of Liberal women will be unable any longer to support the Liberal Party'.[30]

In 1913 the national WLF finally split. Some women attempted to reintroduce a resolution to the annual conference mandating local WLAs to withhold all assistance to anti-suffrage candidates.[31] When this failed, its supporters launched a Liberal Women's Suffragist Union (LWSU), 'to educate Liberal women to work harder for suffragist Liberals and to refrain

27 *Women's Liberal Federation News*, November 1910.

28 *Women's Liberal Federation News*, December 1911.

29 Stewart-Brown, 'Presidential Address to the Lancashire and Cheshire Union of Women's Liberal Associations, 13 March 1912', *Women's Liberal Federation News*, April 1912.

30 *Women's Liberal Federation News*, December 1912.

31 An initial attempt to pass this in 1912 had been defeated when the Liberal Cabinet, panicked by what in effect would be a strike of WLAs, decided to make a concession in the form of pledging support for the White Slave Traffic Bill, a pet concern of many prominent WLF members. The resolution was reintroduced by Tunbridge Wells in 1913. For more details, see WLF Annual Report, 1912. Also Hirshfield, 'Fractured Faith'.

from working for anti-suffragist Liberals'.[32] The LWSU was presented as a voluntary organisation, and membership did not necessarily entail leaving the WLF. However, through the summer of 1913 there was a steady haemorrhage of WLAs from the WLF, with 68 associations, and 18,000 members leaving up to 1914.[33]

Nationally, many who left drifted into the Labour Party. The LWSU considered following NUWSS electoral policy and offering help to individual Labour candidates. The close WLA/NUWSS ties avoided such final partings on Merseyside, as women could help pro-suffrage Labour candidates in elections by channelling their efforts through the NUWSS, as suffragists rather than as Liberals. They continued to work through the WLA for Liberals who supported suffrage. The Women's Citizen's Associations provided a further arena. Still suffrage tensions were not totally absent. In June 1913, Stewart-Brown, so long an opponent of making suffrage a test question, finally parted company with the official WLF position. In a letter addressed to all WLAs affiliated to the Lancashire and Cheshire Union, she announced her resignation from the Presidency of that body. She explained, 'I cannot remain president of an organisation of Liberal women some of whom even now continue to work for anti-suffrage candidates, as I feel that by so doing they are retarding the advance of true Liberalism.'[34] This was not, she hoped, a final parting. 'I shall continue to speak and work for Liberalism… my resignation does not mean that I am severing my connection with the party for which I have worked hard and unceasingly for twenty-five years. But I think I can now serve it better "in a position of greater freedom and less responsibility".'[35] This was a coded way of expressing her desire to be free to criticise the party in public, which she was to do quite effectively within the pages of *Common Cause*.

Stewart-Brown did not simultaneously resign her Chairmanships of Wavertree, Waterloo or West Toxteth WLAs. Indeed, she was re-elected to all of these in 1914, suggesting approval of her actions, although this was not unanimous. Organised opposition to her call for a more progressive policy came mainly from Mrs Alice Holt, who gathered supporters within the West Derby WLA. Holt retained the Presidency of this association. In May 1914 she also inaugurated Liverpool Central WLA. This attracted 50 members, drawn from 'all Liberal women who approve of the policy in assisting the Liberal Party in the constituencies without exacting a pledge to support women's suffrage or refusing to assist the candidate if he were unwilling to give such a pledge'.[36] A similar branch in Wavertree Garden

32 E. Acland, *Women's Liberal Federation News*, August 1913.
33 Hirshfield, 'Fractured Faith', p. 187.
34 *Women's Liberal Federation News*, July 1913.
35 *Women's Liberal Federation News*, July 1913.
36 *Women's Liberal Federation News*, June 1914.

Suburb attracted 32 women. (These were probably dissidents from Stewart-Brown's three associations whose combined membership dropped by 81 between 1913 and 1914.)[37] Despite this opportunity to express public dissent, the remaining 673 Merseyside members stayed in their original branches, unwilling to subordinate the demands of their gender to the ambitions of their party.

One of the features that differentiated the WLF from its contemporary the Primrose League was its ability to offer women an opportunity to organise autonomously in associations that were inaugurated and managed by other women. This difference was particularly strong within Merseyside, where local distinctions had resulted in nearly all of the League's official positions being taken by men. Yet as an auxiliary organisation to a political party whose parliamentary wing was wholly male, the WLF was forced increasingly to make compromises. Initially, women such as Stewart-Brown, who had gained much public political experience through her work for the Federation, were willing to make these. The WSPU was not an option for them, due to its persistent attacks on the government, while the NUWSS, with whom they had close involvement, offered little of significant difference in the way of experience. It was the constant failure of Liberal MPs to deliver on the suffrage question that finally forced Liberal women in Liverpool to abandon blind party loyalty in favour of suffrage work. Even on this they preferred to direct their work through the WLAs whenever they could, altering rather than abandoning the associations that they had painstakingly built over the past two decades.

Socialist Women and the Suffrage Challenge

Although it did not advance as it had done in the 1890s, Liverpool's socialist culture continued in the years leading up to the outbreak of war. Familiar faces from the early movement remained, but for women there was a significant gap in personnel caused by the early death of Eleanor Keeling and the increasingly serious illnesses of Jeannie Mole.[38] The death of Enid Stacy, a popular and regular visitor, further depleted the ranks of women who sought a synthesis between socialism and feminism.[39] Socialism made its first municipal successes during this time, although some of these were short lived and a parliamentary seat remained elusive. The ILP, FS and Trades Council continued to grow, along with independent societies and Clarion groups.

---

37 All figures drawn from WLF Annual Reports.
38 Joseph Edwards and Eleanor Keeling left the area in 1901 and Keeling died in 1903. Jeannie Mole died in 1912.
39 Julia Dawson was just one commentator who recalled Stacy's local visits in her obituary, *The Clarion*, 11 September 1903. In the same article, Dawson also compares Stacy and Keeling and comments on the loss they were to the socialist women's movement.

The Transport Strike of 1911 established syndicalism within the city, and it became a stronghold of the newly formed British Socialist Party, successor to the SDF, which formed a significant national challenge to the ILP in the years immediately prior to the First World War. Women continued to find space within these groups, still broadly within the areas of education, agitation and organisation. However, the emergence of the WSPU from within the ILP offered them alternative sites for activity. The WSPU's ability to provide local women with a separate space to organise meant that socialists were more directly challenged than other political groups by its growth.

The persistence of links between the ILP and the WSPU has been subjected to much historical analysis. There is a general acceptance that at a national level they were severed either at the Cockermouth by-election in April 1906 when Christabel Pankhurst initiated the policy of working *against* Liberal candidates rather than for pro-suffrage ones, or the following year when Christabel and her mother resigned from the ILP.[40] After this, the national WSPU was committed to a policy of political independence, and required that its members stopped their involvement in any party activity until after the vote was won. Yet at local level such demands were often simply ignored, as the particular characteristics of a WSPU branch proved more influential than national policy.[41]

The WSPU offered local socialist women much more than the ILP. It gave them the chance to select their own agenda and guaranteed them space as speakers, whereas within the ILP they always had to compete with men. As late as March 1907, *The Labour Leader* praised Alice Morrissey, not for her work as a political organiser, but for her skill with 'catering arrangements'.[42] By contrast, the WSPU acknowledged her as an agitator, orator, organiser and, following her imprisonment, a martyr. Some socialist women used suffrage as a lever to broader political work. Mary Bamber addressed several local socialist groups on the question, but, although she continued to support the WSPU from the sidelines, she was soon identified more with the question of women workers.[43] Others such as Emma Hillier, Hattie Mahood and Patricia Woodlock continued to work in the ILP and address its meetings, but did so increasingly as socialist suffragettes. However, as the career of

---

40 For Cockermouth see Liddington and Norris, *One Hand Tied Behind Us*, p. 207; Rosen, *Rise Up Women!*, p. 71; Smith, *The British Women's Suffrage Campaign*, p. 31. For further discussion of WSPU/ILP links see Liddington, *The Life and Times of a Respectable Rebel*, p. 140; Smith, *The British Women's Suffrage Campaign*, pp. 31–33; Van Wingerden, *The Women's Suffrage Movement in Britain*, pp. 70–77. Also Cowman, 'Incipient Toryism'.

41 See, for example, the portrait of the Wimbledon branch given in Stanley and Morley, *The Life and Death of Emily Wilding Davison*.

42 *The Labour Leader*, 6 March 1907.

43 *The Clarion*, 2 March 1906. Mary's daughter, Bessie Braddock, later recalled her mother's approval at her childhood support for the WSPU. See Braddock and Braddock, *The Braddocks*.

Alice Morrissey demonstrates, it was possible for local women to be active simultaneously as suffragettes and as socialists.

Although she had been a founding member of the local WSPU, Alice Morrissey continued to work as a socialist in the ILP. She was its local secretary for 1907–8 and its first female delegate to the LRC in 1908–9. She also campaigned publicly for John Hill in the Kirkdale by-election of September 1907. Officially there was no work for WSPU members to do in this contest, as no government candidate was involved. For socialist women, opportunities for public political work materialised as *The Labour Leader* explained:

> Much good and useful work has been done by women. Mrs Bruce Glasier in particular... was one of the most effective speakers taking part... Other women workers who assisted by addressing meetings were Mrs Morrissey, Mrs Cooper, Mrs Cobden-Sanderson and Mrs Bamber... In canvassing and other necessary work in connection with the contest the women workers were [also] very much in evidence.[44]

The Labour Leader then used Morrissey as a stick with which to beat the newly formed Women's Freedom League which had stated that its founders trusted neither 'Liberal, Tory or Labour politicians':

> we know of many hitherto members of the WSPU who are resolved to work definitely with the ILP for the return of labour members pledged to support their cause. The presence of... Mrs Morrissey on Mr Hill's platform this week is an indication of this fact.[45]

Yet Morrissey was no 'hitherto' member and retained her WSPU membership despite her work for Hill. Nor was she the only woman to do this. Throughout 1907, the year in which national WSPU and ILP relations reached an all-time low, socialist women with feet in both the WSPU and ILP camps were welcomed at Liverpool ILP meetings. Miss Labouchere spoke at Wavertree on 'The Relation of the ILP to Women's Suffrage' in February. Patricia Woodlock told of her 'Experiences in Holloway' in July, and Australian suffragette Mrs Martel addressed the Clarion Club in the summer. Socialist or suffragette was not necessarily an 'either/or' question on Merseyside.

The local evidence indicates that whereas links between the national leadership of the WSPU and the ILP may have slackened as the Union grew, in some local areas they were retained by individuals with deep-rooted joint loyalties. Militancy, that multi-faceted suffrage phenomenon, provides one explanation for why so many of Liverpool's socialists continued to support the WSPU. A tradition of public militancy among socialists continued up until the war, and WSPU militancy often reflected socialist actions. Many

44 *The Labour Leader*, 27 September 1907.
45 *The Labour Leader*, 27 September 1907.

early local acts of suffrage militancy were committed by socialist women. When Morrissey was first arrested for suffrage activities in June 1906 along with her husband, who was then a Liverpool councillor, *The Labour Leader* presented this as an attack on two prominent socialists.[46] Although such support began to wane nationally as WSPU militancy increased, it was always forthcoming from Liverpool socialists. In January 1912 prominent socialist John Edwards was invited to open the WSPU's new offices. In so doing, he reminded his audience that 'since the advent of militancy, the suffrage movement [has] improved by leaps and bounds'.[47] Helen Jollie, who extended the invitation, continued to cement links between the WSPU and local socialism until the outbreak of war. When the city council refused to hire Picton Hall for suffrage meetings as the WSPU was not 'respectable', she complained to socialists that 'respectability [has] never been the claim of any reformer of any age', a statement with which they were bound to agree.[48] Constitutional suffrage societies with their largely middle-class membership and pro-Liberal bias received less sympathy. When Cecily Leadley-Brown of the NUWSS and CUWFA claimed 'that the Tory Working Men's Associations were in earnest about women getting the vote', *The Liverpool Forward* mocked her position:

> the audience politely refrained from smiling, [but] now Miss Leadley-Brown has mentioned the fact, we shall be aware and look out for it.[49]

There was a negative side to this. The Liverpool WSPU was far more than an ILP auxiliary organisation. Socialist women who retained their political involvement while active in the WSPU found that the latter increasingly took up more of their time and energy as they were not restricted to a small part of its work. Increasingly, the dual work they undertook developed a single focus, and their activities within the socialist groups were undertaken as suffragettes. Outside of her immediate socialist circles, Morrissey was increasingly seen as a suffragette rather than a socialist.[50] Consequently, her speeches for the ILP became progressively limited to suffrage topics. Similarly, on the Trades Council, Miss Hackey, Trades Council delegate and WSPU activist, developed a high profile through moving suffrage motions. Hence she was perceived on the Council not as a woman trade unionist or as a delegate of her members, but as a suffragette, despite the fact that the WSPU had no affiliate status to the Trades Council. As general support by

---

46 *The Labour Leader*, 29 June 1906; 6 July 1906. See also Mitchell, *The Hard Way Up*, pp. 143–46, 149.
47 *The Liverpool Forward*, 17 January 1912.
48 *The Liverpool Forward*, 7 March 1913.
49 *The Liverpool Forward*, 9 January 1914.
50 See *The Porcupine*, 19 January 1907, 'Even Mrs Morrissey refrained from speaking on the equality of the sexes'; *The Liverpool Weekly Mercury* 8 December 1906, '[She] has distinguished herself as a warm supporter of the demand for woman suffrage.'

local socialists for the WSPU increased public political activities for women within socialism, it paradoxically contributed to their continued marginalisation. Women had been 'women comrades', restricted to catering or squeezed into educating. Now they added socialist suffragette to their list of roles, again remaining slightly apart from full party activity.

A strong local socialist women's section may have overcome this, but none was forthcoming. The women who would have been obvious candidates for dividing their political energies between mixed socialist activities and work for the Women's Labour League were already deeply involved in the WSPU, making work in a third organisation both unnecessary and largely impossible. The limited success of a WLL branch at Wallasey underlines this. A branch was formed there by Claire Stallybrass in 1906.[51] Stallybrass was extremely unusual among local socialist women in her conviction of the necessity for anti-militancy and in her affiliation to the NUWSS. The lower levels of public activity demanded of constitutional suffragists allowed her more time to devote to WLL activities. Interestingly, two of Wallasey's most active WSPU socialists, Helah Criddle and Hattie Mahood, took no recorded part in Stallybrass's organisation. The WSPU and the WLL were not directly hostile to one another, but they appeared incompatible on Merseyside, where socialist militant suffragettes were adequately provided for, in organisational terms.

The WSPU allowed local socialist women to retain the political perspectives they developed through socialism using militant techniques such as rowdy street corner meetings. Their continued joint socialist activity shows that this remained an important part of their work. However, the WSPU also gave them the opportunity to prioritise gender issues, often by working with women of a different class or political affiliation. More importantly, it also allowed women to set their own agenda completely, to determine the direction of an organisation and to take all its official positions. Within the WSPU they no longer had to compete with men for positions, as continued to be the case within the socialist groups.

Women Socialists within their Parties

Not all of Liverpool's women socialists became active suffragettes. For some, socialism remained the entire focus of their political work. As in the earlier period, they continued to struggle against male perceptions and definitions of their political role, but set against the fuller range of opportunities provided for women by suffrage organisations, this contrast became increasingly marked. The socialist view of women, which refused to see anything in the position of their gender other than a parallel with class oppression, became increasingly less attractive to women who looked to socialism to provide emancipation through political activity.

51 Collette, *For Labour and for Women*, Appendix 2, pp. 204–17.

As in the previous decade, the language of local male socialists reveals much about their attitudes to women. A good example appeared in *The Labour Leader* in 1907. The paper recounts events surrounding an accident to a workman outside St George's Hall:

> ... a pretty girl [came] forward to see if she could be of any assistance... The ambulance was late... and the working men... started grumbling 'if he was a rich man they would have sent something soon'.
> The girl, who had... shown her sympathy looked the speaker bravely in the face.
> 'Just remember this accident and what you have now said when the elections come round' she said gently. 'Vote for the Labour Party and the Socialists, and turn the men out who are responsible for making the workers wait.'[52]

The girl, whose attractiveness is her main feature, emerges as a ministering angel from the crowd to tend to the wounded man. Her public speaking has a gentle tone, and she is applauded for her bravery in daring to address the men at all. Socialism is a natural extension of her nurturing femininity. It would appear that the very public roles being undertaken by socialist women had done little to widen perceptions of their work.

Similarly idealised versions of socialist womanhood permeated the language of Liverpool socialism through this period. In 1912, local socialist organisations again began a joint publication, *The Liverpool Forward*, which had a 'Woman's World Column' as a regular feature. Its reception demonstrates how much socialist women's views of their own position in society had altered since the advent of militant suffrage. In 1895, Eleanor Keeling had provided the only voice of criticism against her own inclusion of recipes in her *Clarion* column. Seventeen years on, the domestic content of the new column caused outrage. Miss Norton wrote:

> Surely there is some mistake. The woman's column! Mock turtle soup! Velvet soup! Sponge cake! It can't be that the writer thinks he has catered properly for women's needs.[53]

While D. Mason added:

> Why this implied restriction of woman's sphere?... Do not give subtle encouragement to the tradition that the world of thought, of politics, is a world where women have no place.[54]

In response, the content was slightly modified, but the column never developed the same sense of identity among its readership that earlier

---

52 *The Labour Leader*, 20 September 1907.
53 *The Liverpool Forward*, 11 May 1912.
54 *The Liverpool Forward*, 18 May 1912.

women's pages had done. Friendship networks and political policies among socialist women were now developed through activities, and the need for the space of a newspaper column was much less intense.

Yet domestic ideology continued to have direct bearing on the opportunities that socialism offered women for public political activity. Topics offered to women speakers tended to be restricted and practical experience limited. With the exception of Alice Morrissey, women held no high-profile office even in the smaller socialist branches.[55] The emergence of the British Socialist Party (BSP) branch in 1911 did nothing to challenge this situation. Unlike its predecessor, the SDF, the BSP was at odds with many other local socialists. It took over Kensington Socialist Society. Its members were referred to as 'our opponents' by members of the Clarion Club.[56] Yet on the question of woman's public political role, the BSP shows itself completely in step with other local groups. It built seven branches before appointing two women, Hetty Myer and Mary Claire, to the relatively lowly positions of literature secretary and lecture secretary for Liverpool East branch.

The majority of socialist actions by women remained on the periphery of party activity, channelled through non-aligned socialist societies or groups. Kensington Socialist Society had attempted to form a women's circle in January 1911. This met with initial success, although it faded by October, when the Society was taken over by the BSP. More significant was the women's group which met at the local Clarion Café from 1906. The café had been relaunched in that year as part of an attempt to enlarge the local Clarion Club. Women, 'just as much a part of society as [men]', were specially invited 'to help in any work undertaken by the club and to make use of it'.[57]

Socialist women began meeting in the club on Tuesday afternoons. Following their approaches it was agreed to halve the subscription rates for women from one shilling to sixpence, reflecting their lower economic status. This worked, and the Tuesday meetings, which consisted of a formal paper followed by afternoon tea, ran for a number of years. The subjects provided by the club were wide-ranging. In 1908, for example, papers included Mary Bamber on 'The Feeding of School Children', and Margaret Bondfield on 'Woman's Place in Social Evolution' while WSPU activist Hattie Mahood was able to deviate from her usual topics to speak on 'The Licensing Bill'.[58] However, despite the wide range of papers, the Clarion Club still placed restrictions on women's participation. The presentations were all from invited speakers and the club did not encourage women to take the first steps

---

55 *The Labour Leader* and *The Clarion* carried fairly regular lists of ILP, SDF and Socialist Society branch secretaries.
56 *The Clarion*, 24 November 1911.
57 Julia Dawson in *The Clarion*, 21 December 1906.
58 All details of meetings taken from *The Clarion*.

into public speaking on its platforms. Also, all the meetings were small, and indoor. While the club allowed women to tackle a broader range of subjects than usually came their way, the opportunity to discuss them was reserved for those who were free to attend on Tuesday afternoons.

The Fabian Society

The Fabian Society, still an important local force, was not caught up in the suffrage debate to the same extent as political parties.[59] Locally it allowed women more space than any of the other socialist organisations before the First World War if they were willing to work in the role of educators. As with other socialist groups, Liverpool's Fabian women lived within rigidly defined gender boundaries, as this extract from the 1909–10 Annual Report shows:

> Women members are doing quiet and good work as members of 'After-Care Committees' for feeble minded children, voluntary relief committees, and in promoting and strengthening the life and work of women both as wage earners and mothers.

For those women prepared to work within such frameworks, the educational work of the FS offered the opportunity of public political involvement on an unprecedented scale.

The Clarion Club used educational meetings as a way of promoting fellowship between socialists, but for Fabians, education was paramount. As advocates for socialism, the FS was most concerned with providing expert speakers on particular subjects. This resulted in women being able to lay claim to certain areas as exclusively theirs, due to their gender. An examination of the subjects covered by women speakers indicates this, and shows that other external factors affected their position within the society.

From 1909–10, there were a total of 156 Liverpool Fabians, of whom 36 were women. However, out of a list of 17 lecturers, only two were women, highlighting the difficulties women had in achieving prominence even at a local level. The two women concerned, Mrs Billinge and Mrs M. E. Edwards, between them gave 18 out of the society's 81 lectures that year. Both were well advanced in local Fabian and socialist circles. Billinge was an early woman member of the Liverpool FS EC. She was also active in the Labour Party. Edwards (née Noest) was the second wife of John Edwards whom he married in 1905. She was Dutch, and had translated John Stuart Mill's *Subjection of Women* into her native language.[60] Edwards was also a suffrage

---

59 For details of its national policy on this, see P. Pugh, *Educate, Agitate, Organise: One Hundred Years of Fabian Socialism*, London, Methuen, 1984.

60 See her own entry in the Fabian Summer School's visitors' book, Summer 1912. The edition is J. S. Mill, *De Slaverng der Vrouw: Uit het Engelsch vert door R. C. Nieuwenhuijs, met eee voorrede van A. J. Vitringa. Naar de 4e Engelsche uitg. bew. M. E. Noest*, Amsterdam, 1898.

activist, although she joined no organisation until linking with the US in the war. The range of groups that she and Billinge addressed shows how the FS provided a wide audience for those women who were active in its ranks, and allowed them to present themselves as political activists at a variety of locations. Evidence from subsequent years shows that as the FS advanced, so did its women. By 1911–12, 26 of the 143 lectures given were by Edwards and Billinge. By this stage, their range of subjects had broadened. Edwards tackled 'Edward Carpenter', and Billinge spoke on 'Organisation'. However, the traditional gender view of issues resulted in Billinge also adding 'Motherhood' to her repertoire, while Edwards looked at 'The Driving Force of the Women's Movement'.

So in the field of education, the FS's view of itself as a facilitator for the broader socialist movement, supplying expert speakers on certain subjects, led to its providing real opportunity for political activity for those women who were willing or able to become speakers. Sometimes a lack of self-confidence could hold the women back. In a directory of Fabian speakers in Liverpool, one women stated that she was only willing to address small societies.[61] Yet, as socialist women involved in the WSPU discovered, the roll of subjects that they were allowed to attempt remained at best limited. Marginalisation, it appeared, remained unavoidable in organisations where women and men competed for public roles.

★ ★ ★

Both Liberal and socialist politics continued to provide an important arena for women's political activity on Merseyside in the years leading up to the First World War. However, both ultimately failed to meet the challenge posed by the rise of suffrage organisations in the region in different ways. Liberal women faced an uncomfortable paradox, attempting to retain support for a government that was increasingly dismissing their own demands for equality. As women active in party politics, the public denial of their right to full equality by their male leaders placed unbearable demands on their loyalties, and made it virtually impossible for them to attract the support of women newly politicised through suffrage. Socialist women were finding the sex-class analysis of the WSPU (which gave them political control) much more attractive than the position of their own party, which claimed to see gender oppression as equal to class oppression, but increasingly subordinated the former to the latter. The more they became involved with the WSPU, the more their marginalisation within socialism was thrown into stark relief.

As suffrage organisations continued to expand in the city, it is unlikely that women loyal to either political party could continue to ignore their growth

61 Circular from Liverpool Fabian Society, Fabian Society Papers, Nuffield College, Oxford.

indefinitely. However, the outbreak of the First World War radically altered this political picture. The largest local suffrage organisation collapsed, while the smaller groups rapidly altered the main focus of their work. Political parties faced different challenges both locally and nationally, as the war altered local and national government. Women within these parties shared in these challenges, and continued to develop their work, as the next chapter will demonstrate.

CHAPTER EIGHT

The War

Previous chapters have ended abruptly with the outbreak of the First World War in August 1914. This break is unavoidable. The social effects of the war cannot be denied, especially within a port city. Liverpool's docks saw their share in national imports rise from 25 per cent in the three years before the war to 33 per cent between 1915 and 1920.[1] Thousands of troops poured into camps near the port, raising concerns for the virtue of local girls, and murmurs of the need for a new Contagious Diseases Act. There were demographic changes too. Thousands left the city to fight; 13,500 never returned.[2] As well as these absences, occasional sightings of German submarines less than five miles off the coast and sporadic threats of air raids gave a certain immediacy to local perceptions of war. The loss of the Lusitania, whose sinking caused national outrage, was felt particularly strongly in Liverpool which 'regarded the ship as its own possession'.[3] One eyewitness, local headmistress Ada McGuire, wrote sadly how 'the little street at the side of the Cunard offices was filled with a dense mass of people waiting for news [as the] crew belonged almost entirely to Liverpool'. As the extent of the tragedy unfolded, reaction was fierce; German shops were wrecked and individuals hounded and interned for their own safety against a rioting mob of around 3,000.[4]

The unprecedented effect of the First World War on civilians was felt particularly by women. The cost of living rose dramatically, increasing by 25 per cent in the first months of the war.[5] Regional price variations show that Liverpool suffered disproportionately from inflation, with a standard loaf of bread costing twopence more than in Manchester by 1918.[6] Separation allowances, which were paid directly to the families of servicemen, rarely kept

---

1   Waller, *Democracy and Sectarianism*, p. 271.

2   Waller, *Democracy and Sectarianism*, p. 270.

3   *The Times*, 10 May 1915.

4   Ada McGuire to 'Eva', 9 May 1915, Imperial War Museum Collection, 96/31/1. See also Waller, *Democracy and Sectarianism*, p. 272; *The Times*, 11 May 1915.

5   *The Woman's Dreadnought*, 23 January 1915. The figure concurs with the yearly increase presented in N. Ferguson, *The Pity of War*, London, Allen Lane, 1998, p. 331 although no months are specified.

6   J. M. Winter, *The Great War and the British People*, London, Macmillan, 1985, p. 229.

pace with rising costs.[7] Moreover, these were paid monthly and retrospectively, a system that brought many working-class women close to destitution in September 1914.[8] Simultaneously many industries supplying luxury consumer goods shut down, forcing thousands of women out of work.[9] On Merseyside, dressmakers and needlewomen watched their usual market evaporate.[10] However, there were also fresh opportunities. The unemployment that followed the outbreak of war in August soon gave way to labour shortages, allowing for a refiguration in the gendering of occupations that had been considered exclusively male.[11] Economic hardship combined with this to alter the British workforce.

The popular characterisation of a feminised workforce during the First World War requires careful handling.[12] Although there is compelling evidence for a 10 per cent overall increase in the female workforce between 1914 and 1918, this figure is subject to industrial and regional variation.[13] Many female trades suffered high unemployment rates throughout the war, meaning that much of the labour force was drawn from existing workers.[14] What did alter was the type of work available to women. Its very public nature promoted a new image of working women. 'Women fill vacant places', an American visitor to London noted. 'Girls run elevators, punch tickets and act as post office clerks. Outside one store a girl in high boots and rubber hat calls taxis.' Women were suddenly more visible. In Liverpool, they were also visibly different. Ada McGuire was more struck by their new image than by any different roles:

> We have the women tramguards on the cars here now... Very businesslike they look too, in their uniforms... Bon Marche have a very smart commissionaire in uniform – she looks like a smart naval officer or officeress.[15]

These highly visible changes were rooted more in economic necessity than

---

7 Winter, *The Great War*, p. 241; J. M. Winter and J.-L. Robert, eds, *Capital Cities at War: Paris, London, Berlin 1914–1918*, Cambridge, Cambridge University Press, 1997, table 10.2 p. 294; S. Pedersen, 'Gender, Welfare and Citizenship in Britain during the Great War', *American Historical Review*, vol. 95, no. 4 [1990], pp. 983–1006.

8 For the Liverpool context see Stocks, *Eleanor Rathbone*, p. 73

9 Woollacott, *On Her Their Lives Depend*, p. 23.

10 *Common Cause*, 4 December 1914.

11 For some discussion of unemployment in London see J. Lawrence, 'The Transition to War in 1914', in Winter and Robert, eds, *Capital Cities at War*, pp. 135–63.

12 T. Bonzon, 'The Labour Market and Industrial Mobilization 1915–1917', in Winter and Robert, eds, *Capital Cities at War*, pp. 164–65, especially pp. 186–87.

13 For figures see Woollacott, *On Her Their Lives Depend*, pp. 17–19; Ferguson, *The Pity of War*, p. 268.

14 See I. O. Andrews, *The Economic Effects of the World War upon Women and Children in Great Britain*, New York, Oxford University Press, 1920. G. Braybon makes heavy use of her arguments; see Braybon, *Women Workers and the First World War*, p. 45.

15 Ada McGuire to 'Eva', 7 December 1915, Imperial War Museum Collection, IWM 96/31/1.

in feminism. Some women, like the tram-drivers mentioned above, took over their husbands' jobs and wage packets for the duration of the war, augmenting family finances and securing the job for the man's return.[16] Other women welcomed the fresh opportunities of wartime. Nationally, munitions works offered women a reasonable wage and a job that gave them 'the sense of being somebody of importance in the world, doing something of confidence'.[17] On Merseyside, women were relieved to give up casual employment for more fixed hours.[18]

For politically active women, more was at stake. Sandra Holton has been rightly critical of historical interpretations that present the enfranchisement of women as a 'reward' for their war work.[19] However, this does not mean that feminists did not consciously use the opportunities provided by the war to advance their cause. Many of them viewed their public war work as part of longer term claims on citizenship. Read through their experiences, the war years present a story of continuity more than one of change, in which the war itself appears as an event that postponed rather than hastened the female vote. They were able to direct their activities through familiar organisations that adapted to the new situation. Other women found themselves drawn into new networks as their current groups dissolved. Through these they were often able to renew old acquaintances, and experiment with fresh ways of working as the war progressed. The variety of activities encompassed within these wider claims for citizenship matched the number of organisations. While some women returned to the language of separate spheres to argue for a feminist pacifism based on the maternal instinct, others embraced a chauvinistic patriotism involving a militaristic interpretation of women's war service. Some continued to agitate for the vote, although most who did so were simultaneously involved in other campaigns.

Continuity in the struggle for citizenship displayed various manifestations. Many of these involved performing 'auxiliary' war work of the type that has been credited with achieving women's movement from the private to the public sphere.[20] 'Auxiliary' must not be interpreted as secondary. The First World War brought war to the domestic life of the nation meaning that much of this work had direct bearing on its course. However, while women's war

16 Ada McGuire to 'Eva', 7 December 1915, Imperial War Museum Collection, IWM 96/31/1.

17 M. Hall Caine, *Our Girls: Their Work for the War*, London, Hutchinson & Co, 1916, p. 94. For a discussion of pay rates in these factories see Woollacott, *On Her Their Lives Depend*, chapter 5.

18 *Home Service Corps Review*, 11 April 1916.

19 Holton, *Feminism and Democracy*, p. 130. For the opposite view, see A. Marwick, 'Women and the Family', in H. Cowper, C. Emsley, A. Marwick, B. Purdue and D. Englander, *World War One and its Consequences*, Milton Keynes, Open University Press, 1990, pp. 13–21.

20 See D. Condell and J. Liddiard, *Working for Victory? Images of Women in the First World War 1914–18*, London, Routledge & Kegan Paul, 1987, p. 21, for a further discussion of this point.

work was broadly aimed towards helping an allied victory, it was not all overtly jingoistic. Several groups simultaneously directed women's contributions towards the war effort on Merseyside, each one responding to a different motivation. Although extremes of patriotism bordering on the chauvinistic can be identified here, so too can an embryonic feminist pacifism. Also discernible is a feminist concern to alleviate the suffering that the war caused to local women, demonstrating continuity with woman-centred approaches to public political work.

A partial explanation for some of the shifting alliances at this time lies in the unexpectedness of the First World War. Although there had been ominous portents of war for some time, senior politicians throughout Europe were caught off guard by the rapidity of events.[21] Women's organisations, which had often worked in opposition to the government, were similarly surprised, both at local and national level, and had to make abrupt decisions. Many allied to political parties followed the lead of their parent body and suspended combative inter-party activity for the duration of the war. The suffrage organisations were in a slightly different position, in that they were not closely tied to a combative electoral process now suspended in the interests of national unity. They had to determine how best to reformulate their demands in an altered situation. Unsurprisingly, considering the variety of campaigning methodologies available within the suffrage movement prior to the outbreak of war, there was little consensus as to which way they should now go.

The WSPU leadership immediately decided to suspend militancy and all active campaigning for the duration of the war. A lack of substantial records makes it impossible to recreate what led to this decision.[22] What is retrievable is a picture of total confusion. This is most marked in Liverpool where the WSPU had provided the most successful means of mobilising women into the public sphere. Its unexpected demise left a large vacuum. The final record of the local branch appeared in *The Suffragette* of 7 August 1914. It was buoyant and optimistic, reporting on government attempts to pressurise newsagents to stop stocking *The Suffragette* on pain of prosecution for incitement during the arson campaign:

> [T]he only effect [this] has had in Liverpool has been to increase the sale. A sympathiser has ordered four quires weekly… and is having them distributed from door to door.[23]

---

21 For contrasting European perspectives see, for example, A. Shlyapnikov, 'The Working-class of St Petersberg and War', translated and reproduced in J. Riddel, ed., *Lenin's Struggle for a Revolutionary International: Documents 1907–16*, New York, Monad Press, 1986, p. 127; A. Wiltsher, *Most Dangerous Women: Feminist Peace Campaigners of the Great War*, London, Pandora, 1985, p. 14.

22 Rosen, *Rise Up Women!*, p. 247.

23 *The Suffragette*, 7 August 1914.

The unfortunate sympathiser must have been severely out of pocket, as *The Suffragette* did not appear again until 1915 when it re-emerged briefly, without its suffrage content, before relaunching as *The Britannia*. The local branch closed the shop and sent the remainder of its money down to London.[24] Helen Jollie avoided the fate of many WSPU organisers in Scotland who were forced to borrow their rail fare home.[25] She remained in Liverpool for a short time, but played no leading role in politics again.[26] To this extent, Liverpool suffragettes followed national directives, but they did not embrace the Pankhursts' total capitulation to a chauvinistic war campaign.[27] Instead, some members drifted into other bodies, others concentrated their work in similar locations that they had simultaneously developed such as the Church League, while the majority fell away from traceable public activity with the demise of their union. When the Women's Party (as the WSPU became) formed a branch in Liverpool around 1917, it recruited no former members of the WSPU.

The Home Service Corps

A small local organisation, the Home Service Corps (HSC) became the natural successor to Liverpool WSPU. This Corps, which shared elements of personnel and policy with the WSPU, engaged in a vigorous campaign organising women for war work. It was the brainchild of Phyllis Lovell whose public work previously included being secretary of the Southport CLWS and organiser for both the Merseyside VFWF and US. She also laid claim to a record of activity 'harassing the government' in militant campaigns, presumably through the WSPU.[28] She dissented from WSPU war policy, and continued some low-level suffrage work through the VFWF and the US.[29] Unlike other WSPU dissenters, she believed that feminist pacifism was 'misguided' and agreed with the idea that women should work collectively in the war effort.[30] The HSC coordinated such work, situating it within a framework that prioritised women's claim to citizenship, and frequently echoed the rhetoric of militant suffrage when making its demands.

Lovell launched the HSC immediately after the collapse of the Liverpool WSPU branches in September 1914. She first offered the US branch for war

24 Alice Ker, diary, 14 September 1914.
25 Leneman, *A Guid Cause*, p. 209.
26 Alice Ker's diary mentions Helen Jollie.
27 For a description see M. Z. Doty, *Short Rations: An American Woman in Germany 1915–1916*, London, Methuen & Co., 1917, p. 41.
28 *The Birkenhead News*, 21 August 1915. Although there is no official mention of her in connection with the WSPU or the WFL, her membership of the VFWF makes it more likely that her militant activity took place in the former organisation.
29 *Votes for Women*, 30 January 1914; 12 April 1915.
30 See leading article, *Home Service Corps Review*, 1 October 1915.

work, and was directed to the impoverished Great Homer Street district.[31] Here, the US began a clothing bureau to help relieve 'hundreds of families... living in cellars' and impoverished due to the outbreak of war. Over 1,000 women around Great Homer Street had seen their husbands join up in the first weeks of war and their family incomes diminish drastically. This left them 'suddenly... thrown entirely upon their own resources... with no one to lean on to whom they could go for advice'.[32] This provided the US with a wonderful opportunity to organise a large group of women together, many of whom had previously eschewed public politics. Games and entertainments were the first attempted activities, but Lovell soon realised that the women's situation as fighters' wives demanded something different. She began to infuse the organised games with a sense of purpose and recruited the women into an 'Amazon Army' – a drill squad that 'kept the women from brooding at home and gave them an outlet for their military spirit'.[33] The idea was that they would be physically fit to meet the new challenges of wartime. The choice of name presented this work as equating to a female national service.

The HSC later claimed that it was 'started... simply to meet the need of the moment'.[34] However, its style of organisation shows that if Lovell had no firm plans for the future, she had taken definite lessons from her affiliations of the past. She created a strong women-centred organisation infused with a philosophy that demanded that women should seize any available opportunity towards advancement. Much of this came from the pre-war suffrage connections of some of its key personnel which, while not exclusively WSPU, were oriented more towards militancy. Mrs K. Stanley Clarke, founder and secretary of the Birkenhead CUWFA, was an important member of the HSC. Prominent WSPU recruits included Dorothy Abraham, an ex-WSPU prisoner, and her mother, a long-standing militant activist.

The visual identity so vital to the WSPU was also central to the HSC.[35] Members were expected to wear a uniform of dark navy, including a cap and Sam Brown belt. They welcomed this, not least because it provided a comfortable alternative to 'the mufti which takes so long to arrange... flaps in the wind... [and] soils in the dust'.[36] The military style uniform was matched by a strict military structure. Lovell was Commanding Officer, and below her was a series of ranks ranging from commissioned sub-lieutenants through non-commissioned officers down to privates.[37] This was critical as

31 *Votes for Women*, 25 September 1915.
32 From a leaflet, 'Home Service Corps and Police Aid Detachment', LRO, MD 220/3.
33 From a leaflet, 'Home Service Corps and Police Aid Detachment', LRO, MD 220/3. Also *The Liverpool Weekly Post*, 24 April 1915.
34 *Home Service Corps Review*, 8 May 1917.
35 For visual identity see, for example, Tickner, *The Spectacle of Women*, especially pp. 94–97.
36 *Home Service Corps Review*, 8 May 1917.
37 *Home Service Corps Review*, 14 November 1916. Commissions were obtained through examination.

the HSC's claims for citizenship were based on its work, making it imperative that the organisation appeared as much like an army unit as possible. Furthermore, it was felt that by borrowing certain aspects of militarism previously only available to men, women were able to overcome what were seen as some less desirable facets of femininity such as physical weakness or moral flippancy. Through its regular military drills the HSC felt that women learned 'absolute and prompt obedience, alertness, method and combination... [and] all sense of what is commonly known as "schoolgirl stupidity" is lost'.[38]

Alongside the uniform and drill the HSC also promoted a wide associational culture. Its original social aspects remained important, and it ran cricket and badminton teams. Branch meetings were organised regularly, mainly on Merseyside although the Corps also extended northwards as far as Kirkham and Lytham. Members were expected to attend at least one weekly drill session to retain physical fitness in preparation for 'a crisis should one arise', and to 'fit the recruits for the physical strain of their new duties – the work of men being... heavier than that usually undertaken.'[39] Meetings also fostered a sense of comradeship, which leading members of the HSC felt was crucial in convincing individual members that 'the daily routine of war work, often very hard and most intensely monotonous, is not borne entirely by herself... because the Corps stands behind'. The existence of the *Home Service Corps Review* was as important as the uniform in promoting a sense of community among members. The paper was 'designed to keep members in touch with current events' and also to provide a 'binding influence', a clear reference back to the function and purpose of earlier suffrage papers. Although the *Review* undoubtedly had a limited circulation, it ran as a weekly paper from August 1915 to March 1918. Its eventual demise was not caused by poor sales, but a chronic wartime paper shortage.

The HSC offered its membership the opportunity to participate directly in the war effort in several ways. Its distinctive image proved appealing to local women. The spring of 1915 saw a national directive calling for the establishment of a women's reserve to free men for fighting. The response in Liverpool was particularly poor, with only 300 women replying.[40] By contrast, when the HSC opened an office in Church Street, 2,000 women 'from all classes' registered their names.[41] As well as placing women into jobs, the Corps also provided training for the unskilled including classes in motor and horse driving, gardening and bookkeeping. However, it was much more than a wartime employment and training agency. Much emphasis was laid on the way that the women themselves viewed this work, and how it had

---

38 *Home Service Corps Review*, 11 December 1917.
39 From a leaflet, 'Home Service Corps and Police Aid Detachment', LRO, MD 220/3; *The Birkenhead News*, 21 August 1915.
40 *The Liverpool Courier*, April 1915.
41 From a leaflet, 'Home Service Corps and Police Aid Detachment', LRO, MD 220/3

changed them. Work was frequently compared to military service and always discussed in the wider context of validating the claim to citizenship that this demonstrated. Typical is this description of the 10 HSC members who worked as lift girls in the Royal Liver Building from December 1916. There was

> [an] almost military-like precision and smartness with which these girls flung back the gates, stepped outside and stood at attention. They reminded one irresistibly of soldiers... and, if they had brought their heels together with a sharp click and saluted... it would have only seemed quite the right thing for them to do... [They] are pioneers... [and] those who follow after... reap the benefits which the pioneer has sown.[42]

Although the Corps' leaders believed that their work proved that women were 'ready for unfettered citizenship' they did not accept that the war alone had caused this.[43] They historicised contemporary changes and were particularly defensive of suffrage militancy, arguing strongly against the idea that it was only possible to take feminist demands seriously now that they were no longer 'obscured by the hysteria of the suffragettes'.[44] Militancy, according to the leadership of the HSC, was not hysteria but a manifestation of 'the perpetual world struggle towards good, and the consequent opposition arising therefrom'. In an interesting twist on the old physical force argument, this made women's suffragette activity indistinguishable from men's warmongering:

> Militancy, whether displayed by the woman who sets fire to an unimportant hayrick in a country village, or by the armoured camps of a world of belligerence, is in essence if not in degree the same thing – the outward and visible sign of the pain of growing up.[45]

Yet, while refuting the argument that it was the war that had made women ready for participating in the national political life of the nation, there was also an acceptance that it was 'through the welter of circumstances arising out of the war [that] the nation... discovered that its womenfolk possess ability and talent in hitherto untried spheres of activity'.[46] There was also little consensus as to how women should function as active citizens after the war. Lovell's editorials constantly demanded full political emancipation for women. Clarke, on the other hand, was a strong advocate for women

42 *Home Service Corps Review*, 9 January 1917.
43 *Home Service Corps Review*, 13 February 1917.
44 See, for instance, 'A History Lesson for the "Old Fashioned School"', *Home Service Corps Review*, 12 June 1917; 'Her Service Conquers', *Home Service Corps Review*, 13 February 1917.
45 *Home Service Corps Review*, 1 February 1916.
46 *Home Service Corps Review*, 11 September 1917.

returning to the domestic sphere once the wartime crisis had passed, to avoid the accusation that 'on the hour of the nation's extremity, [women] filched from men their rightful place'. This distinction reflects class as well as political differences. Working women themselves felt differently. An interview that the *Review* carried with some of Liverpool's few women dockers who were briefly employed in 1916 shows them keen to remain in the work. As well as a wage of five shillings and ten pence for a ten-hour day, they appreciated the conditions, which included breaks and 'ample sanitary accommodation', all much more attractive and less arduous than 'hawking vegetables from a barrow', their main alternative source of income.[47]

The HSC's greatest achievement was the work of its Police Aid Detachment (PAD). This forerunner to women police was established in 1915 at the request of Mr Lane, Chief Constable of Lancashire.[48] Its aims and objectives were markedly different from the work of Women's Patrols on Merseyside, discussed later in this chapter. The PAD appears to have been much more similar to the national Women Police Service, both organisations insisting on full uniform and titles of rank for their officers, and both with personal links to militant suffrage.[49]

The PAD was concerned with proving women's ability to undertake all aspects of police work on an equal footing with male police. It did not seek a special space within policing that could only be undertaken by women. The war provided the perfect backdrop against which restrictions on women's employment could be tested. The PAD began by freeing male police for the war by patrolling parks and providing stewards for the numerous free concerts that the city provided for soldiers. In July 1916 members undertook their first piece of detective work and helped to bring a dubious fortune teller to court.[50] Other detective assignments followed, and by 1917 the Birkenhead Watch Committee was so impressed by the work that it decided to employ a female police force, the first town in England to do so.[51] Lovell was drafted as Sergeant in Charge of the 40 recruits captained by Clarke and

47 *Home Service Corps Review*, 8 March 1916.

48 From a leaflet, 'Home Service Corps and Police Aid Detachment', LRO, MD 220/3.

49 See P. Levine, '"Walking the Streets in a Way no Decent Woman Should", Women Police in World War One', *Journal of Modern History*, 66, March 1994, pp. 34–78. Neither the Women Police Service or the Women's Police Volunteers which are discussed in this article formed Merseyside Branches as the PAD appears to have been covering identical ground here. For further discussion of the way that divisions between the Women's Patrols/Police Service/Volunteers rested on earlier interorganisational rivalry within the suffrage movement, see A. Woodsen, 'The First Women Police: A Force for Equality or Infringement?', *Women's History Review*, vol. 2, no. 2, 1993, pp. 217–32, especially p. 223; L. Bland, 'In the Name of Protection: The Policing of Women in the First World War', in C. Smart and J. Brophy, eds, *Women in Law: Explorations in Law, Family and Society*, London, Routledge & Kegan Paul, 1985, pp. 23–49, especially p. 26.

50 *Home Service Corps Review*, 11 September 1917.

51 *Home Service Corps Review*, 9 January 1917; 13 February 1917.

helped by Mrs Abraham.[52] Sergeant Lovell proudly led her volunteers out, remarking:

> There was no jesting, and we were taken quite seriously, as I hoped we should be. I must say the women looked the part. They were all under 30 years of age, healthy and of good physique.[53]

As well as promoting equality with male police and extending employment opportunities for women, the work of the PAD brought public recognition for the HSC, and the *Review* was well aware of the significance of this. When the PAD was called in to guard an exhibition of war 'relics', including a captured Zeppelin, Lovell was proud of her role. She found it

> Satisfying to know that because one has drilled and waited, and carried sacks of waste paper on dark and stormy nights, and never refused to do the dirty work when it has come along, and, moreover, to do it cheerfully and without question, one has become capable of duty of a wider kind.[54]

The Civic Service League and the Women's War Service Bureau

The HSC was not the only organisation to re-situate existing feminist demands in a fresh context during the war. Other local groups from different political traditions also sought both to provide a specifically female public space for women's war work, and to locate this work within their broader campaigns. Two main organisations, the Civic Service League (CSL) and the Women's War Service Bureau (WWSB), continued constitutional suffrage traditions on Merseyside. Their work lacked much of the overt public dimensions of the HSC. They wore no uniform, and operated under a loose network of directors rather than a military-style hierarchy. Also, whereas the HSC attempted to diminish gender differences, both the CSL and the WWSB emphasised them, promoting what they felt to be the unique contributions of women in developing a caring and nurturing response to the war. Many of them were motivated by a strong sense of duty that can be traced back to much of Liverpool's mid-nineteenth century feminist philanthropy.

The Liverpool CSL had formed in 1911 amid the panic surrounding the Transport Strike. It established a Ladies' Branch which would not

---

52 *Home Service Corps Review*, 13 February 1917; *Conservative and Unionist Women's Franchise Review*, January–March 1915. Mrs Abraham's involvement is deduced from her later work for Women's Patrols.

53 P. Lovell in *The Southport Advertiser* quoted in J. Lock, *The British Policewoman: Her Story*, London, Robert Hale, 1979, p. 68.

54 *Home Service Corps Review*, 14 November 1916.

be very heavily called upon, but the experiences of the past strike have shown that it is very desirable to have a competent body of women workers whose services could be relied upon in an emergency.[55]

This had a fixed membership of 100, restricting its public impact. Many of its members were also involved in a variety of different female political networks and included Evelyn Deakin of the NUWSS and CUWFA, Lady Petrie, Chairman of the Liverpool Ladies Unionist Federation, and Mabel Fletcher, also a keen Tory. The membership of Miss Harriet Johnson, President of the Liverpool BWTA, linked the CSL to a further layer of women's public activity. That of Mrs Clifford Muspratt, sister-in-law to Nessie Stewart-Brown, demonstrates again the persistently dynastic quality to much of local female politics.[56]

Before the war, the CSL promoted a secondary and subordinate role for its members, but paradoxically expanded their opportunities for public work. It organised ambulance classes for some of its membership, and encouraged them to take advantage of some of the training courses that it offered in secretarial skills. By 1914 the League would have been the obvious place for respectable, anti-socialist ladies looking for war work had it not been challenged by yet another body, the WWSB. This was formed from two separate ideas which very quickly came together. Immediately following the outbreak of war, the Lady Mayoress, Mrs Herbert Rathbone, issued a public request to all local women to come forward for war work. One of the first respondents was Dr Mary Davies of the NUWSS. She had already had the offer of a large house in Gambier Terrace to serve as a centre for such activity, and the WWSB opened on 7 August 1914.[57] As with the other two organisations, the WWSB largely drew from one particular existing group. Its leading personnel were mainly ex-NUWSS. Dr Davies was the chief officer in charge, aided by Miss Jessie Beavan, the Honorary Secretary of the West Lancashire NUWSS federation. Frances Ivens, MS, Chairman of Liverpool CUWFA, who held joint membership of the NUWSS and had also worked professionally alongside Mary Davies, held classes in first aid.[58]

The CSL felt slighted by Mrs Rathbone's actions which undermined its own efforts. Rathbone claimed that she was unaware of the CSL's existence and of her responsibility to it. The early friction between the two groups

55 Minutes of the Preliminary Meeting of Liverpool Civic Service League Women's Branch, September 1911, LRO.
56 Undated MSS membership list, LRO.
57 Typescript, 'Conference of the Lady Mayoress', Information Bureau and the Committee of the Women's Branch of the Civic Service League, 23 October 1914', LRO; *Common Cause*, 14 August 1914; Women's War Service Bureau Reports, LRO.
58 *Common Cause*, 14 August 1914; *Conservative and Unionist Women's Franchise Review*, October–December 1914.

demonstrates both how personal relief work was felt to be, and how much of it inextricably entwined with feminist activities. Much of the CSL's war work involved producing items – bandages, clothing, food parcels, etc. – to be sent to troops at the front, an activity also undertaken by the WWSB. Disputes over such work were not uncommon during the First World War, as many schemes were seen as a way of constructing links between wives, mothers and daughters at home and husbands, fathers and sons in the trenches.[59] An uneasy compromise was reached between the CSL and the WWSB, and a special room was provided at Gambier Terrace with the CSL's Miss Glynn in charge. All garments made by the CSL were directed there rather than to the main sorting room of the WWSB, and only placed into the WWSB's common stock if not directed for a specific destination by the CSL.[60]

Women who went from the CSL into the WWSB found themselves working with a peculiarly eclectic group. The Bureau's large committee was predominantly drawn from leading members of the NUWSS and WCA, including the familiar figures of Edith Bright, Bessie Shilston Watkins and Lydia Booth. Nessie Stewart-Brown was also involved, as was her sister, Hildegarde Gordon Brown. Their presence and broader organisational loyalties helped to shape the doctrines of the WWSB which aimed at providing a separate and special role for women in wartime that would definitively prove them 'worthy of citizenship, whether their claim be recognised or not'.[61] However, the peculiar circumstances of war also prompted several changes in direction among local feminist organisations. As new questions dominated the political agenda, women from a variety of political groups outside constitutional suffrage were drawn to the WWSB. Annie Billinge of the FS and Women's Co-Op Guild was just one woman from a very different tradition of women's politics who came to play a leading role in the Bureau. So too was Mrs A. C. Abraham, an ex-WSPU member who appears to be the only woman involved in both the WWSB and the HSC. Their presence also diversified the Bureau so that it functioned on two levels, initiating new forms of war service and simultaneously providing a larger coordinating umbrella through which existent groups could direct their efforts in this field. Women could work for the Bureau alone, or could retain older organisational links as well. This meant that while for several women the Bureau represented a first step into the public world of women's politics, for others it was merely a

59 Particular anger in Liverpool greeted Sir Edward Ward's scheme for a county organisation for Lancashire which would result in Liverpool parcels going to Manchester troops. Miscellaneous Documents, Liverpool Council of Women Citizen's papers, LRO.
60 Typescript 'Conference of the Lady Mayoress' Information Bureau and the Committee of the Women's Branch of the Civic Service League, 23 October 1914. Liverpool Record Office.
61 *Common Cause*, 14 August 1914. The quotation here relates to Liverpool WWSB, but was originally made by Mrs Fawcett.

different means of continuing the work of the previous decade. The seemingly contradictory alliances and dual activities by certain individuals show the state of confusion within women's politics prompted by the war.

As well as providing parcels for troops, the WWSB coordinated a Soldiers' and Sailors' Families Association, which ran a number of social clubs for soldiers' and sailors' families. These allowed women to meet together and share fears and experiences in a controlled space, protected from the accusations of disloyalty to which wives of servicemen often laid themselves open if seeking an active social life during their husbands' absence.[62] Feminism and philanthropy intermingled, allowing the clubs to serve as examples of woman-centred relief work aimed at lifting the burden of war that fell on women rather than directly supporting the war effort. There were sometimes problems with attempts to impose organisation. The Lodge Lane Club, which Miss Chubb of the NUWSS and WCA helped to coordinate, had to discontinue its clothing club as 'women [were] indifferent about making their garments at the club' despite the generous provision of two sewing machines. In marked contrast, the club at Bankhall was proud of the fact that its committee came entirely from its working-class membership. Bankhall went from strength to strength, and hoped to continue after the war.[63]

As with the HSC, the WWSB's most public work was performed through its Women's Patrols. These formed as part of a country-wide initiative by the National Union of Women Workers (NUWW). Unlike the PAD, which viewed police work by women as part of wider demands for equality, the Women's Patrols were much more representative of the resurgence in protectionist feminism that has been identified with the war.[64] This resurgence arose amid widespread concern for the welfare of young women, which was especially acute in cities such as Liverpool. Here, numbers of girls flocked to the large canvas towns temporarily housing thousands of young soldiers. 'Khaki fever' affected men and women of all classes, but it was with the women that protectionist feminists concerned themselves, believing that 'withdrawing... girls from the danger zone [was] indeed women's work'.[65] The image of 'women' safeguarding 'girls' reflected the national policy of the Women's Patrols, which would only register women of 27 and over. However, the adherence of the Liverpool Patrol to this policy made for a

---

62 See 'Are Our Tommies' Women True?', *The Liverpool Weekly Courier*, 16 January 1915.

63 Women at Work Collection, Imperial War Museum, 232 1/4 Lodge Lane Club; 232 1/2 Bankhall Club.

64 See Bland, 'In the Name of Protection', especially p. 23.

65 *Conservative and Unionist Women's Franchise Review*, April–June 1915. For a fuller discussion of why some women responded to the perceived crisis in this way see A. Woollacott, '"Khaki Fever" and its Control: Gender, Class, Age and Sexual Morality on the British Homefront in the First World War', *Journal of Contemporary History*, vol. 29, 1994, pp. 325–47.

strong contrast between their rather matronly image and the younger profile of the PAD which recruited women below the age of 30.[66]

The local NUWW established Liverpool's Women's Patrols Movement in November 1914. The NUWW, it may be recalled, had been the site of conflict between socialist and social feminists in the 1890s. The latter group achieved supremacy after which the Union effectively ceased its organisational work, concentrating instead on investigative projects. Social feminists Lydia Booth and Edith Bright were still heavily involved in Liverpool NUWW in 1914 as its president and vice president and took on these positions on a special patrols committee. They were joined by women from a variety of organisations: Mrs A. C. Abraham from the WSPU, Maude Royden of the CLWS and, predictably, Nessie Stewart-Brown. The predominance of women from the municipal elite within the Patrols' leadership ensured that they shared the upper-middle-class image in Liverpool which has been identified with their equivalents elsewhere.[67] There were attempts nationally to contradict this through simultaneously stressing the woman-centredness of the patrols and distancing them from the 'coppers'. One widely publicised anecdote told how

> In a certain district some rough girls were discussing the [Patrol] organiser... and said 'Oh! She's nothing but a woman Copper from London.' The Club girls indignantly repudiated this, saying 'she ain't, she's a working woman like us, she's got it [the NUWW] badge on her arm to show she's a friend to us girls'.[68]

It is uncertain how successful such attempts were nationally, but they would certainly have had little effect in Liverpool considering the composition of the leadership of the local Women's Patrols.

In January 1915, Miss Mabel Cowlin was appointed Patrols Organiser and given an office in the WWSB's Bold Street depot. Cowlin was a trained social worker with strong links to constitutional suffragists. These had in part been established through her work for the Liverpool National Council for Combatting Venereal Disease, a connection that again emphasises the maternalistic character of much of the work of local Women's Patrols. In the PAD, Lovell had resigned her commission in frustration at the refusal to grant her organisation the power of arrest.[69] The Women's Patrols, however, had no interest in attempting to emulate police. They avoided a uniform, aside from

66 Liverpool Council of Women Citizens papers, LRO; *Home Service Corps Review*, 9 January 1917.
67 G. Braybon and P. Summerfield, *Out of the Cage: Women's Experiences in Two World Wars*, London, Pandora, 1987, p. 45. This is upheld by Woollacott in 'Khaki Fever'.
68 *Conservative and Unionist Women's Franchise Review*, April–June 1915.
69 Lock, *The British Policewoman*, p. 77.

a reluctantly adopted armband, and had no interest in moving into detective work like the PAD.[70] They concentrated on work with women and children and were content with their power to remove (but not arrest) those whom they considered in danger.[71] Despite repeated claims from the NUWW that patrols were not involved in rescue work, the ground evidence in Liverpool shows them doing just this. They 'protected' children waiting outside public houses, fetching out their parents if the wait was excessive.[72] They would appeal to prostitutes on the grounds of their common femininity, proudly citing successes such as when

> one of... [the older prostitutes] brought a young girl to the office and begged the patrols to save her from the life she herself found so difficult to leave.[73]

'Saving' and 'protecting' were common motifs in descriptions of patrol work.

While the Women's Patrols may have begun due to 'the special difficulties connected with the newly-formed camps', they soon diversified into broader areas of work.[74] Although they were concerned with rescuing young girls from descending into immorality, they were not overtly condemnatory of the 'natural desire for both sexes for each other's society'.[75] Instead they were keen to provide attractive alternatives to camp following, and set up a number of social clubs to provide a place for soldiers and girls to socialise together. These were often co-run through the SSFA at the WWSB. It was soon recognised that while camp following might be temporary, a larger problem consisted of 'the inimical influences of the common meeting places supplied by the public house... picture palace and the street', which was exacerbated by wartime blackout regulations.[76] Against this, the clubs supplied 'wholesome, well-regulated recreation... [for] both sexes together'.[77] They appear to have been well supported, and involved their membership in organising events. A young member of the Wirral Club, Margaret W., explained that her club

> started near a camp is succeeding well and the girls themselves helping to insist on the Rule being well kept – that they remain half an hour in the club after the bugle has called the men back to camp.

However, she felt that this would change in summer when

---

70 Liverpool Women's Patrols Second Annual Report, 1916, Liverpool Record Office.

71 Anon, untitled typescript history of Liverpool Women Police, Fawcett Library, London.

72 Liverpool Women's Patrols Second Annual Report, 1916, LRO.

73 M. Cowlin, appendix 111, 'Liverpool', in E. Tancred, ed., 'Women Police 1914–50', National Council of Women, 1951, cited in Lock, *The British Policewoman*, p. 75.

74 Liverpool Women's Patrols Second Annual Report, 1916, Liverpool Record Office.

75 Liverpool Women's Patrols Third Annual Report, 1917, Liverpool Record Office.

76 Liverpool Women's Patrols First Annual Report, 1915, Liverpool Record Office.

77 Liverpool Women's Patrols First Annual Report, 1915, Liverpool Record Office.

no power on earth will keep either girls or men in any club room however attractive... So many of the girls come from homes where there is only one living room – a tired (and therefore cross often) father and of course they want to go out – most of them having to sit at machines all day.[78]

The leadership responded with the initiative of open-air concerts and a tea canteen (run by the BWTA) on New Brighton Promenade. Similar recreation schemes evolved at Seaforth and Aintree. The Seaforth Club was particularly successful, and attracted visitors from throughout Britain keen to make it the model for their own clubs.[79]

The streets, rather than just the camps, soon became the more ambitious target for the Liverpool Patrols. They believed that

The streets are great unsupervised clubs. They need supervising. The Women's Patrols are present to supervise, to help raise the standard of conduct, and to be at hand to render any service they can in all that concerns the welfare of women and young people.[80]

Although they did not push the link directly, it was important to the success of this work that the Women's Patrols were registered and approved by the Chief Constable. Patrols acted in close liaison with the police, undertaking work beyond the scope of traditional policing. The names of girls who had come to police attention through unsuitable behaviour would be passed to patrols who would visit the homes and talk directly to the parents and girls themselves. Such involvement was often welcomed, especially in the cases of girls from more 'respectable' backgrounds. One case in 1918, for example, involved a

Pretty, well-dressed girl of 15 seen coming out of music hall with a middle-aged Man. Girl set upon by two older women, one being wife of man. Crowd gathered, girl very frightened, clung to patrols... Visited girl's home. Very respectable. Mother most distressed at story, promised to talk to girl herself.[81]

This case had a happy ending with the girl coming home early in future and the parents full of gratitude to the patrols. Patrol work was 'more concerned with keeping women and girls out of the Police Court than in getting them into it'.[82] Yet the Court remained a last resort, and patrol responses were not always as sympathetic as in the above case, especially when the individual

---

78 Undated letter from 'Margaret W.', Liverpool Council of Women Citizens Papers, Liverpool Record Office.
79 Liverpool Women's Patrols Third Annual Report, 1917, Liverpool Record Office.
80 Liverpool Women's Patrols Fourth Annual Report, 1918, Liverpool Record Office.
81 Liverpool Women's Patrols Fourth Annual Report, 1918, Liverpool Record Office.
82 Liverpool Women's Patrols Fourth Annual Report, 1918, Liverpool Record Office.

concerned was less remorseful. Children of 'drunk and carousing' parents would be handed over to the Liverpool Society for the Prevention of Cruelty to Children and their homes placed under official supervision. Others found begging were sent to the Industrial Schools. One homeless woman 'very dazed, [her] mind affected by [the] desertion of her husband' was 'sent to an institution as [deemed] too weak to be self-supporting'.[83]

Patrols clearly envisaged their work as a continuity of public political activity, and as part of a wider campaign for female citizenship. Much was made of the fact that it was both essential 'for the sake of the honour and good reputation of the city' and beyond the capacity of male police, 'essentially women's work'.[84] Those undertaking it provide further threads of continuity in feminist campaigning during the war. They also demonstrate again the peculiar state of flux that the war occasioned in women's politics. Most of those involved were constitutional suffragists. However, the coexistence of the Women's Patrols and the HSC, although complicating the narrative of local women's police work, also provides further evidence for the mixture of constitutional and militant suffragists who worked side by side in smaller suffrage bodies. One such, the CUWFA, worked with both groups, on a strictly geographical basis. So, although its Birkenhead members were directed into the PAD by Mrs Stanley Clarke, Miss Brassey was attempting to persuade Liverpool members to help the Women's Patrols.[85]

Suffrage Organisations and the War

Other aspects of relief work in Liverpool were filtered through existing societies, or coordinating bodies, often former suffrage organisations. Unlike the WSPU, some suffrage societies were less certain about how to approach the war. The CUWFA, NUWSS and CLWS all ceased active suffrage campaigning during the war, but their branches continued to meet, seeing relief work as an activity that they could do collectively during the conflict. Their claims for political rights were suspended, but their claims to citizenship remained. The CUWFA dropped 'Franchise' from its *Review* in January 1915, as the paper increasingly only covered women's war work. Local branches followed this trend. Birkenhead CUWFA offered its services to the Mayor, and worked with the NUWSS to get a workroom providing employment for dressmakers. Between 30 and 40 women were taken on, with more as outworkers, and the minimum trade board rate (three pence per hour) was offered, plus a long lunch hour. Mrs Stanley Clarke, Secretary of

83 All cases from Liverpool Women's Patrols Third Annual Report, 1917, Liverpool Record Office.
84 All cases from Liverpool Women's Patrols Third Annual Report, 1917, Liverpool Record Office.
85 See, for example, the local reports for both districts, *Conservative and Unionist Women's Franchise Review*, April–June 1915.

Birkenhead CUWFA, also established registration offices in conjunction with both the Women's Local Government Society and the HSC of which she was an active member. These schemes around women's work took up most of the CUWFA's campaigning energy. Again Clarke was anxious that her members did not to appear to be taking men's jobs, stating that it was only

> in this great crisis [that] women have been called upon as citizens to take their place with men in serving their country... [Miss Knowles added] that care would be taken not to disorganize the genuine labour market, but urged all women of leisure who could to register, especially those who have been in some employment previous to their marriage, as they were particularly asked for.[86]

The public work of the Liverpool CLWS was less organised. Some members took 'sewing for the soldiers and [paid] for it to be done by women needing the work' while others were 'sewing and knitting for friends who have enlisted'.[87] To retain a sense of corporate identity, members were urged 'to wear their badges when doing any public work'.[88] Although some joined the HSC, and others the SSFAs, war caused something of a membership crisis for the CLWS. A few stalwarts repeatedly urged 'suffragists to make their organisation as strong in numbers and finance as possible in order that the voices of women may speak with force and power in the social and industrial settlements necessary after the war'.[89] However, the Annual Report of 1916 admitted that 'little direct suffrage work has been done owing to the pressure of other duties caused by the war'.[90] Such events emphasise how difficult it was to retain any form of organisation amid the social disintegration caused by the war.

Constitutional suffragists now formed the largest suffrage organisation on Merseyside. Nationally, the NUWSS feared equal dislocation to the WSPU but managed to avoid it, largely through Mrs Fawcett's view of relief work as a means of uniting those women in her organisation who were broadly in favour of the war, and those who were becoming increasingly involved in the feminist peace movement.[91] On Merseyside the immediate opening of the WWSB helped continuity of public activity without imposing either a pacifist or a jingoistic stance. The NUWSS also continued its work through the Women Citizens' Associations (WCAs) to develop and foster a sense of citizenship.

---

86 *Conservative and Unionist Women's Franchise Review*, July–September 1915.
87 *Church League for Women's Suffrage Monthly Review*, October 1914.
88 *Church League for Women's Suffrage Monthly Review*, September 1914.
89 Miss Janet Heyes, *Church League for Women's Suffrage Monthly Review*, May 1916.
90 Miss Janet Heyes, *Church League for Women's Suffrage Monthly Review*, May 1916.
91 Holton, *Feminism and Democracy*, p. 30. For a full outline of the development of feminist pacifism in Britain during the First World War, see Wiltsher, *Most Dangerous Women*, 1985.

As well as working through the WWSB, the LWSS and its Wirral offshoot initiated its own campaigns aimed more at alleviating the suffering which war placed upon the women of a nation than with augmenting the flow of men to the front.[92] Wirral suffragists ran a social club.[93] They also opened a maternity centre and babies' welcome. This venture, supported by the medical officer of health, was an immediate success, and dealt with over 100 babies in its first four months. As well as providing paediatric examinations and advice to mothers on childcare and feeding, the welcome was a practical venture, offering cheap food for mothers and babies alike. It was so successful that it was taken over by the Public Health Department.[94]

Similar relief work aimed at alleviating suffering was undertaken by a local branch of the Scottish Women's Hospitals' Association (SWHA). This body, formed by Dr Elsie Inglis, the Honorary Secretary of the Scottish NUWSS, established and staffed three hospitals in France, two in Serbia and one in Russia.[95] Her initiative received warm support from Merseyside's constitutional suffragists. Birkenhead held weekly sewing parties while in Liverpool Nessie Stewart-Brown organised fundraising meetings and formed an administrative branch whose 'influential and representative committee' included the Bishop and the French Consul.[96] As well as support work, the SWHA offered the chance of direct involvement at the front to women with medical qualifications. The Liverpool branch felt especially proud of the work done at Royaumont Hospital by Dr Frances Ivens, the former Chief Surgeon of Liverpool's Stanley Hospital for Women who was a member of the LWSS and Chairman of Liverpool CUWFA, who was awarded the *Croix de Guerre* for her work.

Other suffragist initiatives were more overtly patriotic, such as the Patriotic Housekeeping scheme devised by Cicely Leadley-Brown.[97] Her Patriotic Housekeeping Exhibition, which opened in Liverpool in 1915, toured Britain. It covered diverse themes from vegetarian cookery demon-

---

92 Sandra Holton points out that the London Society aimed its war work at providing women workers in order to free men to join up, and at working in munitions factories and associated war trades. See Holton, *Feminism and Democracy*, p. 132. Also Strachey, *The Cause*, p. 340.

93 *Common Cause*, 17 January 1916.

94 *Common Cause*, 16 April 1915; 23 March 1917.

95 See Strachey, *The Cause*, p. 347. For more details on the hospitals see L. Whitelaw, *The Life and Rebellious Times of Cicely Hamilton*, London, Women's Press, 1990; C. Hamilton, *Life Errant*, London, J. M. Dent, 1935; A. de Navarro, *The Scottish Women's Hospital at the Franc Abbey of Royaumont*, London, Allen & Unwin, 1971; M. Lawrence, *Shadow of Swords: A Biography of Elsie Inglis*, London, Michael Joseph, 1971; Crofton, *The Women of Royaumont*.

96 *Common Cause*, 24 April 1917.

97 See K. Cowman, 'The Patriotic Sausage or the Politicisation of Domesticity in Britain during the First Word War', in A. Despard, ed., *A Woman's Place: Women, Domesticity and Private Life*, Kristiansand, Høgskolen I Agder, 1998, pp. 95–105.

strations (including 'the patriotic sausage... a sausage guiltless of pork'), to shoe repairing and child welfare.[98] The old class perspective of the LWSS underpinned the exhibition, with one meeting for 'patriotic servants'

> specially arranged for their benefit, and an appeal made in the press to mistresses to set them free to come.[99]

LWSS members developed a gendered view of patriotism, in which the home became an integral part of war, with allied housewives fiercely guarding the country's resources. This gendered view, although not threatening to demolish existing class barriers, attempted to transcend them by creating a common location for activity, based on gender, so that patriotic house-keeping could be practised in one's own kitchen or in that of one's mistress.

Such initiatives, which often involved working closely with other groups, preoccupied the LWSS in the early years of the war. By 1916, however, the overriding emphasis on war work was beginning to concern some local activists including Eleanor Rathbone. She feared that this was eclipsing the older priorities and jeopardising her work for a national network of WCAs:

> Most suffragists are obeying a sound political instinct which tells them that the present time is more suitable for exercising such functions of citizen-ship as are open to them than for actively pushing their demand for fuller rights. But it is possible to follow that instinct too far and to allow absorp-tion in the tasks of the present to lead to a culpable neglect of the duty of preparing for the future. I believe that many of our societies are, in fact, making this mistake.[100]

Although Eleanor Rathbone acknowledged that suffrage societies were overwhelmed by the volume of war work that they had undertaken, she stressed that the WCAs could play a valuable role in ensuring that women who were entering directly into public life at this time, and through such entries 'had discovered themselves to be citizens for the first time', should have their 'newly aroused consciousness... captured, fostered and directed... [to] become a permanent source of strength to the feminist movement'.[101]

In August 1916, when it appeared likely that a suffrage bill would be placed before the House, the LWSS organised a joint meeting with the CWSS, CLWS and CUWFA at which Mrs Fawcett pointed out that if the govern-

---

98 Report by Elizabeth Macadam on the Liverpool Patriotic Housekeeping Exhibition, *Common Cause*, 20 August 1915.

99 Report by Elizabeth Macadam on the Liverpool Patriotic Housekeeping Exhibition, *Common Cause*, 20 August 1915.

100 E. Rathbone, 'Women Citizens' Associations', *Common Cause*, 30 June 1916. In a foot-note to her own article, Rathbone explains that it was written 'before the rumours about a possible Redistribution Bill threatened to bring the question of the Suffrage into the sphere of immediate practical politics'.

101 Rathbone, 'Women Citizens' Associations', *Common Cause*, 30 June 1916.

ment was willing to discuss 'the immediate enfranchisement of soldiers and sailors, on the grounds of service to their country... women could not allow their service to the country... to pass unrecognised'.[102] This equation of women's war work with men's could be interpreted as opportunistic, but the openings that war presented for breaking down concepts of citizenship as they had been gendered within the Victorian era and recreating them to include women had been previously recognised by the LWSS. In *Common Cause* in January 1915, Eleanor Rathbone sneered openly at the idea that during invasion, women should hide until 'some elderly male civilians and policemen can... herd us... out of the zone of danger'.[103] The suffrage campaign, she argued, had taught women not to accept this role. Working through the WCA, women were now educated to a point where they were no longer willing to be passive:

> In so extreme a national emergency... if there are any functions which can usefully be performed by women, then women have a right to claim these... even if it should mean breaking down the masculine tradition.[104]

The exploration and development of female citizenship became a prime concern. Although it was contextualised within the boundaries of wartime emergency, there was no discussion of returning to the 'masculine tradition' once the national emergency had passed. Eleanor Rathbone continued with this theme and developed a concept of post-war citizenship that would contain feminine as well as masculine characteristics, for the benefit of all:

> Nor is it only upon questions specifically affecting their sex that women have a right to be heard... Have they no interest in the future economics and fiscal system of the country... Must the influence of women, the traditional qualities of women count for nothing in repressing any spirit of national vindictiveness and in bringing about saner and sweeter relationships.[105]

Other suffrage organisations also attempted to 'keep the suffrage flag flying'.[106] Smaller groups such as the US, the Independent Suffragettes and the Suffragettes of the WSPU who '[thought] it right to continue suffrage propaganda through the war', remained active.[107] Women who continued to

102 *Common Cause*, 18 August 1916.
103 E. Rathbone, 'In Case of Invasion', *Common Cause*, 1 January 1915.
104 Rathbone, 'In Case of Invasion', *Common Cause*, 1 January 1915.
105 *Common Cause*, 18 August 1916.
106 The phrase was in common usage by the US and WFL during the war. Work on franchise campaigns during the war includes Stanley with Morley, *The Life and Death of Emily Wilding Davison*; Cowman, 'A Party Between Revolution and Peaceful Persuasion', pp. 77–88.
107 Subheading of the occasional *Suffragette News Sheet* published by the Suffragettes of the WSPU.

demand the vote on Merseyside often did so through newer groups, although the longer-established WFL became less marginalised with the demise of competition from the WSPU. Old barriers again broke down or were transcended, old friendships reactivated and new alliances forged as women sought to adapt their demands to an altered climate.

The VFWF, in common with other branches throughout England, was scheduled to become a US branch in August 1914, when *Votes for Women* was to become the US's official paper.[108] The outbreak of war postponed this, and in Lancashire and elsewhere VFWF branches lost direction as suffrage organisations. In March 1915, Phyllis Lovell as local secretary called 'a meeting of all of those who are anxious to keep up suffrage work'.[109] At the meeting a US branch was formed; Miss Isabel Buxton, a CLWS and WSPU activist, was appointed secretary and an appeal issued to 'all who are ready to help in the work of the branch'.[110]

Predictably, the US attracted some of the more active members of the WSPU who opposed the official order to cease campaigning. Annie Marks, Ada Broughton and Helah Criddle were quick to involve themselves. Old links between the WSPU and socialists were rekindled. Meetings were held at the Clarion Café again and John Edwards, in semi-retirement due to ill health, became a familiar speaker to the branch. His wife actually joined the US, her first formal link to any suffrage society.[111] Other WSPU tactics were revived. Paper sales were restarted and a fund opened to pay for a US poster to be displayed at Central, Lime Street and Exchange Stations. Through this the US was able to reclaim something of the very public profile of the WSPU before the outbreak of war. As its levels of activity were lower, it also attracted women such as Phyllis Lovell and Dr Alice Ker who wished to be involved both in war work and in separate suffrage agitation. Ker had stopped her suffrage work in August 1914 and concentrated on using her medical skills to organise bandaging and ambulance classes at the WWSB. By 1916, she was among her former colleagues as vice president of the US.

Liverpool US enjoyed remarkable success for a branch that was not founded until after the outbreak of the war. It was also helped by a strong alliance with the WFL. The WFL, it may be remembered, had never really succeeded in taking away ground from the WSPU in Merseyside, and had restricted much of its operation there to surrounding districts. In May 1914, local WFL members were confident that there was sufficient interest in the suburban groups to attempt a Liverpool branch again, but the war postponed this.[112] This meant that the WFL was as keen to be helped by the US as it

108 For a discussion of the effect of the war on the US see Cowman, 'A Party Between Revolution and Peaceful Persuasion'.
109 *Votes for Women*, 12 March 1915.
110 *Votes for Women*, 12 March 1915.
111 *Votes for Women*, 25 June 1915.
112 *The Vote*, 22 May 1914.

was to help the new organisation, and by the summer of 1915 the two groups were working in tandem in a vigorous programme of weekly outdoor meetings at which suffrage arguments were once again aired on the streets of Merseyside, and literature sold.[113] The US continued to act as a coordinating organisation, but certain individuals began to direct much more of their public work through the WFL. Ada Broughton had actually joined the WFL early in 1915, before the formation of the local US branch.[114] The WFL formed its first Liverpool branch early in 1915, and continued to organise, although the northern branches at Aintree and Waterloo were always more active. Interestingly, these continued to recruit, albeit in small numbers, throughout the war. There were always fresh women ready to be convinced by the suffrage argument and join the ranks of suffragists in Merseyside, it appears, right up to the end of the conflict.[115]

Other significant wartime suffrage work was carried out in Liverpool by the CWSS, which continued to proclaim itself 'suffragist' whenever possible. The relatively later appearance of its newspaper, *The Catholic Suffragist*, in 1915 may have driven its struggle to retain a separate identity. Certainly, the Liverpool branch felt that the war did not demand the suspension of suffrage work. Indeed, its members called for the opposite, and stated that as 'the burden of war falls heavily on women... we hope all will help to keep the suffrage flag flying that we may be powerful to get wrongs realised when peace is restored'.[116] This was not merely speculative talk. Some local CWSS work during the war was indistinguishable from relief work. Many members worked through the SSFA, and the CWSS made garments for the SSFA to distribute.[117] Members also ran a club in Burlington Street via the Women's Patriotic League which was identical to the SSFA clubs apart from its Catholic identity. What is unique about the CWSS is its determination not to lose its identity as a suffrage organisation through its broader involvement in this work. This was publicly acknowledged by one member, Mrs Anderson, who spoke at a special meeting to 'urge... upon [members] the necessity of keeping the society together'.[118] In this the religious identity of the society was probably a great help. There appears to have been some sympathy for its aims among local Catholics. *The Catholic Times* office helped to distribute *The Catholic Suffragist* and many local churches permitted paper sales before services. The novelty of paper selling for many of the women involved must also have helped. A few CWSS members had done this for the WSPU, but most were new to this type of public work.

In October 1915 the CWSS and US, together with the WFL, established

---

113 *Votes for Women*, 11 June 1915.
114 *The Vote*, 22 January 1915.
115 *The Vote*, 9 November 1917, mentions three new members at a local meeting.
116 *The Catholic Suffragist*, February 1915.
117 *The Catholic Suffragist*, January 1915.
118 *The Catholic Suffragist*, October 1915.

a Suffrage Club which met weekly at 18 Colquitt Street, with a committee taken from one member of each society. The club was a forum where members of different societies could meet informally 'on common ground'.[119] It also provided a meeting room for separate societies on a rota basis. The US had the second Tuesday in each month for an 'At Home' evening. Other societies hosted events on specific evenings. These joint initiatives helped to retain some semblance of a suffrage campaign, but did not remove organisational divisions which re-emerged around individual activists. In September 1915, for instance, Mr and Mrs Cousins emigrated from Liverpool to India. Both had been active campaigners. Mrs Cousins had addressed several meetings for both the WFL and the WSPU, and had been chosen by the latter group to address the local memorial service for Emily Wilding Davison.[120] When she left, both *Votes for Women* and *The Vote* carried reports of a farewell social that concentrated on the affiliation of those attending. *The Vote* claimed that Alice Ker attended as a representative of the WSPU, the first mention of the Union within local suffrage circles for 12 months.[121] This episode demonstrates that even within the state of flux associated with the war, personal organisational identities continued to be guarded fiercely by individuals. The Suffrage Club provided a common meeting ground but it did not represent a new organisation.

Sadly little else is known of the work of the Suffrage Club, although it continued to meet at least until February 1918.[122] The significance of the club, or of wartime suffrage campaigns more generally, must not be overstated. For every Merseyside woman who visited the club on Mondays, or attended suffrage meetings, many more preferred to situate their claims for political rights within the broader framework of war work. But it is important to note that on Merseyside many activists were determined not to give up their suffrage work simply because national leaders demanded it. The work they undertook was difficult. Their numbers were also depleted. Many long-term activists left Merseyside during the war for a variety of reasons. Alice Ker moved to London in autumn 1916. Nurse Lupton of the WSPU went to work in France as a VAD nurse. The Pankhursts' refusal to release funds or membership records to women who wished to carry on the WSPU's original work meant that for the second time women like Ada Broughton and Annie Marks faced the task of building an organisation from more or less nothing. This time, without such a large national campaign behind them, their efforts were smaller. Their existence can only really be regarded as a footnote to the preceding chapters on suffrage campaigns, yet they merit attention, representing as they do continuity with a strand of independent

119 *The Catholic Suffragist*, November 1915.
120 *The Suffragette*, 20 June 1913.
121 *Votes for Women*, 24 September 1915; *The Vote*, 24 September 1915.
122 *The Catholic Suffragist*, February 1918.

suffrage activity on Merseyside that never displayed blind allegiance to a national leadership.

In August 1914 suffrage organisations were by far the largest and most visible female political groups on Merseyside. Their national collapse forced local activists to make difficult choices about how to continue public work. Some enthusiastically supported the war. Others concentrated on relief work from a position that neither supported nor condemned the war itself. Others found new ways of working through bodies such as the HSC and the Women's Patrols. In all of these cases, the background of the war stretched the boundaries of acceptable behaviour for women. However, in a local context it becomes clear that much of this stretching was undertaken by women with a long history of pushing back such boundaries, their actions demonstrating continuity with older feminist campaigns rather than an abrupt break with the past.

CHAPTER NINE

Conclusion – The Erasure of a Way of Life?

By 1920, Merseyside women had seen their situation and their region undergo several permanent changes. Geographical expansion had brought new districts to the east and west into the city boundaries, while cross-river transport continued to open up the Wirral. The local political map had also altered. In 1918 the extension of the parliamentary franchise to all men and most women over 30 quadrupled the electorate to 344, 816.[1] There were also more subtle alterations. Many of the 'old families' who dominated the political and social circles of pre-war Merseyside found that heavy taxes and changing social mores altered their position. 'The erasure of a traditional way of life' occurred as values such as deference gave way to a new social order.[2] Position was no longer enough to secure political power.

Women were equally affected by these changes. Many who had devoted much of the two decades to suffrage campaigns were now enfranchised, and seeking a place in the new political order with little inclination to continue to work for an equal franchise. Some women found their social position improved. Domestic service began to decline with 'man girls' finding positions for themselves in the new service industries, or as professionals such as teachers or clerks.[3] Other women suffered as unemployment swept the region. By 1921, the local branch of the National Unemployed Workers' Movement (NUWM) was organising regular demonstrations to mobilise the estimated ninth of the local population seeking work.[4] Women suffered too from a strong local feeling that they had taken men's jobs.[5] Despite their participation in innumerable demonstrations, they were unable to gain a

1 Waller, *Democracy and Sectarianism*, p. 281.
2 Waller, *Democracy and Sectarianism*, p. 277.
3 See G. Anderson, 'A Private Agency for White-Collar Workers Between the Wars: A Study of the Liverpool Clerks' Association, 1918–39', *International Review of Social History*, vol. XXXI, 1986, pp. 19–39.
4 Braddock and Braddock, *The Braddocks*, p. 31; W. Hannington, *Unemployed Struggles 1919–36*, London, Lawrence & Wishart, 1977 [1936].
5 Braddock and Braddock, *The Braddocks*, p. 31.

foothold in the local leadership of the NUWM.[6]

The three models of women's political activity outlined in the introduction to this book had seen mixed achievements by 1920, with many short-lived victories. At this point, with thirty years of women's political activities described, it is worth considering if any conclusions can be drawn as to which proved most successful once the vote was won. Of all the organisations discussed, the WSPU with its 'sex-class' model that excluded men from all positions and gave women complete freedom in arranging their work had proved most successful at bringing large numbers of women into political work. The mass campaign that the WSPU delivered on Merseyside brought its participants into contact with innumerable other women from different class, religious and political backgrounds through its insistence that gender was a more important identity than any of these. Yet this major reason for its success concealed the seeds of its own destruction. The WSPU was correct to assume that gender would unify women around an issue such as their exclusion from the franchise which affected all women equally. However, it was naive in its underestimation of the appeal of other identities or loyalties when the franchise was achieved. Once it ceased its suffrage work, the WSPU ceased to function on Merseyside. Some of its activists did move into other suffrage societies or other areas of public work as the previous chapter has shown. However, the majority simply stopped political work. The only possible explanation for this is that they were primarily attracted to the single-issue politics of the WSPU, and did not feel the urge to participate in more general campaigns. Writing of national politics, Susan Kingsley Kent has argued that the devastating psychological effect of the war brought the end of 'sex-class' politics, as

> In the aftermath of the Somme… a conflict between the sexes could not be tolerated: it conjured up images of the battlefield horrors that so gripped the country's imagination.[7]

However, the Merseyside evidence points to something much more mundane, namely that the demise of 'sex-class' politics had been inevitable all along. Much of the WSPU's success stemmed from its ability to locate a campaign among a broad base of women, emphasising unity rather than differences. Now, in the 'utter chaos' of post-war Liverpool without the unifying call for the vote, differences were thrown into stark relief.[8] The

---

6   For accounts that present an implicitly male-dominated picture see, for example, J. Arnison, *Leo McGree: What a Man, What a Fighter*, London, Union of Construction, Allied Trades and Technicians, 1980; T. Lane, 'Some Merseyside Militants of the 1930s', in Hikins, ed., *Building the Union*, pp. 153–80; J. Rawlings, 'Stormy Petrel: Struggle or Starve', unpublished typescript, Ruskin College, Oxford.

7   S. Kingsley Kent, *Making Peace: The Reconstruction of Gender in Inter-war Britain*, Princeton, Princeton University Press, 1993, p. 91.

8   Braddock and Braddock, *The Braddocks*, p. 31.

totality of the collapse of sex-class politics on Merseyside can be gauged in 1919 when Christabel Pankhurst's failure to secure nomination for the parliamentary seat of West Derby was barely noticed.[9] By contrast, the 1919 police strike attracted great support from local workers. During associated demonstrations the Riot Act was read in Liverpool, an event that would be repeated throughout the next decade. The class war, it would appear, had returned to supersede any thought of 'sex-classes' and women were once again polarised. Ideas about the unity of gender had little to say to the working-class women of Merseyside who found their lives open to the scrutiny of women on the Public Assistance Committee, nor did they appeal to middle-class women who found themselves unable to afford or obtain domestic service.

The activities of various women's organisations during the Great War indicate that the ideology of separate spheres remained influential. It was clearly an important factor in much relief work, emphasising women's 'special' contribution to the war effort and relying heavily on a belief that women were essentially a non-combatant, nurturing sex. During the war the WCAs also drew on this ideology as they struggled to develop a gendered concept of citizenship that would guarantee enfranchised women a specific role in post-war reconstruction. Members consciously used the war to argue for this, claiming that through 'this great crisis, women have been called upon as citizens to take their place in serving their country'.[10] However, as with the demise of sex-class politics, this claim did not represent a dramatic change in direction for women's politics as a result of the war. Rather, it again offers evidence for a continuity of thought discernible among constitutional suffragists locally as they attempted to draw feminists away from class and sex conflict.

The Liverpool WCA attempted to retain some form of political organisation based on gender alone. Initially, it was unconcerned with losing some members to groups with different priorities. As Eleanor Rathbone explained of the NUWSS, 'those of us who would wish to work for other ends can do so for other agencies'.[11] Within the WCA, members attempted to unite a significant body of local women in an organisation that would allow what they continued to argue was women's unique influence to be felt through all levels of the state. They attempted this through the formation of the Liverpool Council of Women Citizens (LCWC), a body 'composed of representatives of practically all women's societies in the city' to 'give public expression... upon questions specifically affecting the interests of women'.[12]

9   Waller, *Democracy and Sectarianism*, p. 283.
10 Mrs Stanley Clarke, Birkenhead CUWFA Secretary, *Conservative and Unionist Women's Franchise Review*, Issue 23, July–September 1915.
11 E. Rathbone, letter to NUWSS council, *Common Cause*, 21 May 1915.
12 Liverpool Council of Women Citizens/Liverpool Women Citizens' Association, Joint Statement of Aims, 1919. Liverpool Women Citizens' Association Papers (hereafter LWCA Papers), LRO.

However, as with the sex-class model, this attempt to unite women was thwarted by the conflicting interests of its membership outside the organisation itself. In October 1921, Edith Eskrigge, the LCWC secretary, laid out policy for the forthcoming local elections where, as the three main political parties were each fielding female candidates, she called for workers for each candidate.[13] The idea was that women could separate from the WCA for election work for their preferred candidate, then reunite in the WCA and count each successful female candidate as a victory. What would have occurred had women candidates been opposing one another in the same ward was unclear, although the following year brought an indication that such gender-based alliances would flounder when party political interests became involved. Nessie Stewart-Brown, fighting the parliamentary constituency of Waterloo for the Liberal Party, was furiously attacked by Janet Harrison, a prominent local woman, for her opposition to a forthcoming Divorce Law Reform Bill.[14] In responding, Stewart-Brown was unable to keep party politics out of her argument, despite a brave attempt to appeal to all women in the electorate:

> If women voters do not support me on the ground of my long services to the women's suffrage movement, I must abide by the consequences of my views... *Mrs Harrison, if I mistake not, is already an active worker on behalf of the Conservative Candidate.*[15]

Political affiliations proved stronger than those of gender, with the majority of women with party loyalties returning to their parties. By the 1930s, the LCWC was so distanced from local politics that it was unable to name local women councillors.[16] A gendered concept of citizenship that reserved a public role for women could make little headway against the enduring appeal of party. This is best evidenced through Eleanor Rathbone's own attempts to enter Parliament as an Independent. Although the WCA enthusiastically supported her campaign in East Toxteth in 1922, the electorate rejected her in favour of a party-affiliated candidate. It was only within the limited electorate of the Combined English Universities that she met with success in 1929.

With the increased prominence of class politics in inter-war Liverpool, the socialist model of organisation, which had not done particularly well before the war, fared slightly better. The local LRC had continued to support the sporadic attempts by women to unionise, but during the war they added to this with concerted efforts to recruit women workers into the Labour Party.

---

13 Liverpool Women Citizens' Association Annual Report, 1919–20, LWCA Papers, LRO.
14 Unidentified Press Cutting, January/February 1922, LWCA Papers, LRO.
15 Unidentified Press Cutting, January/February 1922, LWCA Papers, LRO, my italics.
16 LCWC minutes, June 1937, LWCA Papers, LRO. The names are filled in in a different hand and ink in the minutes.

Women socialists initiated this campaign. Mary Bamber had unionised the largely female workforce at the Garston bobbin works prior to its large strike in 1912. In 1915, she requested permission to establish a workplace Labour Party branch, a step that Jeannie Mole would have approved of, had she lived to see it.[17] However, the war also augmented opportunities for women. Mrs Hardcastle, ILP delegate to the LRC since 1912, was elected as a Poor Law Guardian in Wavertree in 1915 where she 'assured the committee that she would do her best to carry the banner of Labour'.[18] Her selection was undoubtedly due in part to the absence of many male socialists during the war. This also opened the way for a steady increase in the numbers of women active in the LRC, culminating in a local record of three female executive committee members by 1918.

However, socialist women still found their activities largely controlled by men, and often marginalised. By 1918 there was a WLA in Liverpool, which subsequently gave way to Women's Sections within the Labour Party in 1922.[19] Yet, despite this apparent move to encourage women, they were still treated with suspicion and refused any degree of autonomy. In June 1918, for example, Sarah McArd of the WLA was summoned before the Executive of the LRC and reprimanded for her action in submitting an account for literature without first requesting permission. Ironically, much of the Executive's concern stemmed from the fact that there would be 'overlapping as in this case the (LRC) secretary had secured 1000 copies of the same leaflet for the women's use'.[20] The male secretary received no admonishment for ordering literature to be used by the WLA without first consulting the women themselves.

Pat Thane has argued that despite such instances of male dominance in the inter-war Labour Party, it is still important to include 'women who chose to work for feminist... goals in a mixed-sex organisation' in an analysis of inter-war women's politics.[21] The tenacity of Merseyside's socialist women remaining in their party organisation supports this. Furthermore, some socialist women did manage to build careers through party politics, with a steady trickle emerging as council candidates up to the Second World War. And, although according to Sam Davies only 8 per cent of Labour's municipal candidates between 1905 and 1937 were women, this compares well with the figure for the Liberal (4 per cent) and Conservative (3 per cent) parties.[22]

---

17 LRC minute book, September 1915, LRO.
18 LRC minute book, September 1915, LRO.
19 LRC minute book, September 1918, LRO. See also Davies, 'Class, Religion and Gender', pp. 217–46.
20 LRC Executive Committee Minutes, June 1918, LRO.
21 P. Thane, 'The Women of the British Labour Party and Feminism, 1906–45', in H. L. Smith, ed., *British Feminism in the Twentieth Century*, Aldershot, Edward Elgar, 1990, pp. 124–43.
22 Davies, 'Liverpool Labour Party and Women', pp. 241–43.

In terms of enabling women to gain access to the public political arena, the socialist model might therefore be argued to have delivered more over the long term than its initially more successful contemporaries.

The careers of women in other Merseyside political parties in the 1920s also demonstrate the influence of the socialist model beyond its obvious forum of socialist politics. Those elements of socialist ideology that emphasised the commonality interests of male and female socialists within their parties can be discerned within Liberal and Conservative politics in the inter-war period as gender-based alliances faltered. In both cases, women began to see themselves as primarily Liberal or Conservative rather than as female politicians. The WLF began to revive slowly.[23] Similarly, although no local figure remained, national records display a rising female membership within Conservative organisations, and it is possible to infer a similar trend in Liverpool from the slow but steady increase in female candidates. Although small in comparison with the numbers of male candidates, female politicians had come a long way from their first reception in the Guardians' elections of 1893.

The failure of local feminists to sustain a unified political movement after 1918 was as responsible for the small advances by women within political parties as were the actions of party activists themselves. Furthermore, when speaking of the limited success of the socialist model of organisation and the adaptation of similar methodologies within Liberal and Conservative politics, it must be acknowledged that inter-war Merseyside witnessed a decline in feminist politics. The majority of the large, combined membership of the suffrage organisations did not find a new home either in the LCWC or in the slightly reconstructed political parties. The reasons for this are as varied as the individuals themselves. Hattie Mahood gave up the WSPU, socialism and political life following a breakdown in health in 1912.[24] Cecily Leadley-Brown continued some association with the WCA but concentrated mainly on her career in law, working in the chambers of Nessie Stewart-Brown's husband.[25] Other key figures including Lydia Booth and Dr Alice Ker left the area, along with many other prominent citizens. Much more difficult to explain, but also most common, was the route followed by Patricia Woodlock who went from addressing two to four public meetings a week to participating in no recorded political activity for the remainder of her life.[26] Many of her fellow activists were every bit as swift to drop out of activity. It would

---

23 M. Pugh, *Women and the Women's Movement in Britain 1914–59*, Basingstoke, Macmillan, 1992, table 5.6, p. 140.

24 Pembroke Chapel Minute Book, 21 April 1912.

25 'Liverpool Women who Take Control', *The Liverpool Daily Post*, undated cutting, LWCA Papers, LRO.

26 *Kelly's Directory* records her as living in Liverpool in 1931, but no record of her death, or of her later life, can be found.

appear that the suffrage campaign possessed a unique appeal that was not to find its equal between the wars. There are no obvious answers as to why this should be so, but the Merseyside evidence does appear to favour certain explanations. Much of the success of the WSPU came from its style of campaigning. The variety and novelty of the many elements that made up suffrage militancy possessed a unique attraction that no other organisation matched. Similar campaigning styles have been attempted up to the present day through organisations such as the Campaign for Nuclear Disarmament and the Anti-Poll Tax Federation, which have succeeded in uniting a disparate membership behind one demand for a short period of time. The denial of difference inherent in single-issue politics appears to make this possible. However, as yet no organisation has succeeded in acknowledging or removing deeply rooted differences of class, gender or politics, or in over-coming them once they rear their heads.

Although my focus on public political activity has shown a decline in women's participation after the First World War, I do not wish this to be interpreted as the end of the story. Running throughout this book has been a conviction that an important degree of political power within a democracy rests within the elected institutions of the state, its parliament, municipal authorities and other governing bodies. I have demonstrated how Merseyside women demanded access to these bodies and slowly penetrated them prior to achieving the parliamentary franchise. Although their influence after 1918 remained small, it gradually increased as the three main political parties, the major vehicles for achieving political power, became more open to women members. In 1927 Liverpool elected its first female Lord Mayor, Margaret Beavan, and in 1945 Bessie Braddock became the first local female MP. Although there is still a temptation to consider these examples as 'tokens', this has not been my intention. Rather, I cite them as inheritors of a long-standing political tradition in which women always played an important role, albeit one for which they frequently had to battle. As I began by saying, the purpose of a local study is not to create an alternative 'total' picture; rather, I believe that my narrative throws further light on our understanding of the results of nationally developed theories about the nature of women's polit-ical involvement as they were implemented in a local context. Although further local studies need to be undertaken before larger conclusions can be drawn, the Merseyside evidence serves to broaden our understanding of exactly what political involvement meant to the many women who under-took it between 1890 and 1920.

Bibliography

Primary Material

1 Manuscript Collections, Papers of Organisations and Unpublished Typescripts

Autograph Letter Collection, Women's Library, London
Liverpool Conservative Party Papers, Liverpool Record Office
Criddle Family Papers, Merseyside Record Office
Emily Wilding Davison Papers, Women's Library, London
Fabian Society Papers, Nuffield College, Oxford
Joseph Edwards Papers, Liverpool Record Office
Joseph Edwards Papers, Nuffield College, Oxford
Glasier Papers, Liverpool University
Kelly's Directories, 1890–1910
Alice Ker diaries, private collection
Legge Papers, Liverpool Record Office
Liverpool Town Clerks' Cuttings Books, 1900–1910, Liverpool Record Office.
Liverpool Trades Council and Labour Party Papers, Liverpool Record Office
Liverpool & District British Women's Temperance Association Papers, Liverpool Record Office
Ada McGuire correspondence, Imperial War Museum
Dora Marsden Papers, microfilm, University of York
Melly Papers, Liverpool Record Office
National Society for Women's Suffrage Occasional Papers, microfilm
Marjorie Patmore Papers, Liverpool Record Office
Pembroke Chapel Papers, Regents Park College, Oxford
Primrose League Papers, Bodleian Library, Oxford
Rathbone Literary Club Minute Book, Liverpool Record Office
Suffragette Fellowship Collection, Museum of London
Wallasey Independent Labour Party minute book, National Museum of Labour History
West Derby Coroner's Inquest Register, Lancashire Record Office
Women's Co-operative Guild Papers, University of Hull
Liverpool Women Citizens' Association Papers, Liverpool Record Office
Women at War Collection, Imperial War Museum
Women's Liberal Federation Papers, Bristol University
Women's Labour League Papers, microfilm
Women's Suffrage Collection, Manchester Public Library
Women's Trade Union League Papers (microfilm) incorporating Women's Provident and Protection League Annual Reports; Women's Trade Union League Annual Reports

2   Annual Reports and Yearbooks

Catholic Women's Suffrage Society Annual Reports, 1912–20, Women's Library, London

Church League for Women's Suffrage Annual Reports, 1910–18, Women's Library, London

Fabian Society Annual Reports, 1897–1920, Nuffield College, Oxford

The Labour Annual, 1895–1900

Liverpool Fabian Society Annual Reports, 1910, 1911, 1912, 1915, 1918, 1923, Nuffield College, Oxford

Liverpool Kyrle Society Annual Reports, Merseyside Record Office

Liverpool Ladies' Work Society Annual Reports, Merseyside Record Office

National Union of Women's Suffrage Societies, West Lancashire, West Cheshire & North Wales Federation Annual Reports, 1912, 1913, Women's Library, London

The Reformers' Yearbook, 1901–09

Women's Liberal Federation Annual Reports, 1888–1929, Bristol University

Women's Social and Political Union Annual Reports, 1907–14, Women's Library, London

Women's Trade Union League Annual Reports, microfilm

3   Newspapers and Magazines

Aigburth Parish Magazine
The Birkenhead News
The Birkenhead and Wirral Herald
The Britannia
Calling All Women
The Catholic Suffragist
Church League for Women's Suffrage Monthly Paper
The Clarion
Common Cause
Conservative and Unionist Women's Franchise Review (later *Conservative and Unionist Women's Review*)
Daily Express
Daily Mail
The Daily News
Fabian News
The Fortnightly Review
The Free Church Suffrage Times
The Freewoman
The Friend
The Home Service Corps Review
The Independent Suffragette
Justice
The Kensington Pioneer
The Labour Leader
The Labour Prophet
The Liver
The Liverpolitan
The Liverpool Courier

Liverpool Daily Post
The Liverpool Forward
The Liverpool Labour Chronicle (later *Liverpool Labour Chronicle and Trades Union Reporter*)
The Liverpool Mercury
The Liverpool Pulpit
The Liverpool Review of Politics, Society, Literature and the Arts
The Liverpool Weekly Courier
The Liverpool Weekly Mercury
The Liverpool Weekly Post
The Men's League for Women's Suffrage Newsletter
The New Penny Magazine
The Porcupine
The Primrose League Gazette
The Southport Advertiser
The Suffragette
The Suffragette News Sheet
The Times
The Vote
Votes for Women
The Wallasey and Wirral Chronicle
The Westminster Review
Womanhood
The Women's Dreadnought
Women's Franchise
Women's Freedom League News
Women's Liberal Federation News
Women's National Liberal Association Quarterly Leaflet
Women and Progress
Women's Suffrage Journal
Women's Trade Union League Review
Women's Tribune, later *Women and Progress*
Women's Union Journal
The Woman Worker

Works Published before 1930

Andrews, I. O., *The Economic Effects of the World War upon Women and Children in Great Britain*, New York, Oxford University Press, 1920

Anon., 'Wealth and Want – Glitter and Grime', *The New Penny Magazine*, no. 216, vol. XVII, 1903, pp. 301–05

Anon., *Robert Weare of Bristol, Liverpool and Wallasey: An Appreciation and Four of his Essays*, Manchester, C.W.S. Printing Works, n.d. (1920?)

[Anon.], *Rules of the Liverpool Upholstresses' Union Established November 11 1890*, British Library of Economic and Political Sciences

Anon., *Women's Suffrage: Opinions of Leaders of Religious Thought*, London, Central Society for Women's Suffrage, 1895

Armstrong, R. A., *The Deadly Shame of Liverpool*, Liverpool, G. Philip and Son, 1890

Bebel, A., *Women in the Past, Present and Future*, London, Swan Publications, 1988 [1879]

Bell, Revd M., *The Church and Women's Suffrage: Sermon Before the Inaugural Meeting of the Church League for Women's Suffrage*, London, Church League for Women's Suffrage Pamphlet no. 1, 1909

Caine, M. H., *Our Girls: Their Work for the War*, London, Hutchinson and Co., 1916

Clarke, A., *Working Lives of Women in Seventeenth Century London*, London, Routledge and Sons, 1915

Clayton, J., *Votes for Women – The Appeal to Catholics*, London, Catholic Women's Suffrage Society Pamphlet, n.d.

de Alberti, L., 'History of the Catholic Women's Suffrage Society', *Catholic Citizen*, vol. XIV, no. 9, 15 October 1928, pp.77–81

Doty, M. Z., *Short Rations: An American Woman in Germany 1915–16*, London, Methuen and Co., 1917

Drake, B., *Women in Trade Unions*, London, Labour Research Department, 1920

Engels, F., *The Origins of the Family, Private Property and the State*, Chicago, Charles H., Kerr, 1902 [1884]

Fawcett, M. G., *What I Remember*, London, Fisher and Unwin, 1924

—*Women's Suffrage: A Short History of a Great Movement*, London, T. C. and E. C. Jack, 1912

Holt, A., ed., *Merseyside: A Handbook to Liverpool and District prepared on the occasion of the meeting of the British Association for the Advancement of Science*, Liverpool, Liverpool University Press, 1923

Hutchins, B. L., *Women in Modern History*, London, G. Bell and Sons, 1915

Joff, T., *Coffee House Babble*, Liverpool, privately published, n.d.

Kempthorne, Revd J. A., *Speech to Queen's Hall*, London, The Collegium, 1912

Kenney, A., *Memories of a Militant*, London, Arnold, 1924

Liverpool Ladies' Union of Workers among Women and Girls, ed., *Women Workers: Papers Read at a Conference by the Liverpool Ladies Union of Workers Among Women and Girls, November 1891*, Liverpool, Gilbert G. Walmsley, 1892

Liverpool Women's Industrial Council, *How the Casual Labourer Lives: Report of the Liverpool Joint Research Committee on the Domestic Condition and Expenditure of the Families of Certain Liverpool Labourers*, Liverpool, Liverpool Women's Industrial Council, 1909

—*Liverpool Women's Industrial Council Report on Homework in Liverpool*, Liverpool, Liverpool Women's Industrial Council, 1909

Lytton, C., *Prisons and Prisoners: Some Personal Experiences by Constance Lytton and Jane Warton, Spinster*, London, William Heinemann, 1914

Manson, R. T., *Wayward Fancies of R. T. Manson*, Liverpool, Lyceum Press, 1907

Marx Aveling, E., 'The Woman Question', *The Westminster Review*, New Series, LXIX, January, 1886, pp. 207–22

Maurice, C. E., *The Life and Work of Octavia Hill*, London, Macmillan, 1913

Mill, J. S., *De Slaverng der Vrouw: Uit het Engelsch vert door R. C. Nieuwenhuijs, met eee voorrede van A. J. Vitringa. Naar de 4e Engelsche utig. bew. M. E. Noest*, Amsterdam, 1898

Muir, R., *History of Liverpool*, London, Liverpool University Press, 1907

Muspratt, E. K., *My Life and Work*, London, John Lane, 1917

Nott-Bower, W., *Fifty Two Years a Policeman*, London, Edward Arnold, 1926

Orchard, B. G., *Liverpool's Legion of Honour*, Birkenhead, published by the author, 1893

Pankhurst, E., *My Own Story*, London, Eveleigh Nash, 1914

Pankhurst, E. S., *The Suffragette*, London, Gay and Hancock Ltd., 1911

Pease, E. R., *The History of the Fabian Society*, London, A. C. Fifield, 1916

Picton, J. A., *Liverpool Improvements and How to Accomplish Them*, Liverpool, E. Howell, 1853

—*Memorials of Liverpool, Historical and Topographical*, London, Longmans, 1875

—*Memorials of Liverpool, Historical and Topographical Including a History of the Dock Estate. Second Edition Continued to the Reign of Queen Victoria*, Liverpool. Gilbert G. Walmsley, 1903

Pike, W. T., *A Dictionary of Edwardian Biography: Lancashire*, Edinburgh, Peter Bell, 1986 [1903]

—*Liverpool and Birkenhead in the 20th Century*, Brighton, W. T. Pike / Pike's New Century Series, 1911

Pinchbeck, I., *Women Workers and the Industrial Revolution, 1750–1850*, London, Routledge, 1930

Rathbone, E., *A New Form of Suffrage Propaganda*, London, NUWSS Pamphlet, n.d. (1913?)

Roberts, H. D., *Hope Street Church Liverpool and the Allied Nonconformity*, Liverpool, Liverpool Booksellers Company, 1909

Stanton, T., ed., *The Woman Question in Europe*, New York, Source Book Press, 1970 [1884]

Strachey, R., *The Cause: A Short History of the Women's Movement in Great Britain*, London, Virago, 1988 [1928]

Temple, Revd W., *The Religious Aspect of the Women's Movement*, London, The Collegium, 1912

Tooley, S., *Ladies of Liverpool*, n.p. 1895

Webster, V., 'What Women are Doing in Liverpool', *Womanhood*, vol. 3, no. 16, March 1900, pp. 279–81; 6, no. 32, July 1901, pp. 103–07; vol. 6, no. 34, September 1901, pp. 273–76

Whitting, H. A., *Alfred Booth: Some Memories, Letters and other Family Records Arranged by his Daughter Harriet Anna Whiting*, Liverpool, Henry Young and Sons, 1917

Williams, Revd G., *Women's Rights: A Sermon*, Glasgow, Candlish Memorial U. F. Church, 1914

Works Published after 1930

Alberti, J., *Eleanor Rathbone*, London, Sage, 1996

Alexander, S., *Becoming a Woman and Other Essays in Nineteenth and Twentieth Century Feminist History*, London, Virago, 1994

Anderson, G., 'A Private Agency for White-Collar Workers Between the Wars: A Study of the Liverpool Clerks' Association 1918–39', *International Review of Social History*, vol. XXXI, 1986, pp. 19–39

—*The Service Occupations of Nineteenth Century Liverpool*, Salford, Salford Papers in

Economics, 1981

Angerman, A., G. Binnema, A. Keunen, V. Poels and J. Zirkzee, eds, *Current Issues in Women's History*, London, Routledge, 1989

Arnison, J., *Leo McGree: What a Man, What a Fighter*, London, Union of Construction, Allied Trades and Technicians, 1980

Atkinson, D., *The Purple, White and Green: Suffragettes in London 1906–14*, London, Museum of London, 1992

Banks, O., *Becoming a Feminist: The Social Origins of First Wave Feminism*, Brighton, Wheatsheaf, 1986

—*A Biographical Dictionary of British Feminists*, Brighton, Harvester, 1985–90

—*Faces of Feminism*, Oxford, Martin Robertson, 1981

Barrow, L., and I. Bullock, *Democratic Ideas and the British Labour Movement 1880–1914*, Cambridge, Cambridge University Press, 1996

Bartley, P., *Prostitution: Prevention and Reform in England 1860–1914*, London, Routledge, 2000

Bealey, F., and H. Pelling, *Labour and Politics 1900–1906: A History of the Labour Representation Committee*, London, Macmillan, 1958

Bean, R., 'Aspects of New Unionism in Liverpool 1889–91', in H. Hikins, ed., *Building the Union: Studies of the Growth of the Workers' Movement: Merseyside 1756–1967*, Liverpool, Toulouse Press, 1973, pp. 99–120

Bellamey, J., and J. Saville, eds, *The Dictionary of Labour Biography*, London, Macmillan, 1972–93

Belchem, J., *Merseypride: Essays in Liverpool Exceptionalism*, Liverpool, Liverpool University Press, 2000

Belchem, J., ed., *Popular Politics, Riot and Labour: Essays in Liverpool History 1790–1940*, Liverpool, Liverpool University Press, 1992

Belchem, J., and N. Kirk, eds, *Languages of Labour*, Aldershot, Ashgate, 1997

Bell, E. Moberley, *Storming the Citadel: The Rise of the Woman Doctor*, London, Constable, 1953

Bisson, R. F., *The Sandon Studios and the Arts*, Liverpool, Parry Books, 1965

Blake, C., *The Charge of the Parasols: Women's Entry into the Medical Profession*, London, Virago, 1990

Bland, L., 'In the Name of Protection: The Policing of Women in the First World War', in C. Smart and J. Brophy, eds, *Women in Law: Explorations in Law, Family and Society*, London, Routledge and Kegan Paul, 1985, pp. 23–49

Bohstedt, J., 'More than One Working Class: Protestant and Catholic Riots in Edwardian Liverpool', in J. Belchem, ed., *Popular Politics, Riot and Labour: Essays in Liverpool History 1790–1940*, Liverpool, Liverpool University Press, 1992, pp. 173–216

Bonzon, T., 'The Labour Market and Industrial Mobilization 1915–17', in J. Winter and J.-L. Robert, eds, *Capital Cities at War: Paris, London, Berlin 1914–1918*, Cambridge, Cambridge University Press, 1997, pp. 164–95

Boston, S., *Women Workers and the Trade Unions*, London, Lawrence and Wishart, 1987

Bowers, A., J. Sharples and M. Shippobottom, eds, *Charles Reilly and the Liverpool School of Architecture 1904–33*, Liverpool, Liverpool University Press, 1996

Braddock, B., and J. Braddock, *The Braddocks*, London, Macdonald and Co., 1963

Brady, L. W., *T. P. O'Connor and the Liverpool Irish*, London, Royal Historical

Society, 1983

Braybon, G., *Women Workers and the First World War*, London, Routledge, 1989

Braybon, G., and P. Summerfield, *Out of the Cage: Women's Experiences in Two World Wars*, London, Pandora, 1987

Bridenthal, R., C. Koonz and S. Stuart, eds, *Becoming Visible: Women in European History*, Boston, Houghton Mifflin and Co, 2nd edn, 1987

Briggs A., and J. Saville, eds, *Essays in Labour History 1886–1923*, London, Macmillan, 1971

Brogden, M., *On The Mersey Beat: Policing in Liverpool Between the Wars*, Oxford, Oxford University Press, 1991

Brown, H., A. Kaloski and R. Symes, eds, *Celebrating Women's Friendship Past, Present and Future*, York, Raw Nerve Press, 1999

Caine, B., *Destined to be Wives: The Sisters of Beatrice Webb*, Oxford, Clarendon Press, 1986

Callahan, K., '"Performing Inter-Nationalism" in Stuttgart in 1907: French and German Socialist Nationalism and the Political Culture of an International Socialist Congress', *International Review of Social History*, vol. 45, part 1, April 2000, pp. 51–88

Campbell, B., *Iron Ladies: Why Women Vote Tory*, London, Virago, 1987

Chandler, G., *Liverpool*, London, Batsford, 1957

Chew, D. Nield, ed., *Ada Nield Chew: The Life and Writings of a Working Woman*, London, Virago, 1982

Cole, M., 'Guild Socialism and the Labour Research Department', in A. Briggs and J. Saville, eds, *Essays in Labour History 1886–1932*, London, Macmillan, 1971, pp. 260–83

—*The History of Fabian Socialism*, London, Heinemann, 1961

Collette, C., *For Labour and For Women: The Women's Labour League 1906–18*, Manchester, Manchester University Press, 1989

Condell D., and J. Liddiard, *Working for Victory? Images of Women in the First World War 1914–18*, London, Routledge and Kegan Paul, 1987

Cowman, K., '"Incipient Toryism?" The Women's Social and Political Union and the Independent Labour Party, 1903–14', *History Workshop Journal*, 53, Spring 2002, pp. 128–48

— 'The Patriotic Sausage or the Politicisation of Domesticity in Britain during the First World War', in A. Despard, ed., *A Woman's Place: Women, Domesticity and Private Life*, Kristiansand, Høgskolen I Agder, 1998, pp. 95–105

—'"A Party Between Revolution and Peaceful Persuasion": A Fresh Look at the United Suffragists', in J. Purvis and M. Joannou, eds, *The Women's Suffrage Movement: New Feminist Perspectives*, Manchester, Manchester University Press, 1998, pp. 77–88

—'"Crossing the Great Divide": Inter-organisational Suffrage Relationships on Merseyside, 1895–1914', in C. Eustance, J. Ryan and L. Ugolini, eds, *A Suffrage Reader: Charting Directions in British Suffrage History*, London, Leicester University Press, 2000, pp. 37–52

— '"We Intend to show what Our Lord has done for Women": The Liverpool Church League for Women's Suffrage 1914–18', *Studies in Church History*, vol. 34, 1998, pp. 475–86

—'The Battle of the Boulevards: Class, Gender and the Purpose of Public Space in

Later Victorian Liverpool', in S. Gunn and R. Morris, eds, *Making Identities; Conflicts and Urban Space 1800–2000*, Aldershot, Ashgate, 2001

Cowman, K., and H. Brown, 'Exploring Suffrage Friendship', in H. Brown, A. Kaloski and R. Symes, eds, *Celebrating Women's Friendship Past, Present and Future*, York, Raw Nerve Press, 1999, pp. 121–54

Cowper, H., C. Emsley, A. Marwick, B. Purdue and D. Englander, *World War One and its Consequences*, Milton Keynes, Open University Press, 1990

Crawford, E., *The Women's Suffrage Movement: A Reference Guide*, London, UCL Press, 1999

Crofton, E., *The Women of Royaumont, a Scottish Women's Hospital on the Western Front*, East Lothian, Tuckwell Press, 1997

Davidoff, L., *Worlds Between: Historical Perspectives on Gender and Class*, Cambridge, Polity Press, 1995

Davidoff, L., and C. Hall, *Family Fortunes: Men and Women of the English Middle Class 1750–1850*, London, Hutchinson, 1987

Davies, S., 'Class, Religion and Gender: The Liverpool Labour Party and Women 1918–39', in J. Belchem, ed., *Popular Politics, Riot and Labour: Essays in Liverpool History 1790–1940*, Liverpool, Liverpool University Press, 1992, pp. 217–46

Davin, A., 'Foreword', in D. Nield Chew, ed., *Ada Nield Chew: The Life and Writings of a Working Woman*, London, Virago, 1982, pp. ix–xxiv

Despard, A., ed., *A Woman's Place: Women, Domesticity and Private Life*, Kristiansand, Høgskolen I Agder, 1998

Dowse, R. E., *Left in the Centre: The Independent Labour Party 1893–1940*, London, Longmans, 1966

Duby, G., and M. Perrot, eds, *A History of Women in the West, Vol. IV: Emerging Feminism from Revolution to World War*, Cambridge, MA, Belknap Press/Harvard University Press, 1993

Dyhouse, C., *No Distinction of Sex? Women in British Universities, 1870–1939*, London, UCL Press, 1995

Eustance, C., 'Meanings of Militancy: The Ideas and Practice of Political Resistance in the Women's Freedom League', in J. Purvis and M. Joannou, eds, *The Women's Suffrage Movement: New Feminist Perspectives*, Manchester, Manchester University Press, 1998, pp. 51–64

Eustance, C., J. Ryan and L. Ugolini, eds, *A Suffrage Reader: Charting Directions in British Suffrage History*, London, Leicester University Press, 2000

Evans, R., *Comrades and Sisters: Feminism, Socialism and Pacifism in Europe, 1870–1945*, Brighton, Wheatsheaf, 1987

Faue, E., *Community of Suffering and Struggle: Women and the Labour Movement in Minneapolis, 1915–45*, London, University of North Carolina Press, 1991

Ferguson, N., *The Pity of War*, London, Allen Lane, 1998

Fidler, G., 'The Liverpool Labour Movement and the School Board: An Aspect of Education and the Working Class', *History of Education*, vol. XIV, 1979, pp. 43–61

—'The Work of Joseph and Eleanor Edwards, Two Liverpool Enthusiasts', *International Review of Social History*, vol. XXIV, 1979, pp. 293–379

Fletcher, S., *Maude Royden: A Life*, Oxford, Blackwell, 1989

Frances, H., 'Dare to be Free! The Women's Freedom League and its Legacy', in J. Purvis and S. Stanley Holton, eds, *Votes for Women*, London, Routledge, 2000, pp. 181–202

Fulford, R., *Votes for Women*, London, Faber and Faber, 1957

Garcia, M. A., 'The Gender of Militancy: Notes on the Possibilities of a Different History of Political Action', *Gender and History*, vol. 11, no. 3, November 1999, pp. 416–74

Garner, L., *A Brave and Beautiful Spirit: Dora Marsden, 1882–1960*, Aldershot, Avebury, 1990

Gawthorpe, M., *Uphill to Holloway*, Penebscott, ME, Travisty Press, 1966

Goldie, G. Wyndham, *The Liverpool Repertory Theatre 1911–34*, Liverpool, Liverpool University Press, 1935

Golding, J. A., 'An End to Sweating? Liverpool's Sweated Workers in Legislation', *North West Labour History*, 21, 1996–97, pp. 3–29

Gordon, E., *Women and the Labour Movement in Scotland*, Oxford, Clarendon Press, 1991

Gourvish, T. R., and A. O'Day, eds, *Later Victorian Britain 1867–1900*, London, Macmillan, 1988

Grant, L., 'Women's Work and Trade Unionism in Liverpool 1890–1914', *North West Labour History*, 7, 1980–81, pp. 65–83

Green, B., *Spectacular Confessions: Autobiography, Performative Activism and the Sites of Suffrage 1905–38*, London, Macmillan, 1997

Gunn, S., and R. Morris, eds, *Making Identities; Conflicts and Urban Space 1800–2000*, Aldershot, Ashgate, 2001

Hall, C., *White, Male and Middle-Class: Explorations in Feminism and History*, Oxford, Blackwell, 1992

Hamilton, C., *Life Errant*, London, J. M. Dent, 1935

Hamling, W., *A Short History of the Liverpool Trades Council, 1848–1948*, Liverpool, Liverpool Trades Council and Labour Party, 1948

Hanmer, J., C. Lunn, S. Jeffreys and S. McNeill, 'Sex Class – Why is it Important to call Women a Class?', *Scarlet Women*, vol. 5, pp. 8–10, n.d.

Hannam, J., '"I had not been to London": Women's Suffrage: A View from the Regions', in J. Purvis and S. Stanley Holton, eds, *Votes for Women*, London, Routledge, 2000, pp. 226–45

—'Women and the ILP 1890–1914', in D. James, T. Jowitt and K. Laybourn, eds, *The Centennial History of the Independent Labour Party*, Halifax, Ryburn Academic Publishing, 1992, pp. 205–28

— *Isabella Ford*, Oxford, Blackwell, 1989

Hannington, W., *Unemployed Struggles 1919–36*, London, Lawrence and Wishart, 1977 [1936]

Harrison, B., 'Women in a Men's House: The Women MPs, 1919–45', *Historical Journal*, 29, no. 3, 1986, pp. 623–54

—*Prudent Revolutionaries: Portraits of British Feminists Between the Wars*, Oxford, Oxford University Press, 1987

Heeney, B., *The Women's Movement in the Church of England, 1850–1930*, Oxford, Oxford University Press, 1988

Hikins, H., *Strike! 1911*, Liverpool, Toulouse Press, 1981

Hikins, H., ed., *Building the Union: Studies of the Growth of the Workers' Movement: Merseyside 1756–1967*, Liverpool, Toulouse Press, 1973

Hilden, P., *Working Women and Socialist Politics in France, 1800–1914: A Regional Study*, Oxford, Clarendon Press, 1986

Hirshfield, C., 'Fractured Faith: Liberal Party Women and the Suffrage Issue in Britain 1892–1914', *Gender and History*, vol. 2, no. 2, Summer 1990, pp. 173–97

Holcombe, L., *Wives and Property*, Oxford, M. Robertson, 1983

Hollis, P., *Ladies Elect: Women in English Local Government, 1865–1914*, Oxford, Clarendon Press, 1987

Holton, R., *British Syndicalism 1900–1914*, London, Pluto Press, 1976

Holton, S. Stanley, *Feminism and Democracy: Women's Suffrage and Reform Politics in Britain 1900–1918*, Cambridge, Cambridge University Press, 1986

—*Suffrage Days: Stories from the Women's Suffrage Movement*, London, Routledge, 1996

Howell, D., *British Workers and the Independent Labour Party 1888–1906*, Manchester, Manchester University Press, 1983

Hume, L. Parker, *The National Union of Women's Suffrage Societies 1897–1914*, New York, Garland, 1982

Hunt, F., ed., *Lessons for Life? The Schooling of Girls and Women 1850–1950*, Oxford, Blackwell, 1987

Hunt, K., 'Fractured Universality: The Language of British Socialism Before the First World War', in J. Belchem and N. Kirk, eds, *Languages of Labour*, Aldershot, Ashgate, 1997, pp. 65–80

—*Equivocal Feminists: The Social Democratic Federation and the Woman Question 1884–1911*, Cambridge, Cambridge University Press, 1996

—*Socialist Women: Britain, 1890s to 1920s*, London, Routledge, 2001

Hunt, K., and J. Hannam, 'Propagandising as Socialist Women: The Case of the Women's Columns in British Socialist Newspapers 1884–1914', in B. Taithe and T. Thornton, eds, *Propaganda: Political Rhetoric and Identity 1300–2000*, Stroud, Sutton, 1999, pp. 167–82

Ireland, I., *Margaret Beavan of Liverpool: Her Character and Work*, Liverpool, Henry Young and Sons, 1938

James, D., 'Researching the History of the ILP', in D. James, T. Jowitt and K. Laybourn, eds, *The Centennial History of the Independent Labour Party*, Halifax, Ryburn Academic Publishing, 1992, pp. 337–64

James, D., T. Jowitt and K. Laybourn, eds, *The Centennial History of the Independent Labour Party*, Halifax, Ryburn Academic Publishing, 1992

John, A. V., ed., *Unequal Opportunities: Women's Employment in England 1800–1918*, Oxford, Blackwell, 1986

John, A. V., and C. Eustance, eds, *The Men's Share: Masculinities, Male Support and Women's Suffrage in Britain, 1890–1920*, London, Routledge, 1997

Jones, D. Caradog, *A Social Survey of Merseyside*, London, University Press of Liverpool/Hodder and Stoughton, 1934

Jones, J., 'A Liverpool Socialist Education', *History Workshop Journal*, 18, Autumn 1984, pp. 92–101

Jordanova, L., *History in Practice*, London, Arnold, 2000

Josephson, H., ed, *The Biographical Dictionary of Modern Peace Leaders*, Westport, CT, Greenwood Press, 1984

Judt, T., *Socialism in Provence 1871–1914: A Study in the Origins of the Modern French Left*, Cambridge, Cambridge University Press, 1979

Kanya-Forstner, M., 'Defining Womanhood: Irish Women and the Catholic Church in Victorian Liverpool', in D. M. MacRaild, ed., *The Great Famine and Beyond:*

Irish Migrants in Britain in the 19th and 20th Centuries, Dublin, Academic Press, 2000, pp. 166–88

Kean, H., *Deeds not Words*, London, Pluto Press, 1990

Kent, S. Kingsley, *Making Peace: The Reconstruction of Gender in Inter-War Britain*, Princeton, NJ, Princeton University Press, 1993

—*Sex and Suffrage in Britain 1860–1914*, London, Routledge, 1987

Kerber, L., 'Separate Spheres, Female Worlds, Women's Place: The Rhetoric of Women's History', *Journal of American History*, vol. 75, 1988, pp. 3–39

Kirk, N., *Change, Continuity and Class: Labour in British Society 1850–1920*, Manchester, Manchester University Press, 1998

Lane, T., 'Some Merseyside Militants of the 1930s', in H. Hikins, ed., *Building the Union: Studies of the Growth of the Workers' Movement on Merseyside 1756–1967*, Liverpool, Toulouse Press, 1973, pp. 153–80

—*Liverpool, Gateway of Empire*, London, Lawrence and Wishart, 1987

Larkin, E., *James Larkin, Irish Labour Leader*, London, Pluto Press, 1989

Lawrence, J., 'The Transition to War in 1914', in *Capital Cities at War: Paris, London, Berlin 1914–1918*, Cambridge, Cambridge University Press, 1997, pp. 135–63

Lawrence, M., *Shadow of Swords: A Biography of Elsie Inglis*, London, Michael Joseph, 1971

Lawton, R., and R. Lee, eds, *Urban Population in Western Europe from the Late Eighteenth Century to the Early Twentieth Century*, Liverpool, Liverpool University Press, 1989

Leneman, L., *A Guid Cause: The Women's Movement in Scotland*, Aberdeen, Aberdeen University Press, 1991

Levine, P., '"Walking the Streets in a Way no Decent Woman Should." Women Police in World War One', *Journal of Modern History*, 66, March 1994, pp. 34–78

— *Victorian Feminism*, London, Hutchinson, 1987

Lewenhak, S., *Women in Trade Unions*, London, Ernest Benn, 1977

Lewis, J., *Women in England, 1870–1950: Sexual Divisions and Social Change*, Brighton, Wheatsheaf, 1984

Leydesdorff, S., 'Politics, Identification and the Writing of Women's History', in A. Angerman, G. Binnema, A. Keunen, V. Poels and J. Zirkzee, eds, *Current Issues in Women's History*, London, Routledge, 1989, pp. 9–20

Liddington, J., *The Life and Times of a Respectable Rebel: Selina Cooper 1864–1946*, London, Virago, 1984

Liddington, J., and J. Norris, *One Hand Tied Behind Us: The Rise of the Women's Suffrage Movement*, London, Virago, 1978

Lock, J., *The British Policewoman: Her Story*, London, Robert Hale, 1979

Mappen, E. F., 'Strategists for Change: Social Feminist Approaches to the Problems of Women's Work', in A. V. John, ed., *Unequal Opportunities: Women's Employment in England 1800–1918*, Oxford, Blackwell, 1986, pp. 235–60

— *Helping Women at Work: The Women's Industrial Council 1889–1914*, London, Hutchinson, 1985

Marwick, A., 'Women and the Family', in H. Cowper, C. Emsley, A. Marwick, B. Purdue and D. Englander, *World War One and its Consequences*, Milton Keynes, Open University Press, 1990, pp. 13–21

— *Women at War*, London, Fontana, 1977

Mason, F. M., 'The Newer Eve: The Catholic Women's Suffrage Society in England,

182   MRS BROWN IS A MAN AND A BROTHER

1911–1923', *Catholic Historical Review*, vol. 72, 1986, pp. 620–38

McKenzie, M., *Shoulder to Shoulder*, New York, Vintage Books, 1988

McPhee, C., and A. Fitzgerald, eds, *The Non-Violent Militant: Selected Writings of Teresa Billington Grieg*, London, Routledge, 1987

Mitchell, D., *The Fighting Pankhursts: A Study in Tenacity*, London, Jonathan Cape, 1967

— *Women on the Warpath: The Story of Women of the First World War*, London, Jonathan Cape, 1966

Mitchell, H., *The Hard Way Up*, London, Virago, 1987 [1968]

Mommsen, W. J., and H. G. Husung, eds, *The Development of Trade Unionism in Britain and Germany 1880–1914*, London, George Allen and Unwin, 1985

Morris, R. J., *Class, Sect and Party: The Making of the British Middle Class, Leeds 1820–1850*, Manchester, Manchester University Press, 1990

Murphy, M., *Molly Murphy, Suffragette and Socialist*, University of Salford, Institute of Social Research, 1998

Navarro, A. de, *The Scottish Women's Hospital at the Franc Abbey of Royaumont*, London, Allen and Unwin, 1971

Neal, F., *Sectarian Violence: The Liverpool Experience 1819–1914: An Aspect of Anglo-Irish History*, Manchester, Manchester University Press, 1988

Nolan, M., *Social Democracy and Society: Working-Class Radicalism in Dusseldorf, 1890–1920*, Cambridge, Cambridge University Press, 1981

O'Mara, P., *The Autobiography of a Liverpool Slummy*, repr. Liverpool, Bluecoat Press, n.d.

Osterud, N. G., 'Gender Divisions and the Organisation of Work in the Leicester Hosiery Industry', in A. V. John, ed., *Unequal Opportunities: Women's Employment in England 1800–1918*, Oxford, Blackwell, 1986, pp. 45–70

Pankhurst, C., *Unshackled: The Story of How We Won the Vote*, London, Cresset Library Reprints, 1987 [1959]

Pankhurst, E. S., *The Suffragette Movement*, London, Virago, 1977 [1931]

Parnell, N. Stewart, *The Way of Florence Barry, 1885–1965*, London, St Joan's Alliance, 1973

Pedersen, S., 'Gender, Welfare and Citizenship in Britain during the Great War', *American Historical Review*, vol. 95, no. 4, 1990, pp. 983–1006

Pelling, H., *The Origins of the Labour Party*, Oxford, Oxford University Press, 1965

Pethick-Lawrence, E., *My Part in a Changing World*, London, Victor Gollancz, 1938

Pethick-Lawrence, F., *Fate Has Been Kind*, London, Hutchinson, 1942

Pollard, S., 'The New Unionism in Britain: Its Economic Background', in W. J. Mommsen and H. G. Husung, eds, *The Development of Trade Unionism in Britain and Germany 1880–1914*, London, George Allen and Unwin, 1985, pp. 32–54

Povey, M., *Uneven Developments: The Ideological Work of Gender in Mid-Victorian England*, London, Virago, 1989

Power, M., 'The Growth of Liverpool', in J. Belchem, ed., *Popular Politics, Riot and Labour: Essays in Liverpool History 1790–1940*, Liverpool, Liverpool University Press, 1992, pp. 21–37

Pugh, M., *The Tories and the People 1880–1935*, Oxford, Blackwell, 1985

— *Women and the Women's Movement in Britain 1914–59*, Basingstoke, Macmillan, 1992

Pugh, P., *Educate, Agitate, Organise: One Hundred Years of Fabian Socialism*, London,

Methuen, 1984

Purvis, J., ed., *Women's History in Britain 1850–1945*, London, UCL Press, 1995

Purvis, J., and M. Joannou, eds, *The Women's Suffrage Movement: New Feminist Perspectives*, Manchester, Manchester University Press, 1998

Purvis, J., and S. Stanley Holton, eds, *Votes for Women*, London, Routledge, 2000

Pye, D., *Fellowship is Life: The National Clarion Cycling Club 1895–1995*, Bolton, Clarion Publishing, 1995

Raeburn, A., *The Militant Suffragettes*, London, Michael Joseph, 1973

Ramelson, M., *Petticoat Rebellion: A Century of Struggle for Women's Rights*, London, Lawrence and Wishart, 1972

Rathbone, E., 'Changes in Public Life', in R. Strachey, ed., *Our Freedom and its Results by Five Women*, London, Hogarth Press, 1936

Rendall, J., 'Women and the Public Sphere', *Gender and History*, vol. 11, no. 3, November 1999, pp. 475–88

Rendall, J., ed., *Equal or Different: Women's Politics 1800–1914*, Oxford, Blackwell, 1987

Reynolds, K. D., *Aristocratic Women and Political Society in Victorian Britain*, Oxford, Clarendon Press, 1998

Richardson, M., *Laugh a Defiance*, London, Weidenfeld and Nicolson, 1953

Riddel, J., ed., *Lenin's Struggle for a Revolutionary International: Documents 1907–16*, New York, Monad Press, 1986

Robb, J., *The Primrose League*, New York, Armstrong Press, 1968 [1942]

Rose, S. O., 'Gender Antagonism and Class Conflict: Exclusionary Strategies of Male Trade Unionists in Nineteenth Century Britain', *Social History*, vol. 13, no. 2, May 1988, pp. 191–207

—*Limited Livelihoods: Gender and Class in Nineteenth Century England*, London, Routledge, 1992

Rosen, A., *Rise up Women! The Militant Campaign of the Women's Social and Political Union 1903–14*, London, Routledge and Kegan Paul, 1974

Ross, E., 'Survival Networks: Women's Neighbourhood Sharing in London Before World War One', *History Workshop Journal*, 15, Spring 1983, pp. 4–27

Rowbotham, S., *Hidden from History: 300 Years of Women's Oppression and the Fight Against It*, London, Pluto Press, 1974

—*Women, Resistance and Revolution*, Harmondsworth, Penguin, 1972

Royle, E., *Radicals, Secularists and Republicans*, Manchester, Manchester University Press, 1980

Rubinstein, D., *A New World For Women: The Life of Millicent Garret Fawcett*, New York, Harvester Wheatsheaf, 1991

— *Before the Suffragettes: Women's Emancipation in the 1890s*, Brighton, Harvester, 1986

Sarah, E., 'Christabel Pankhurst: Reclaiming Her Power', in D. Spender, ed., *Feminist Theorists: Three Centuries of Women's Intellectual Traditions*, London, Women's Press, 1983, pp. 256–85

Sellers, I., 'Nonconformist Attitudes in Later Nineteenth Century Liverpool', *Transactions of the Historical Society of Lancashire and Cheshire*, vol. CXIV, 1962, pp. 215–39

Shoemaker, R., and M. Vincent, eds, *Gender and History in Western Europe*, London, Arnold, 1998

Simey, M. B., 'Eleanor Rathbone', *Social Science Quarterly*, vol. XI, no. 3, 1966–67, pp. 109–11

Simey, M., *Charitable Effort in Liverpool*, Liverpool, Liverpool University Press, 1951

Smart, C., and J. Brophy, eds, *Women in Law: Explorations in Law, Family and Society*, London, Routledge and Kegan Paul, 1985

Smith, H. L., *The British Women's Suffrage Campaign 1866–1928*, London, Longmans, 1998

Smith, H. L., ed., *British Feminism in the Twentieth Century*, Aldershot, Edward Elgar, 1990

Smith, L., *Religion and the Rise of Labour*, Keele, Keele University Press, 1993

Solden, N. C., *Women in British Trade Unions 1874–1976*, London, Gill and Macmillan, 1978

Sowerwine, C., 'The Socialist Women's Movement from 1850 to 1940', in R. Bridenthal, C. Koonz and S. Stuart, eds, *Becoming Visible: Women in European History*, Boston, Houghton Mifflin and Co, 2nd edn, 1987, pp. 399–428

— *Sisters or Citizens? Women and Socialism in France since 1876*, Cambridge, Cambridge University Press, 1982

Spender, D., ed., *Feminist Theorists: Three Centuries of Women's Intellectual Traditions*, London, Women's Press, 1983

— ed., *Women of Ideas and What Men have Done to Them*, London, Routledge, 1982.

Stanley, L., with A. Morley, *The Life and Death of Emily Wilding Davison*, London, Women's Press, 1988

Stansell, C., *City of Women: Sex and Class in New York, 1789–1860*, New York, Alfred A. Knopf, 1986

Steedman, C., *Childhood, Culture and Class in Britain: Margaret Macmillan 1860–1931*, London, Virago, 1990

Stocks, M. D., *Eleanor Rathbone*, London, Victor Gollancz, 1949

Strachey, R., ed., *Our Freedom and its Results by Five Women*, London, Hogarth Press, 1936

Taaffe, P., and Mulhearn, T., *Liverpool: A City that Dared to Fight*, London, Fortress Books, 1988

Taithe B., and T. Thornton, eds, *Propaganda: Political Rhetoric and Identity 1300–2000*, Stroud, Sutton, 1999

Taplin, E., *Near to Revolution: The Liverpool General Transport Strike of 1911*, Liverpool, The Bluecoat Press, 1994

Thane, P., 'Late Victorian Women', in T. R. Gourvish and A. O'Day, eds, *Later Victorian Britain 1867–1900*, London, Macmillan, 1988, pp. 175–208

— 'The Women of the British Labour Party and Feminism, 1906–45', in H. L. Smith, ed., *British Feminism in the Twentieth Century*, Aldershot, Edward Elgar, 1990, pp. 124–43

Thom, D., 'The Bundle of Sticks: Women, Trade Unionists and Collective Organization Before 1918', in A. V. John, ed., *Unequal Opportunities: Women's Employment in England 1800–1918*, Oxford, Blackwell, 1986, pp. 261–89

Tickner, L., *The Spectacle of Women: Imagery of the Suffrage Campaign 1907–14*, London, Chatto and Windus, 1987

Tosh, J., *What is History? Present Aims, Methods and New Directions in the Study of Modern History*, London, Longmans, 1984

Turbin, C., *Working Women of Collar City: Gender, Class and Community in Troy,*

New York, 1864–86, Chicago, University of Illinois Press, 1992

Van Wingerden, S. A., *The Women's Suffrage Movement in Britain 1866–1928*, Basingstoke, Macmillan, 1999

Vellacott, J., *From Liberal to Labour with Women's Suffrage: The Story of Catherine Marshall*, Montreal, McGill-Queen's University Press, 1993

Vicinus, M., *Independent Women*, London, Virago, 1985

— *Suffer and Be Still: Women in the Victorian Age*, London, Methuen, 1980

Vickery, A. J., 'Golden Age to Separate Spheres: A Review of the Categories and Chronology of English Women's History', *Historical Journal*, vol. 36, no. 2, 1993, pp. 383–414

Vickery, A., *The Gentleman's Daughter: Women's Lives in Georgian England*, London, Yale University Press, 1998

Wainwright, D., *Liverpool Gentlemen: A History of Liverpool College, an Independent Day School from 1840*, London, Faber and Faber, 1960

Walker, L., 'Party Political Women: A Comparative Study of Liberal Women and the Primrose League', in J. Rendall, ed., *Equal or Different: Women's Politics 1800–1914*, Oxford, Blackwell, 1987, pp. 165–91

Waller, P. J., *Democracy and Sectarianism: A Political and Social History of Liverpool 1869–1939*, Liverpool, Liverpool University Press, 1981

Warhurst, E., *Liverpool Women Citizen's Association*, Liverpool, n.d.

Waters, C., *British Socialists and the Politics of Popular Culture 1884–1914*, Manchester, Manchester University Press, 1990

Whitelaw, L., *The Life and Rebellious Times of Cicely Hamilton*, London, Women's Press, 1990

Whittingham-Jones, B., *The Pedigree of Liverpool Politics: White, Orange and Green*, Liverpool, privately published, 1936

Wiltsher, A., *Most Dangerous Women: Feminist Peace Campaigners of the Great War*, London, Pandora, 1985

Winter, J. M., *The Great War and the British People*, London, Macmillan, 1985

Winter, J. M., and J.-L. Robert, eds, *Capital Cities at War: Paris, London, Berlin 1914–1918*, Cambridge, Cambridge University Press, 1997

Woodsen, A., 'The First Women Police: A Force For Equality of Infringement?', *Women's History Review*, vol. 2, no. 2, 1993, pp. 217–32

Woollacott, A., '"Khaki Fever" and its Control: Gender, Class, Age and Sexual Morality on the British Homefront in the First World War', *Journal of Contemporary History*, vol. 29, 1994, pp. 325–47

— *On Her Their Lives Depend: Munition Workers in the Great War*, Berkeley, CA, University of California Press, 1994

Yeo, S., 'A New Life: The Religion of Socialism in Britain 1883–1896', *History Workshop Journal*, 4, autumn 1977, pp. 5–56

Unpublished Works

Anon., untitled typescript history of Liverpool Women Police, Fawcett Library, London

Cowman, K., 'Engendering Citizenship: The Political Involvement of Women on Merseyside, 1890–1920', unpublished DPhil thesis, University of York, 1994

Eustance, C., '"Daring to be Free": The Evolution of Women's Political Identities in the Women's Freedom League, 1907–1930', unpublished DPhil thesis, University of York, 1993

Frances, H., '"Our Job is to be Free": The Sexual Politics of Four Edwardian Feminists from c.1910 to 1935', unpublished DPhil thesis, University of York, 1996

Maddocks, S., 'The Liverpool Trades Council and Politics 1878–1918', MA thesis, Liverpool University, 1959

Place, Dorothy Foster (neé Abraham), 'Autobiographical Notes', unpublished typescript, private collection

Rawlings, J., 'Stormy Petrel: Struggle or Starve', unpublished typescript, Ruskin College Oxford

Sellers, I., 'Salute to Pembroke', unpublished typescript, Liverpool Record Office

—'An Experiment in Humanism: Windsor Street Ethical Church, Liverpool, and its Founder, Rev. Harry Youlden', unpublished typescript, Liverpool Record Office.

Index